Flying Off Course

Flying Off Course

The Economics of International Airlines

RIGAS DOGANIS
Director, Transport Studies Group,
Polytechnic of Central London

London
GEORGE ALLEN & UNWIN
Boston   Sydney

George Allen & Unwin (Publishers) Ltd,
40 Museum Street, London WC1A 1LU, UK

George Allen & Unwin (Publishers) Ltd,
Park Lane, Hemel Hempstead, Herts HP2 4TE, UK

Allen & Unwin, Inc.,
8 Winchester Place, Winchester, Mass. 01890, USA

George Allen & Unwin Australia Pty Ltd,
8 Napier Street, North Sydney, NSW 2060, Australia

First published in 1985.
Second impression 1986

British Library Cataloguing in Publication Data

Doganis, Rigas
   Flying off course: the economics of international airlines
1. Aeronautics, Commercial
I. Title
387.7'1 HE9782
ISBN 0-04-387004-X (Hb)   ISBN 0-04-387005-8 (Pb)

Library of Congress Cataloging in Publication Data

Doganis, Rigas.
   Flying off course.
Bibliography: p.
Includes index.
1. Aeronautics, Commercial   2. Air lines.
I. Title.
HE9780.D64   1985   387.7'1   85-4028
ISBN 0-04-387004-X (Hb)   ISBN 0-04-387005-8 (Pb)   (alk. paper)

Type set in 10 on 11 point Times by
Mathematical Composition Setters Ltd, Salisbury, UK
and printed in Great Britain by
Billing and Sons Ltd, London and Worcester

Contents

Acknowledgements

The international airline industry is complex, dynamic and subject to rapid change and innovation. To understand its economic and operational features one must be close to its pulse-beat. In this I have been fortunate: for over a decade I have been lecturing at the Royal Aeronautical Society's Air Transport Course held annually at Oxford and the similar course in Manila organized for the Orient Airlines Association by the Asian Institute of Management. These courses bring together each year a group of managers with wide international experience from various fields of air transport and from many airlines. They provide an open forum for frank discussion of airline trends and problems, where established truths are constantly questioned. I am indebted to the numerous participants at Oxford and Manila who, through their comments and questions, have helped me gain deeper insight into the workings of the airline business. For the same reasons I would like to thank my former students at the Polytechnic of Central London and the participants of the various air transport courses I have given in-house to several airlines, such as Singapore Airlines (SIA), Malaysian Airlines (MAS) and Cathay Pacific.

In the many years of my involvement with air transport there have been so many who have influenced my thoughts that it is difficult to mention them all. But I would like to single out four, Stephen Wheatcroft, Hugh Welburn, Peter Smith and Alan Snudden. They have freely given me the benefit of their wide airline experience and have always been willing to discuss new ideas and concepts. In addition I would like to thank the Polytechnic of Central London and, through them, the Inner London Education Authority for granting me study leave to complete the research on which this book is based; my colleagues at the Polytechnic who took on my workload while I was away; and Alan Jessop and Anne Graham for their valuable comments on the forecasting chapter. Thanks are also due to Josie Binns for her excellent typing of a difficult manuscript.

Finally, I am grateful to my wife Sally, who, with her television journalist's flair and abandon − 'don't let the facts get in the way of a good story' − discussed various aspects of the book with me, and to Dimitri and Chloe for their understanding and support.

Introduction

In the last 30 years the airline industry has undergone an expansion unrivalled by any other form of public transport. Its rate of technological change has been exceptional. This has resulted in falling costs and fares which have stimulated a very rapid growth in demand for its services: a seemingly insatiable demand. In addition, for much of the period scheduled airlines have enjoyed considerable protection from both internal and external competition. Any other industry faced with such high growth of demand for its products while cushioned from competition would be heady with the thought of present and future profits. But not the airline industry. It is an exception to the rule. High growth has for the most part spelt low profits. Increased demand has not resulted in financial success. While some airlines have consistently managed to stay well in the black, the industry as a whole has been only marginally profitable.

The conundrum of high growth and poor financial performance, which characterizes the airline industry, is the background to this book. It is partly explained by some of the problems facing the industry recently. The most dramatic have been the increase in fuel prices in 1974 and 1978–9 and the world economic recession which followed. The recession coincided with the easing of many of the economic regulations and controls on air services. This happened most dramatically in the United States from 1978 onwards, though many other nations also caught the bug. Deregulation affected most of the major international air markets. Its effects even spilled over into countries that viewed deregulation with disfavour. While coping with these external difficulties the international airline industry was itself undergoing structural changes. The late 1960s onwards saw a dramatic growth in charter services and the emergence of large but low cost charter airlines. Equally worrying for the established scheduled carriers was the emergence during the latter part of this period of new dynamic and low cost airlines in some Third World countries, notably in South East Asia.

There is no simple explanation to the apparent contradiction between the industry's rapid growth and its marginal profits. But for the individual airline financial success depends on matching supply and demand in a way which is both efficient and profitable. This is the underlying theme and focus of the book. While airline managements have considerable control over the supply of air services they have relatively little control over the demand. Hence the matching process is not an easy one. To help in understanding the process the present book provides a practical insight into key aspects of airline operations and planning within the conceptional framework of economics.

The book works through the issues logically. Any understanding of the economics of the industry must start with the regulatory framework which circumscribes and constrains airlines' freedom of action (Chs 2 and 3). To match the supply of air services successfully with the demand it is essential to understand airline costs and the factors that affect them (Chs 4 and 5) and the nature of the demand (Ch. 7). A thorough appreciation of demand must be used to develop traffic and other forecasts, since every activity within an airline ultimately stems from a forecast (Ch. 8). Supply and demand are brought together in a number of ways but most crucially through the pricing mechanism. Alternative airline pricing policies and strategies need to be considered (Ch. 9). While the emphasis throughout is on scheduled operations a large part of international air transport is now provided by charter or non-scheduled services. The particular characteristics and advantages of such services require special attention (Ch. 6) as do certain aspects of air freight (Ch. 10). But the book begins by examining the underlying trends in the airline industry, including its rapid technological change, the high growth rates and the marginal profitability.

The book is concerned primarily with international air transport, which accounts world wide for about half the industry's output. Only for the airlines of a few large countries such as the USA, the Soviet Union, Brazil and China are domestic operations of greater significance than international. United States airlines and Aeroflot alone account for three-quarters of the world's domestic operations. As a result the airlines of most countries are primarily concerned with international air services while several of them operate only internationally.

There is no magic wand to ensure success within the international airline industry. This book attempts to flesh out the economic and operational issues which must be understood in order to match supply and demand. Only when this has been done can there be some measure of success in this most dynamic of industries. So come, fly with me.

1
Characteristics and Trends in Airline Operations

1.1 Rapid technological change

In the last 50 years technological innovation in air transport has far outstripped that in any other transport mode. The only comparable innovations elsewhere have been the emergence of the supertankers in shipping and the development of high speed trains, though the impact of the latter is still only marginal. Innovation in aviation has centred on the development of the jet engine for civil use, first in a turbo-propellor form and later as a pure jet. Successive developments in the jet engine have consistently improved its efficiency and propulsive power. The emergence of larger and more powerful engines in association with improvements in airframe design and in control systems has resulted over the last 50 years in successive improvements in aircraft speed and size. Higher speeds and larger aircraft have resulted in significant jumps in aircraft productivity. This is evident in Table 1.1. Even in the era of the piston engine dramatic improvements were made so that the hourly productivity of the Super Constellation was seven times greater than that of the Douglas DC-3. The early turbo-prop aircraft also significantly improved productivity. Though the Viscount's productivity was less than that of the Super Constellation, as a DC-3 replacement the Viscount's productivity was four times as great. Likewise, the Britannias were a significant improvement on the Super Constellations they were meant to replace.

The arrival of the turbo-jet engine had a twofold impact. In the early 1960s the turbo-jets led to a dramatic increase in speeds, while the size of the aircraft did not increase appreciably. In the later 1960s and early 1970s there was no appreciable increase in speeds, because existing speeds were approaching the sound barrier, but there was a significant increase in the size of aircraft. The earlier increases in speeds and the later increases in aircraft size together produced major improvements in aircraft productivity so that while the Boeing 720B in 1960 was producing 11,000 tonne-km per flying hour only 10 years later the hourly productivity of the Boeing 747 was three times as great.

The next major breakthrough was the production of civil aircraft

Table 1.1 Impact of technological advance on aircraft productivity

	Aircraft type	Year of entry into service	Mean cruise speed (km/h)	Maximum payload*	Passenger payload	Hourly productivity (t-km/h)	Annual production† (t-km × 10³)
Piston	DC-3	1936	282	2·7	21	527	1,581
	Lockheed 1049 Super Constellation	1952	499	11·0	47–94	3,790	11,370
Turbo-prop	Viscount 700	1953	523	5·9	40–53	2,100	6,300
	Britannia 310	1956	571	15·6	52–133	6,048	18,144
Turbo-jet	Caravelle VI R	1959	816	8·3	52–94	4,600	13,800
	Boeing 720 B	1960	883	18·7	115–149	11,256	33,770
	Douglas DC-8-63	1968	935	30·6	259	19,500	58,470
	Boeing 747	1969	948	49·5	340–493	31,935	95,805
	Douglas DC-10	1971	915	38·8	400	24,130	72,400
	Airbus A300	1974	891	31·8	245	19,270	57,811
	Boeing 747-300	1983	948	67·8	660	44,350	133,050
	Concorde	1976	2,236	12·7	110	19,346	58,040

*Later versions or developments of these aircraft may have had different maximum or passenger payloads.
†Calculated on the basis of an average block speed assumed to be about 68–69 per cent of the cruise speed. This is likely to be an underestimate for aircraft on medium or long-haul sectors. Assume 3,000 flying hours.

flying faster than the speed of sound. The Anglo-French Concorde which entered service in 1976 flies more than twice as fast as its predecessors yet is able to do this only through a very significant reduction in size. Because of this penalty, supersonic aircraft have a lower hourly productivity than their competitors on long-haul routes. It is this factor which makes their commercial viability so problematical.

In the second half of the 1970s and the first half of the 1980s the rate of technological innovation slackened. Attention switched from the long-haul end of the aircraft market to the development of more efficient short- to medium-haul aircraft such as the Boeing 767 and the Airbus A-310. Developments here were based essentially on existing engine and airframe technology, though there were major developments in avionics, the use of composite materials and other areas. At the same time, the trend towards larger aircraft flying at the same speeds continues. Examples include the Boeing 747-300 with its stretched upper deck and the projected Airbus A320 which is larger than the aircraft it is intended to replace. Thus important gains in hourly productivity continue to be made.

1.2 Impact of technological change

These developments described so briefly above, which were matched by equally rapid innovations in other areas of aviation technology in the air and on the ground, were due primarily to the increasing efficiency of the jet engine. For a given level of propulsive thrust successive engines were able to carry a larger payload and to carry it faster as well. This, combined with other economies arising from the greater size of aircraft, resulted in ever-decreasing costs per capacity tonne-kilometre. Herein lies the significance of the technological improvements in aviation and of the increase in aircraft productivity which they made possible. They enabled airlines to cut their costs of production steadily throughout the 1950s and 1960s both in current values and in real terms (Fig. 1.1). During the 1970s airline unit costs expressed in current values began to rise rapidly as a result of world inflation. They rose particularly sharply following the fuel crises of 1973 and 1978. The airlines tried to counteract the upward pressure on costs by the accelerated introduction of more modern and usually larger jet aircraft and by more effective cost control. As a result, airline costs did not rise as rapidly as world prices so that in real or constant value terms airline costs during the 1970s remained stable or moved slowly downwards (Fig. 1.1). Trying to reduce costs in real terms will be a major preoccupation of airline managements during the next five years.

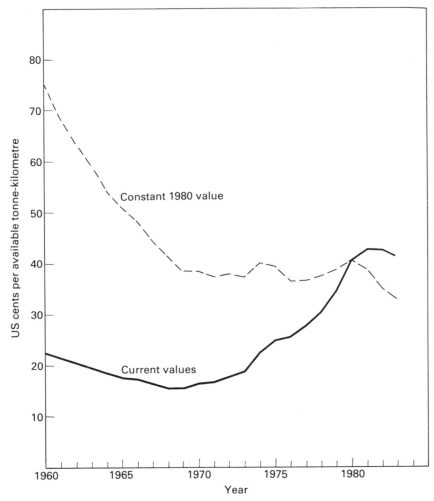

Figure 1.1 Trends in unit operating costs 1960–1983 (all services of ICAO scheduled airlines). Current values are adjusted to constant 1980 values using the OECD retail price index.

The technological developments in aviation, while they were beneficial in their impact on operating costs and in improving safety, also created problems. The increasing size and capacity of aircraft and the speed with which new, larger aircraft were introduced, often in reaction to competition from other airlines, created a strong downward pressure on load factors. Average load factors of ICAO scheduled airlines dropped from a level of around 60 per cent in the early

1950s to levels below 48 per cent by 1969 (Fig. 1.2). There was a significant fall in load factors between 1960 and 1963 with the widespread introduction of the first generation jets and then again between 1968 and 1971 with the introduction of the early wide-bodied

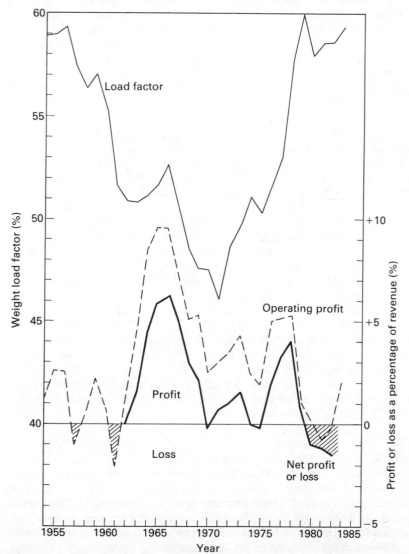

Figure 1.2 Load factors and profit margins of ICAO scheduled airlines 1954–83. (Net profit is after the inclusion of interest and other non-operating items.)

jets. Both these periods of over-capacity were marked by sharply falling profit margins. The airlines did not learn their lesson until 1973 or 1974. It was only then that, in a major effort to counteract the effects of cost inflation, airlines cut their frequencies, often dramatically as more Boeing 747s, DC-10s or Lockheed Tristars were introduced into service. By the late 1970s load factors began to approach the 60 per cent level again. But deregulation of air services, particularly on the North Atlantic and the trans-Pacific routes, with the resultant increase in the number of carriers in many markets combined with a general world recession, meant that that magical 60 per cent was not to be achieved. More than two seats in every five continued to remain empty!

The technical innovations also posed the problem of financing the new capital investments which they made necessary. While the operating costs per capacity tonne-kilometre were falling there was a very rapid escalation in the capital cost of new aircraft. Whereas up to the mid-1950s, with aircraft costing up to $2 million, airlines had been able to finance their purchases either by borrowing from the banks or from their governments or through the world's stock markets, this became increasingly difficult as aircraft prices escalated. By 1974, a 189-seater Boeing 727-200 cost the airlines $8–9 million. (*Note*: throughout this book all references to dollars are US dollars unless otherwise specified.) Ten years later, in 1984, the same airlines were having to pay around $45 million for a 265-seater Airbus A310 with spares to replace their 727s. In the early 1970s a fleet of five small short-haul aircraft would have cost about $45 million. A similar fleet 10 years later cost over $200 million. In 1978 Singapore Airlines placed an order worth $900 million for twelve Boeing 747-7Q aircraft and six Boeing 727s. Three years later the same airline ordered eight Boeing 747-SUDs and six Airbus A300s at a total cost of $1,800 million. These figures are indicative of the scale of investment necessary by the end of the 1970s for a large international airline. Not only did aircraft prices escalate but interest rates also escalated from 4–6 per cent per annum at the beginning of the decade to a peak of over 16 per cent by the late 1970s, though they decreased subsequently and were around 9–12 per cent by 1984.

Two developments eased the problem of raising capital on this scale. First, the aircraft manufacturers became increasingly involved with raising capital for their customers, either through the commercial banks in their own country or through special export trade banks, such as the United States Export–Import Bank. Manufacturers vied with each other in trying to get better financing arrangements for their clients and the terms of such purchase loans became an increasingly important factor for airlines in making a choice between aircraft. Secondly, there emerged consortia of banks which purchased aircraft and then leased them to the airlines. The consortia enjoyed tax concessions and also retained ownership of the aircraft which was a valuable security at a time when the resale value of aircraft was high.

Even when the industry as a whole was doing badly or a particular airline's results were poor, the manufacturers' need to sell inevitably ensured that finance would be forthcoming. But for the airlines this was a mixed blessing. It pushed them to invest when they should have been holding back. The result was that by the early 1980s many major airlines were heavily over-indebted. In other words, the ratio of their debts to their equity capital became much too high. When traffic failed to reach the forecast levels, airlines were no longer able to service these huge debts. Several carriers, such as Braniff and Laker in 1982, collapsed suddenly as their creditors ran out of patience and refused to reschedule debt repayments. By 1981 British Airways had capital debts of just over $1,600 million, yet was under pressure from manufacturers to buy yet more new aircraft for its European operations, each one of which would have cost over $45 million.

1.3 High growth industry

Compared to most industries the annual growth rate achieved by civil aviation has been staggering. In the 15 years between 1955 and 1969 the annual growth in tonne-kilometres performed by the world's scheduled airlines averaged about 14 per cent and only twice during that period, in 1958 and 1961, did the annual increase drop to less than 10 per cent. This consistently high growth rate was unmatched by any other transport mode during this period with the possible exception of international shipping, and that for a short time only. Since 1970 air transport growth has slackened. In the 10-year period from 1970 to 1979 the average annual growth rate fell to just below 10 per cent, though this was still high compared to other industries.

Adapting to lower growth became a key task for airline managers. The years 1980–3 were not encouraging. Average annual growth dropped to around 3 per cent. Was this a short-term phenomenon or did it represent a dramatic slowing down of the industry's rate of growth? If the latter was the case many airlines would find themselves with considerable over-capacity as the decade progressed.

The consistently high growth rates, at least until very recently, mask quite diverse growth patterns on particular routes or in particular countries or geographical areas. Long-term regional variations in growth trends are illustrated in Table 1.2. This shows that, in terms of both international and domestic tonne-kilometres performed, the European and North American airlines have experienced the lowest growth rates in the 10 years from 1972 to 1982. In terms of inter-

Table 1.2 Average annual growth rates in scheduled tonne-kilometres performed from 1972 to 1982 by region

Region of airline registration	Average annual percentage increase in	
	International tonne-kilometres	Domestic tonne-kilometres
Asia and Pacific	17·7	9·4
Middle East	13·4	21·1
Africa	12·1	10·8
Latin America and Caribbean	10·1	10·7
Europe	7·9	5·4
North America	5·1	4·5
World	9·6	5·4

Source: ICAO (1983c).

national traffic the Asian and Pacific airlines have achieved an annual growth rate almost double the world average. Some airlines within this region achieved exceptionally high average growth rates on their international traffic – for Singapore Airlines growth was + 45 per cent per annum; for Korean Airlines + 29.9 per cent and for Thai International + 25.2 per cent. The only airline outside this region to achieve comparable growth rates was Saudia with + 33.7 per cent (ICAO, 1983c). The very rapid growth of Asian airlines completely changed the structure of the international airline industry. In 1970 European and North American airlines generated three-quarters of international air traffic. This dominant position has been significantly eroded. By the mid-1980s their joint share was down to little more than 50 per cent while Asian and Pacific airlines alone now account for over 25 per cent of the world's international traffic. It is the North American airlines in particular that have lost market share, falling behind Asian carriers.

The reasons for the relatively rapid overall growth rate of air transport are not difficult to find. The falling level of operating costs, previously described, enabled airlines to offer tariffs that were lower in real terms. The yield or average fare charged per passenger-kilometre declined up to 1970 in real terms, that is in relation to the cost of other goods and services. This decline in the real cost of air transport was especially marked on international services (Fig. 1.3). It occurred at a time when the per capita incomes in the developed countries of the world were increasing at a rate of 8 per cent per annum while discretionary incomes were growing at an even faster rate. As a consequence the demand for non-business air travel rose rapidly. At the same time the 20 years to 1970 saw a boom in world trade which

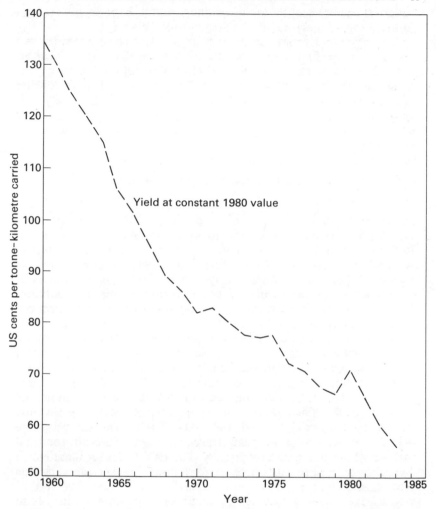

Figure 1.3 Trends in unit revenues 1960–1983. (International services of ICAO scheduled airlines.) Constant 1980 value is based on the OECD retail price index.

generated an increase both in business travel and in the demand for air freight facilities. The fall in the real cost of freight charges was even more marked than the decline in the real value of passenger fares.

During the 1970s the real cost of air transport in many markets continued to decline and disposable incomes also rose, though less rapidly then before. It was not until 1980 and the two or three years that followed that the economic recession affecting many developed countries began seriously to undermine demand. Even then it was not so in all major markets, as is evident from Table 1.2.

The very rapid growth in air transport was characterized by two features. In the first place, the rate of growth of non-scheduled air transport was much higher than that of scheduled, and as a consequence non-scheduled services now account for a significant share of the international airline industry's total output. Secondly, the profitability of airlines during the last 20 years has been fairly marginal despite the rapid growth of demand for their services.

1.4 Rapid growth of non-scheduled operations

In the early postwar years non-scheduled operations were relatively unimportant. Reliable figures are not available, but it is estimated that in the 1950s only about 3–5 per cent of the total tonne-kilometres produced each year by the world's airlines was generated on non-scheduled operations. These early non-scheduled operations were largely associated with military and government charters and with single-entity charters, that is where single persons or organizations were chartering aircraft for their own exclusive use.

In the early 1950s developments were taking place which would dramatically accelerate the development of non-scheduled traffic after 1960. American scheduled and supplemental, that is charter, carriers inaugurated what came to be known as 'affinity charters' across the North Atlantic. These subsequently spread to other long-haul markets. Such affinity charters arose when societies or clubs, whose total membership was normally limited to 20,000 members and whose prime purpose was other than travel, chartered aircraft for their members who shared the cost equally. The 1938 Civil Aeronautics Act had allowed non-scheduled operations under a general exemption from regulations which affected scheduled carriers. But in 1962 Public Law 87-528 confined the role of supplemental carriers exclusively to non-scheduled operations and authorized the Civil Aeronautics Board (CAB) to certify supplemental carriers to operate in designated geographical areas. In time, thirteen supplemental carriers were certified. The final breakthrough came in 1968 with the Inclusive Tour Charter Bill which empowered the CAB to authorize the operation of inclusive tour charters (ITCs), though the CAB had already been doing this for two years. Rapidly developing new holiday markets with affinity group charters and ITCs and bolstered by the operation of substantial military charters in support of the Vietnam war, United States non-scheduled operations grew at a phenomenal rate. Between 1964 and 1967 total passenger miles operated by the US supplementals quadrupled. High growth continued until about 1971 when military charters began to decline (McDonnell Douglas, 1968).

The European airlines meanwhile, had based their own non-scheduled operations on developing ITCs, and were less dependent than their American counterparts on affinity group or military charters. The development of ITCs by the British private airlines in the early 1950s was followed by the formation of charter companies in Scandinavia and later in Germany and elsewhere. These and other companies concentrated on the carriage of high-density ITC traffics between northern and western Europe and the resorts of the Mediterranean, especially those of Spain and Italy, and, to a much lesser extent, those of Greece, Yugoslavia and Tunisia. Growth was rapid, especially after 1965 when the charter companies began to introduce the most modern jet equipment. Between 1965 and 1973 ITC traffic in Europe grew at an average annual rate of 25 per cent, which was more than double the growth rate of scheduled intra-European traffic (Cambau and Lefevre, 1981). The European airlines, both scheduled and non-scheduled, began to develop long-haul charters across the Atlantic and, to a limited extent, to Africa and the Far East. These were to a large extent affinity group charters though ITCs also played a part.

The growth of non-scheduled services was facilitated in the early 1970s by the trend in the United States and some countries in Europe towards the liberalization of often arbitrary regulations limiting passenger access to charter flights. Growing much more rapidly than scheduled services, non-scheduled operations captured a growing share of the total international air traffic. By 1972 it was estimated that 31 per cent, or nearly one-third, of international passenger traffic was carried on non-scheduled services (ICAO, 1974). That was the peak penetration achieved by non-scheduled carriers. During the latter part of that decade the charter share of the total market gradually declined to a level of about 16–20 per cent. In 1982 it was 18.3 per cent (ICAO, 1983c).

This relative decline of non-scheduled traffic in the 1970s can be explained by two parallel developments. First, because as previously mentioned, in the years after the fuel crisis of 1974 the highest growth rates were experienced in markets where non-scheduled services were basically not permitted, namely in the Middle East and in the Asia-Pacific region. High growth was thereby concentrated on scheduled services. Secondly, because the further development of non-scheduled traffic in its two major markets either slowed down, which was the case in Europe, or actually went into decline, which happened on the North Atlantic route.

Liberalization of charter regulations had resulted in a rapid growth of non-scheduled traffic on the North Atlantic route (Table 1.3).

Table 1.3   Scheduled and non-scheduled growth rates on the North Atlantic route 1973 to 1982*

Year	Annual percentage change in passengers on: Scheduled services	Non-scheduled services	Non-scheduled as a percentage of total passengers
1973	+ 5·7	+ 11·6	26·3
1974	− 6·4	− 14·3	24·6
1975	− 5·5	+ 3·1	26·2
1976	+ 10·9	+ 12·8	26·6
1977	+ 5·3	+ 20·2	29·2
1978	+ 23·4	− 17·9	21·6
1979	+ 15·5	− 24·8	14·8
1980	+ 5·2	− 30·2	10·4
1981	+ 3·5	− 7·6	9·4
1982	− 5·2	+ 22·4	11·8
1983	+ 6·4	+ 5·7	11·7
1983 Passengers (000)	17,388	2,301	

*From January 1979 Miami flights included as North Atlantic.
Source: International Air Transport Association, Geneva.

Despite a hiccup in 1974, charter traffic grew faster than scheduled traffic until 1977, when it represented 29.2 per cent of the total passenger traffic on the route. Then in 1978 the charter market collapsed. This was a direct result of deregulation of fares and entry on many North Atlantic scheduled routes. Several new low-cost airlines, such as Laker Airways, began operating scheduled services. Competitive pressure pushed both new and existing scheduled carriers to offer fares which were charter competitive. With little price advantage to offer, charter airlines found their traffic shrinking rapidly. It was not until 1982 that they managed to halt the decline. Yet even in 1983 charter airlines' passenger numbers on the North Atlantic route were less than half what they had been six years earlier and their market share was only 11.7 per cent.

In Europe the much higher rate of growth of non-scheduled traffic, mentioned earlier, had gradually pushed up the charter airlines' share of international passenger traffic. By 1973 for the first time non-scheduled passenger-kilometres on international charters in Europe exceeded passenger-kilometres generated by international scheduled services (Cambau and Lefevre, 1981). But in 1974 the first oil crisis hit the non-scheduled sector of the market much harder than the scheduled sector. The ITC passengers were more price sensitive and more sensitive to the economic situation than the up-market tourists and the businessmen who travelled on scheduled services. The high charter growth rates of earlier years disappeared. Between 1974 and the end of the decade charter and scheduled international traffic grew at fairly similar rates and it was not until the end of the decade that charter traffic growth began to accelerate again. On a number of European air routes charter carriers have captured over 80 per cent and sometimes over 90 per cent of the total air market to the virtual exclusion of scheduled operations. This is the case on air routes between Spain and Scandinavia, the UK, Germany and the Netherlands and between Greece and the UK or Scandinavia. In 1983, 7.2 million passengers flew on charter flights between the UK and Spain and they represented 87 per cent of the total traffic between the two countries. This, one of the largest international air markets in the world, is totally dominated by charter airlines. Overall within Europe around 55 per cent of international passenger-kilometres are generated by non-scheduled carriers (Cambau and Lefevre, 1981). Non-scheduled operations have been characterized by particular features. First, in the period up to the mid-1970s, non-scheduled traffic grew much more rapidly than scheduled. Secondly, non-scheduled operations are strongly international in character. Almost 90 per cent of the total tonne-kilometres generated on non-scheduled services are on international flights (ICAO, 1983c). Finally, scheduled airlines play a major role in non-scheduled operations. In the early postwar years the bulk of the world's non-scheduled traffic was carried by the scheduled airlines. Then the rapid expansion of the supplemental carriers in the United States and of the large charter airlines in Europe and elsewhere pushed the scheduled carriers out of non-scheduled markets. Scheduled carriers were for a time constrained from entering such markets because of regulations imposed by the International Air Transport Association (IATA) or by their own governments. Some scheduled airlines, especially those in Europe, set up charter subsidiaries to circumvent such regulations. Lufthansa set up Condor, Air France and Air Inter jointly created Air Charter International, British European Airways set up British Airtours, which later became a subsidiary company of British Airways, and the SAS member airlines established Scanair.

Most of these charter companies are now owned 100 per cent by their scheduled parent airlines. But in some cases the parent company is not the sole owner. Thus Swissair owns 57 per cent of Balair and KLM has a 25 per cent stake in Martinair. In the United States, where scheduled airlines could not by law establish charter subsidiaries, airlines such as Pan American Airways (Pan Am) entered charter markets in their own right, and competed directly with US supplemental (charter) carriers in those markets where the CAB allowed them to. Outside Europe and North America few countries enjoyed the luxury of separate charter and scheduled carriers. The national scheduled airlines carried charter traffic as necessary. While several very large independent non-scheduled airlines have emerged, such as Britannia (UK) or Wardair (Canada), about 55 per cent of the total non-scheduled traffic is carried either by charter subsidiaries of scheduled airlines or by airlines that operate both scheduled and non-scheduled services (Table 1.4).

The rapid growth of non-scheduled traffic after 1965 dramatically changed the structure of the airline industry and its pattern of operations. A major problem facing airlines and governments in the second half of the 1980s will be how to adapt to the changes and pressures created by the growth of non-scheduled operations on routes where they have been allowed to develop. In three major international air markets, the North Atlantic, the Europe–Mediterranean area and, to a lesser extent, the North Pacific charter competition has been and remains a worrying fact of life for the scheduled airlines. As a result of such competition the operational and other distinctions between scheduled and non-scheduled have become increasingly blurred and difficult to maintain.

1.5 Marginal profitability

In an industry characterized by falling unit costs and an unusually high rate of growth in the demand for its products one would expect firms to obtain substantial profits. While this has been the case for many individual airlines, the profitability of the airline industry worldwide during the last 20 years has been marginal. Only in the period 1963–8 were significant profits achieved.

The traditional measure of profitability, namely the rate of return on assets employed, cannot be applied to the airline industry as a whole. This is because of the difficulty of estimating real asset values for airlines with varied depreciation policies, using varying proportions of leased equipment and often receiving direct or indirect government subsidy in a variety of forms. The measures of profitability normally used among airlines are either the annual operating profit or loss expressed as a percentage of the total annual operating revenue, or the total operating revenue expressed as a percentage of the total operating expenditure. The latter measure is known as the 'revex ratio'. The former, operating profit as a percentage of operating revenue, is calculated annually for the world's airlines by ICAO and is shown diagrammatically in Figure 1.2 above. The operating profit is before interest charges and other non-operating items. Net profit is after payment of interest and inclusion of these other items.

Table 1.4 International traffic (passenger-kilometres) of major non-scheduled operators in 1981

Independent non-scheduled airline	Non-scheduled subsidiaries of scheduled airlines	Non-scheduled services of airlines operating scheduled and non-scheduled services	Non-scheduled inter-national passenger-kilometres (millions)
1 Britannia (UK)			7,156
2 Wardair (Canada)			5,446
3 LTU (Germany			5,213
4	Condor (Lufthansa)		5,044
5 Sterling (Denmark)			3,895
6 Hapag-Lloyd (Germany)			3,856
7		Transamerica* (USA)	3,646
8		Dan Air (UK)	3,608
9		World* (USA)	3,060
10		Laker (UK)	3,014
11		Flying Tigers (USA)	2,899
12	Airtours (British Airways)		2,866
13		Aviaco (Spain)	2,731
14	Scanair (SAS)		2,343
15 Monarch (UK)			2,019

Total (15 largest carriers)	56,796
Total international non-scheduled passenger-kilometres (millions)	98,700
Top 15 carriers as a percentage of total non-scheduled passenger-kilometres	57·5%

*Transamerica and World were primarily US Supplemental (i.e. charter) airlines that moved into scheduled operations following deregulation in 1978.
Source: ICAO (1983c).

Since the mid-1950s the world airline industry has experienced five distinct phases in its financial fortunes.

(a) *Up to about 1960*, profit margins were very low and in a number of years there were net losses. Despite the high load factors compared to later years, financial results were poor because unit operating costs were high (see Fig. 1.1 above).

(b)   *During most of the 1960s* as unit costs declined there was a dramatic improvement in profit margins despite the fall in load factors. Fares and, more important, revenue yields were also falling during this period but less rapidly than the fall in costs.

(c)   By 1968 load factors on scheduled services had fallen to less than 50 per cent and continued to decline. This, together with rising unit costs from 1970 onwards, began to bite into the profit margins. *The period 1968–75* is characterized by poor financial results, particularly in 1970 and 1971. As a reaction to these poor results the airlines made determined efforts to improve load factors and were partially successful in this.

Attempts to improve financial results were completely upset by the fuel price crisis which followed the Arab–Israeli war of October 1973. The years 1974 and 1975 were traumatic for the world's airlines. In the first place, the price of fuel escalated at an alarming rate. The average fuel price paid by IATA airlines doubled in the four months between September 1973 and January 1974 and continued to increase thereafter, but at a slower rate. By mid-1975 airlines were paying three times as much for fuel as they had been paying two years earlier. Second, the widespread inflation in most of the world's economies pushed up other areas of operating costs, especially those that were labour-intensive. Finally, the downturn in economic growth, particularly in Europe and the United States, resulted in declining or very low rates of increase in real disposable income which adversely affected the demand for both passenger and freight transport.

The effect of these trends was a large increase in unit costs in 1974 and 1975 (Fig. 1.1). Cost escalation, combined with a worldwide recession in traffic development, pushed many airlines into a struggle for financial survival. Airlines operating on the North Atlantic route and in Europe were particularly badly hit. In Britain, the Civil Aviation Authority concluded in its annual report that 'the financial year 1974–5 was the worst in living memory – both for the civil aviation and air travel industries'. But worse was to come!

(d)   In the *three years 1975–8* the world's airlines did reasonably well. The price of fuel and other costs declined in real terms, while demand was buoyant and load factors remained at around 55 per cent. This period of well-being was short-lived.

(e)   *From 1979 onwards* the international airlines entered a period of deepening crisis. They were in the anomalous position of enjoying the highest load factors for more than 20 years, while facing increasing losses. Dramatic increases in fuel prices in 1978 combined with stagnating demand and falling yields all helped to bring this about. The high load factors were themselves symptomatic of the crisis for they resulted from the industry's attempt to compensate for the downward pressure on fares and freight tariffs. They did not compensate enough. In 1980 the world's airlines as a whole made an operating loss before paying interest for the first time since 1961.

The curves in Figure 1.2 mask the real size of the losses incurred. After paying interest, IATA member airlines (together with Pan Am) collectively lost $350 million on their international scheduled services in 1979. In 1980 the net loss was $1,850 million; the following year it was $1,900 million, and in 1982 it was marginally lower, at $1,800 million. The loss was about $300 million in 1983 but profits of $1,200 million were projected for 1984 and of $1,500 million for 1985. Much of each year's loss was due to high interest payments on loans for aircraft or for bank overdrafts. IATA members' overall financial results including domestic and charter services were somewhat better than the above figures, which refer solely to international scheduled services. Nevertheless, overall IATA losses in the three years 1980–2 totalled over $4·5 billion. While all airlines were under pressure during this period, many continued to operate profitably, either by achieving higher than average load factors or by reducing their costs in real terms or both. This was the case with several of the newer Third World airlines that were able to benefit from their low labour costs and from the high growth rates in the markets in which they operated. Singapore Airlines (SA), for example, was very profitable throughout this period.

The declining fortunes of the international airlines from 1979 onwards coincided with the period of liberalization of international regulations, particularly on routes to and from the United States. A major issue of controversy within the airline industry is the degree to which, if any, deregulation can be blamed for the industry's financial plight. Resolution of this question one way or the other will have important repercussions on future regulatory developments and thereby on the industry itself.

In the meantime, an industry which has enjoyed uniquely rapid growth over the last 30 years finds that it has been unable to generate enough funds to finance its interest charges, let alone renew its assets. IATA estimated in 1984 that its 124 member airlines required to spend $50 billion (at 1981 prices) during the 1980s to renew and expand their aircraft fleets. To finance this, the IATA airlines would need to achieve an operating profit before interest of 6 per cent (IATA 1983).

They have not done this since 1969. The continuing marginal profitability of the industry, while needing to finance major capital investments, is the major problem facing the airlines during the 1980s.

1.6   The nature of the airline product

As far as passenger services are concerned, there are several contrasting aspects to the airline product. On the one hand, the air journey is seen not as an end in itself, but as part of a business trip or of a two-week summer holiday or of a weekend visit to watch a sports fixture. The air journey is a part of a variety of other products or services. A number of important considerations flow from this. The demand for passenger air services is a derived demand in that it is dependent on the demand for these other activities, business trips, two-week holidays, trips to sports fixtures and so on. This means that to forecast the demand for air services one must forecast the demand for all these other types of expenditure. It also means that there has been strong pressure on the airlines to expand vertically into other areas of the travel industry, such as hotels, travel agencies, car hire or tour organizers, in order to gain greater control over the total travel product. There is also a direct effect on airline marketing techniques in the sense that these are frequently oriented towards selling and promoting the total product, whether it be a business or a holiday trip or a weekend excursion, rather than selling a particular airline. In newspaper and television advertisements many airlines try to interest the reader or viewer in a particular destination or a particular type of trip, and only as an afterthought almost do they suggest the airline which might be used.

On the other hand, airlines have to face the realization that one airline seat is very much like another and that there is from the passenger's viewpoint little difference between one jet aircraft and another, if they achieve similar journey times. Equally, for the freight forwarder the major decision will be whether to ship by air or surface and having taken the decision to use air he may have difficulty in perceiving any difference between one airline and the next serving a particular route. Thus, while air journeys may be only one part of a variety of heterogeneous products or services with different market structures, the air service part of these various products is itself fairly homogeneous. One airline seat *is* very much like another and one freight hold *is* no different from the next. Even those differences which might exist have often been minimized through international or bilateral agreements aimed at standardizing the airline product and the quality of service provided. Even where such external constraints do not exist competitive and economic forces and the fact that they are flying similar or identical aircraft have meant that airlines often end up offering very similar products.

The consequences of the homogeneous nature of the airline product are twofold. First, in competitive markets, it pushes airlines into making costly efforts to try and differentiate their product from that of their competitors. They do this by being first to introduce new aircraft types, by increasing their frequency of service, by spending more on in-flight catering and by advertising. Moreover, much of the advertising is aimed at trying to convince passenger or freight agents that the product they offer can be differentiated from that of their competitors because of the friendliness of the hostesses or the ability of their chefs, or because of other claims which are dubious and difficult to assess.

Second, the homogeneous nature of the airline product makes the emergence of entirely new airlines or the incursion of new airlines on existing routes relatively easy. In other words, in the absence of regulations or other non-economic barriers to entry, airline markets would tend to be characterized by considerable competition between existing carriers and new entrants.

This dichotomy between the heterogeneity of the various products of which the air service is only a part and the homogeneity of the air services themselves is a constant constraint in airline planning, a constraint which often results in apparently contradictory decisions and actions by airline managements.

1.7 Passengers, freight or mail

It is generally assumed that airlines are primarily concerned with carrying passengers and that freight and mail traffic are relatively unimportant both in terms of output and of revenue. This is far from being the truth. In 1982 a quarter of the world's scheduled airline output was concerned with the carriage of freight and mail (Table 1.5). Passenger traffic accounted for the rest. On international routes, where distances are greater and air transport becomes more competitive, freight and mail's share rises to around one-third of output. Conversely, their share is much less on domestic air services.

These global figures hide considerable variations between airlines. A few large international airlines, such as Flying Tigers in the USA or Tradewinds in Britain, are exclusively or almost exclusively concerned with the carriage of freight. They are the exceptions. Most international airlines carry both freight and passengers. At one end of the scale are airlines such as Korean Airlines, JAL, Air France or KLM, for whom air freight represents between 40 and 50 per cent of their production in terms of tonne-kilometres. For Sabena and for the French airline UTA the freight figure in 1983 was 50 per cent, so that

Table 1.5   Distribution of traffic and revenue on scheduled services of ICAO airlines

| | Tonne-kilometres in 1983 | | | Revenue (1982), all services (%) |
	International (%)	Domestic (%)	All services (%)	
Pasengers	63·7	83·7	73·6	87·1
Freight	34·0	13·1	23·6	11·1
Mail	2·3	3·2	2·8	1·7
Total	100·0	100·0	100·0	100·0

freight and mail taken together came to over half their total output. At the other end there are many airlines, such as Eastern in the USA or the Polish airline LOT, where freight and mail together account for only 5–10 per cent of total tonne-kilometres generated.

It is significant that while freight accounts for about a quarter of total airline production it generates only about one-eighth of total operating revenue. This means that the average revenue per tonne-kilometre of freight and, incidentally, of mail, must be very much lower than the average revenue or yield generated by passenger tonne-kilometres. Despite this, freight revenues make an important contribution to many airlines' overall profitability.

Over the airline industry as a whole, the carriage of freight is a significant factor, both in terms of the amount of productive resources absorbed by it and in terms of its contribution to overall revenues. For an individual airline the split of its activities between passengers and freight clearly affects both its marketing policy and the structure of its revenues. The importance of mail revenue, however, is very limited and declining. In the early 1960s mail revenue was about 5 per cent of total revenue, whereas now it is below 2 per cent. Inevitably, much of the discussion which follows concentrates on the passenger aspects of both supply and demand. But this should not mask the significance of air freight for the international airline industry as a whole.

2

The Regulation of International Air Transport

Airline managers are not free agents. Their actions are circumscribed by a host of national and international regulations. These are both economic and non-economic in character and may well place severe limitations on airlines' freedom of action. An examination of the scope and impact of such regulations is crucial to an understanding of the economics of international air transport. For more than three decades the regulatory framework remained largely unchanged. It was three-sided, based on bilateral air services agreements, inter-airline agreements and the tariff agreements of IATA. The present chapter examines this traditional framework of economic regulation, which in many respects remains unchanged. Subsequently Chapter 3 considers the arguments for and against economic regulation and evaluates the so-called period of deregulation which began in the late 1970s with significant economic repercussions on the airline industry.

2.1 Non-economic regulations

The advanced level of aviation technology, the need to ensure passenger safety, despite the rapidity of technological innovation, and the international nature of much of the airline industry have all tended towards the introduction of more complex and more wide-ranging external controls and regulations than are found in most industries. These regulations are broadly of two kinds. First, there is a whole host of technical standards and regulations whose prime objective is to achieve very high levels of safety in airline operations. Such regulations cover every aspect of airline activity and, broadly speaking, they fall into one of the following categories:

(a) Regulations which deal with the airworthiness of the aircraft not only in terms of its design and production standards but also in terms of its performance under different operating conditions such as when there is an engine failure during take-off.
(b) Regulations covering the timing, nature and supervision of maintenance and overhaul work and the training and qualifications of the engineers who carry out such work.

(c)   Regulations governing the numbers and type of flight and cabin crew, their duties, training, licensing and their work-loads and schedules.

(d)   Detailed regulations covering both the way in which aircraft are operated, that is aspects such as flight preparation and in-flight procedures, and also the operation of the airlines themselves. In all countries, air transport operators must be licensed by the relevant civil aviation authority and must satisfy certain criteria and operating standards.

(e)   Finally, there is a complex profusion of regulations and recommended standards dealing with aviation infrastructure, such as airports, meteorological services, *en-route* navigational facilities and so on.

Many of the technical and safety requirements are general, that is not specific to a particular aircraft type, and are promulgated as regulations of the civil aviation directorates or the relevant ministries of each country. In the United States they are known as Federal Aviation Regulations, while in the United Kingdom such regulations appear in the Air Navigation Order (CAA, 1981). While regulations may vary in particular detail from one country to another they are generally based on a whole series of 'International Standards and Recommended Practices' produced by ICAO as seventeen annexes to the 'Convention on International Civil Aviation'. For instance Annex 8 deals with the 'Airworthiness of Aircraft' and Annex 1 with 'Personnel Licensing'. These are constantly revised. As a result there tends to be considerable uniformity in the technical regulations of most member states of ICAO. Operational and safety requirements specific to an aircraft type are contained in its flight manual. But the operational constraints and practices recommended in the flight manuals conform to the more general regulations mentioned above and are approved by the relevant national airworthiness authorities. Among other things, the flight manual will impose payload limitations on an aircraft at airports with high temperatures or inadequate runway length. In this and numerous other ways airworthiness and other technical regulations have direct economic repercussions.

These various technical standards and safety procedures undoubtedly constrain airline managers and, at the same time, impose cost penalties on airline operations. But such external controls are inevitable if high safety standards are to be maintained and significantly all airlines are equally affected by them. No major international airline can enjoy a competitive advantage by operating to lower technical standards since there are no 'flags of convenience' in air transport to enable airlines to circumvent national or international safety or manning regulations.

In addition to the various technical regulations and rules, international air transport is circumscribed by a multitude of national, bilateral and multilateral regulations and agreements whose objective is the economic and, sometimes, political regulation and control of the industry. Such economic controls, unlike the technical standards outlined above, do not affect all airlines equally and therein lies their importance.

2.2 The growth of economic regulation

When the Paris Convention, signed in 1919, accepted that states have sovereign rights in the air space above their territory, direct government intervention in air transport became inevitable. A country's airspace became one of its valuable natural resources. As a result, the free-trade *laissez-faire* approach towards air transport of the early years of aviation was gradually replaced by an incomplete pattern of bilateral agreements between countries having airlines and the countries to or through which those airlines wished to fly. But the restrictive character of 'bilateralism' was soon apparent. Even before the Second World War was over, fifty-two states met in Chicago in 1944 to consider some form of multinational agreement on three critical aspects of international transport: (a) the exchange of air traffic rights, or 'freedoms of the air'; (b) the control of fares and freight tariffs; (c) the control of frequencies and capacity.

From an economist's viewpoint these three aspects together effectively determine the nature of any industry for they regulate entry of firms into each market (through traffic rights), price and level of output.

At Chicago there were two conflicting approaches. The United States, whose civil aviation industry was going to emerge from the Second World War largely unscathed and much larger and better equipped than anyone else's, wanted no control of tariffs or capacity and the maximum exchange of traffic rights including fifth freedom rights. (See Appendix A for explanation of traffic rights). This 'open skies' policy was supported by states such as Netherlands or Sweden whose airlines would have to depend on fifth freedom traffic because their home base was so small. On the other hand, the United Kingdom and most European countries were more protectionist, understandably so since their civil airlines had been decimated in the war. They supported tight controls on tariffs and capacity and the limitation of fifth freedom rights. These two conflicting views could not be reconciled. No multilateral agreement was reached on the three key issues of traffic rights, tariff control and capacity.

The participants at Chicago did manage to agree on the mutual exchange of the first two freedoms, the right to overfly while on an agreed service and the right to land in each other's country. This was done through the 'International Air Services Transit Agreement' signed in December 1944 and to which many more states have subsequently adhered. But no agreement was reached on the mutual exchange of the commercial traffic rights. These are the third and fourth freedoms which allow for the mutual exchange of traffic rights between two countries enabling their respective airlines to carry passengers and freight between them. There is also the fifth freedom which is the right granted by country B to an airline(s) from country A to carry traffic between B and countries other than A (see Appendix A).

The most significant result of the Chicago Conference was the signing of the 'Convention on International Civil Aviation' known subsequently as the Chicago Convention. This provided the framework for the orderly and safe development of international air transport. It did this through its various articles and the Annexes, mentioned earlier, which deal with every aspect of the operation of aircraft and air services both in the air and on the ground. The Convention also set up ICAO, an inter-governmental agency which provided the forum for further discussion of key aviation issues and the basis for the worldwide co-ordination of technical and operational standards and practices. ICAO also provided crucial technical aid and assistance to many countries, helping them to establish airport and air navigation facilities and to organize other aspects of civil aviation infrastructure.

A further attempt at a multilateral agreement on traffic rights, pricing and capacity was made at the Geneva Conference of 1947, but this also failed. In time governments and airlines together found a way of circumventing the failures of Chicago and Geneva. The exchange of traffic rights became a matter for bilateral agreement between states; the control of capacities and frequencies became a matter for inter-airline agreements, and sometimes for bilateral state agreements; and tariffs came to be regulated by IATA. The international regulation of air transport has since been based on these three separate but interlinked elements.

2.3   Bilateral air services agreements

Over the years each country has signed a series of bilateral air services agreements (known as 'bilaterals') with other states aimed at regularizing the operation of air transport services between them. There are three distinct parts to such agreements.

First, there is the bilateral itself. This consists of a number of articles dealing with a variety of questions such as exemption from customs duties on imports of aircraft parts, airport charges, transfer abroad of airline funds and so on. The two key articles are those dealing with the regulation of tariffs and capacity. Most bilaterals specify that passenger fares and cargo tariffs should be agreed by the designated airlines, 'due regard being paid to all relevant factors, including cost of operation, reasonable profit, and the tariffs of other airlines' (Martin, 1984), but both governments must approve such fares and tariffs. In other words, ultimate control on tariffs rests with governments. On capacity, some bilaterals require very strict control and sharing of capacity by the airlines of the two countries while others have minimal control.

Underlying bilateral agreements is the concept of reciprocity, of an equal and fair exchange of rights between countries very different in size and with airlines of varied strengths. This is usually enshrined in an article containing the words 'There shall be fair and equal opportunity for the airlines of both Contracting Parties to operate the agreed service on the specified routes between their respective territories' (Martin, 1984).

The second part of the bilateral is the annex containing the 'schedule of routes'. It is here that the traffic rights granted to each of the two states are made explicit. The schedule specifies the routes to be operated by the 'designated' airline(s) of each state. Airlines are never mentioned by name. It is up to each state to designate its airline or airlines subsequently. The points (towns) to be served by each designated airline are listed or, less usually, a general right might be granted such as from 'points in the United Kingdom'. The routes or points granted to the designated airline of one state are not necessarily the reverse image of those granted to the airline of the other state signing the bilateral. If a town or country is not specifically listed in the route schedule, a designated airline cannot operate services to it unless the bilateral is amended.

The schedule will also indicate whether the designated airlines have been granted rights to pick up traffic in other countries or points lying between or beyond the two signatory states. These are the fifth freedom rights. But they cannot be used unless the third countries involved also agree. Thus the UK–Singapore bilateral grants the Singapore designated airline fifth freedom rights between Athens and London on its services between Singapore and London. The Athens–London rights cannot be exercised unless Greece agrees to this in its own air services agreement with Singapore.

The final part of the bilateral may consist of one or more 'memoranda of understanding' or 'exchange of notes'. These are agreements, often confidential, that amplify or subsequently modify particular aspects of the basic air services agreement.

Many bilateral agreements reflect protectionist attitudes. They insist on prior agreement on the capacity to be provided on the route and also specify that the agreed capacity should be shared equally by the designated carriers of the two states. Some go further and specify that services must be operated in 'pool' by the airline concerned. At the same time few if any fifth freedom rights are granted. Most bilaterals with Eastern European countries tend to be very protectionist and also make pooling mandatory.

A more liberal type of bilateral agreement is frequently referred to as the Bermuda type, after the agreement signed in 1946 between the United Kingdom and the United States in Bermuda (HMSO, 1946). This was significant because it represented a compromise between the extreme positions taken at the 1944 Chicago Conference, and because both the United States and the United Kingdom undertook to try to model all future agreements on the Bermuda pattern. As a result, Bermuda-type agreements have become widespread. They differ from the protectionist or 'predetermination' type of agreements described above in two respects. First, fifth freedom rights are more widely available, provided that the total capacity offered by the airline concerned on fifth freedom sectors is related to the end-to-end traffic potential of the routes. Second, there is no control of frequency or capacity on the routes between the two countries concerned. However, there is one safeguard on capacity: if one airline feels that its interests are being too adversely affected by the frequencies offered by the other, there may be an *ex post facto* review of capacity.

The other significant clause of the Bermuda Agreement was that on tariffs. While both governments maintained their ultimate right to approve or disapprove the tariffs proposed by the airlines, they agreed that where possible such tariffs should be arrived at using the procedures of IATA. For the United States this was a major compromise. It agreed to approve tariffs fixed by an association of producers, the international airlines, even though such price-fixing was illegal under United States domestic anti-trust legislation. In essence, IATA tariff decisions were exempted from the provisions of such legislation. Subsequently, the tariffs article of most bilaterals included wording to the effect that tariff agreement should 'where possible be reached by the use of the procedures of the International Air Transport Association for the working out of tariffs'. Even states such as Singapore, whose national airlines were not members of IATA agreed in their bilaterals to approve where possible IATA tariffs (HMSO, 1971). Thus approval for the IATA tariffs procedures was enshrined in the majority of bilateral agreements. It was this that gave the IATA tariffs machinery such force until deregulation set in from 1978 onwards.

Bermuda-type agreements became widespread, but the effect is not as liberal as their terms might suggest. This is because they do not preclude airline pooling agreements which effectively restrict capacity competition. Nor do they preclude subsequent capacity restrictions imposed arbitrarily by governments to prevent foreign carriers from introducing a new aircraft type or to limit increases in frequencies.

Today each international airline is faced by a complex web of bilateral air services agreements signed by its home state. Such agreements will specify which points can be served and what traffic rights have been granted. Some may impose capacity controls, others will not. Some may even insist that services must be operated in 'pool'. It is the bilateral which tells the airline where it can and cannot fly and how.

Following the United States government's decision in 1978 to liberalize regulations affecting international air services, many United States bilaterals were renegotiated. In the process several new concepts were introduced into the regulatory framework and these are discussed in the following chapter. But the majority of bilaterals around the world have remained largely unaffected by the wind of liberalization blowing through the United States and a few other countries.

2.4 Inter-airline pooling agreements

On the vast majority of international sectors there are two major carriers, the designated airlines of the two countries involved. There may, in addition, be one or more fifth freedom carriers, though in most cases the latter supply only a relatively small part of the total capacity available. As in many duopolistic situations, there is a strong incentive for formal or informal agreements between the duopolists to share out the market. Where one of the two airlines is much weaker or smaller, then pooling is a way of guaranteeing its share of capacity and revenue when faced with a much stronger or well established rival. When the two carriers are of similar strength then pooling is a way of pushing up load factors by removing frequency competition. It also helps to reduce costs and rationalize schedules. Without a pooling agreement competing airline departures tend to bunch at peak periods of demand. If all revenue is shared then airlines do not mind operating some flights at less attractive times. Pool partners can plan their schedules so as to offer a good range of departure times throughout the day. This benefits the passengers and stimulates demand.

Pooling agreements have been forbidden to United States airlines by that country's anti-trust legislation. But they are very widespread in Europe, where 75–80 per cent of intra-European tonne-kilometres are operated on pooled services, and to a lesser extent in certain other parts of the world. (See ECAC, 1982, for analysis of intra-European pools.) Agreements can cover a single route or sector or more normally, all the routes on which the two signatory airlines operate between their two countries. Thus the 1980 British Airways–SAS pool covered virtually all services between Scandinavia and the United Kingdom operated by the two airlines even though only one of the two airlines was operating on some sectors. In general, airline pools cover third and fourth freedom traffics. But fifth freedom traffic may be included on long-haul pools such as the long established one between British Airways and Qantas covering services between the United Kingdom and Australia. While most pool agreements involve two airlines three or four airline pools are not uncommon especially in South East Asia. Although it is often known airlines are operating in pool, the terms of any pooling agreement are closely guarded commercial secrets.

In some instances where the traffic is not considered to be adequate for two-airline operation, there may be a *revenue cost* pool. This means that one airline alone operates the service on behalf of all the airlines in the pool, but costs and revenues are shared between them on a prearranged basis. On the London–Genoa route, there is an operating agreement between Alitalia and British Caledonian under which only the latter airline operates services and revenue and costs are pooled and shared equally, with some minor exceptions. About one in ten pool agreements between West European airlines are of this type. A revenue/cost pool involving three airlines was launched in 1982 on the Hong Kong–Manila–Port Moresby route. The twice weekly service was operated by Air Niugini, but costs and revenues were shared between Air Niugini, Cathay Pacific and the Philippine airline PAL. In revenue/cost pools all partners have an incentive to market and sell the service even if they are not operating it themselves.

More commonly, airlines contract *revenue-sharing* pools in which all revenue on a route or sector is shared by the participating airlines in proportion to the capacity they offer on the route. In a two-airline pool, each airline will normally want a half share of the revenue and hence will expect to provide half the capacity. Imbalances in capacity may be permitted by mutual agreement if one carrier cannot or does not wish to increase its own capacity. If an airline does provide 50 per cent of the capacity but obtains only 47 per cent of the revenue compared to its pool partner's 53 per cent, then the pool partner will hand over 3 per cent of the revenue. The principle of sharing revenue in proportion to capacity is simple, its application becomes rather complex.

The first step in negotiating a pool agreement is to establish how much capacity each airline will be putting into the pool. On a single sector route capacity usually means the number of seats offered but if several sectors are involved then seat-kilometres may be used in order to take account of different sector lengths. On services with several intermediate stops *en route*, such as UK to Australia, it becomes quite a complex problem to identify each carrier's capacity input to the pool. On any one flight only a part of the aircraft's capacity will be on the pooled service. If there are fifth freedom rights at some of the *en route* stops, the difficulties of calculating pooled capacity are compounded.

The second key item is to agree the pool accounting unit. This is the notional fare or revenue which each airline earns from one passenger on each pool sector. The number of revenue passengers carried on each sector by an airline are multiplied by the pool accounting unit for that sector to produce the revenue which that airline has to put into the pool. It is this notional revenue which is pooled not the actual revenue collected. Such a system is less open to cheating because each airline need not know its pool partner's actual revenue, only the number of passengers carried, which is easy to verify. But it also provides an incentive to keep up fares and a strong disincentive to undercut the market. If an airline sells a ticket for $220 when the pool accounting unit is $200 it can keep $20 and only $200 is credited to the pool. Conversely, if it has sold a ticket for $150 then it still has to contribute $200 for that passenger to the pooled revenue. Though a notional figure used purely for accounting purposes, the pool accounting unit is normally related to the average revenue per passenger in the preceding period.

Some revenue-sharing pools allow for an unlimited transfer of funds from the one airline to the other, provided that the final adjusted revenue of each airline is proportional to its share of capacity offered. About one in five of the pools between European airlines are of this type (ECAC, 1982). Such agreements remove all competitive incentive. In practice most pools have a limit to the revenue that may be transferred from one airline to the other. This transfer limit may be expressed as a percentage of the total pooled revenue, or as a percentage of the donor's or the recipient's revenue. Alternatively the transfer limit may be a maximum sum of money. Many pool agreements will have fairly low transfer limits. Thus the 1982/3 pool agreement between Malaysian Airlines and British Airways had a transfer limit of only 1 per cent of total revenue. Yet an earlier British Airways pool with Pakistan's PIA had a transfer limit of 7 per cent of the donor's revenue.

The aim of the transfer limit is to ensure that an airline which is very successful in marketing and selling its service does not end up transferring large sums of money to its inefficient pool partner. In the pool negotiations the more successful airline will try to have a very low transfer limit while the weaker operator will want a high limit or no limit at all. Once transfer limits are imposed, particularly if they are very low, then competition begins to creep back, for the more passengers a pool carrier can carry the more revenue he can keep. But there is still no competition in terms of frequencies or capacities.

In some pool agreements, especially those covering complex route structures, pool partners have an 'entitlement' to a certain amount of revenue and only the balance is pooled. This entitlement (or 'retention') may be expressed as a fixed sum or usually as a percentage of the revenue. Usually the entitlement is around 10–30 per cent. Its aim is to cover certain elements of sales costs such as agents' commissions, sales office costs and so on. There seems little point in having an entitlement if there is a low transfer limit.

Revenue-sharing pool agreements are usually for a minimum period of 3–5 years, though capacities to be provided and the pool accounting unit are renegotiated annually or for each season. Pool accounts are settled monthly.

Pool agreements may also cover freight. Freight revenue pools are based on the same principles and have the same features as the passenger revenue pools described above. They may relate to all-freighter services or to freight carried on passenger aircraft or both. British Caledonian (BCal) and Nigerian Airways had a cargo as well as a passenger pool for many years on their London–Nigeria services. Originally there was no transfer limit and BCal found it was paying so much of its freight revenue to Nigerian Airways that it withdrew from the agreement. Later a new agreement included a transfer limit of 10 per cent of total revenue, which was still very high and disadvantageous to BCal. Eventually, in 1982, BCal pulled out of the pool since it found it was still paying too much to Nigerian Airways.

Among some airlines a pool agreement can become a comprehensive agreement covering much more than rationalizing of schedules and capacity control. One logical step is to develop a common tariffs policy for the pooled routes and for the IATA tariff conferences. Other aspects of the agreement may involve joint sales promotion and advertising, use of each other's reservation systems, sharing of ground handling facilities at airports and so on.

The effect of all pooling agreements, once entered into, is to reduce the freedom of action of the airlines involved and to blunt any competitive tendencies. Collectively the effect of the bilateral air services agreements and of inter-airline agreements is to delimit the routes on which airlines can operate and to determine the capacity shares of the two (or occasionally three) designated carriers in these markets. This is particularly so in the European area, though revenue pool agreements are also widespread in South East Asia and elsewhere but not on routes involving United States carriers.

2.5 Inter-airline royalty agreements

When airlines have wanted to pick up fifth freedom traffic from points where they did not have fifth freedom rights under the existing bilaterals, they have sometimes been able to 'buy' such rights by making royalty payments to the airline of the country concerned. It was pointed out earlier that SIA has fifth freedom rights between Athens and London under the terms of the UK–Singapore bilateral, but could not use these rights unless they were also granted in Singapore's bilateral with Greece. This was not the case, so when in 1977 SIA operated from Singapore to London via Athens it agreed to pay Olympic Airways a royalty for any local traffic picked up between Athens and London. In other words, SIA bought the Athens–London fifth freedom rights from the Greek government by paying the Greek airline for them. The royalty in this case was expressed as 20 per cent of the revenue generated from fifth freedom traffic. Despite the royalty, SIA began to carry so much traffic between Athens and London that Olympic cancelled the royalty agreement a year later in 1978.

Royalty agreements for fifth freedom traffic are fairly common. But in some cases, airlines have been forced into making royalty agreements to cover the carriage of 'sixth' freedom traffic. The concept of sixth freedom has rarely appeared in any bilateral agreement, though the expression has been widely used for many years. It involves the carriage of traffic between two points, between which an airline does not have fifth freedom rights, by the use of two sets of third and fourth freedom rights. Malaysian Airlines (MAS) can carry traffic between London and Kuala Lumpur using their UK third and fourth freedom traffic rights. MAS can carry those passengers on to Australia using the third and fourth freedom rights, granted under the Australia–Malaysia bilateral. Traditionally, attempts have been made to limit such through traffic between London and Australia by the imposition of various controls such as the need to make stop-overs in Kuala Lumpur. KLM in Europe and SIA, Thai International and MAS in South East Asia have been so successful in generating sixth freedom traffic that the various regulatory controls, such as the necessity for stop-overs *en route*, have been slowly eroded.

Sixth freedom traffic carried by MAS or Thai between London and Australia respresents a loss of traffic for the third and fourth freedom carriers on the route, namely British Airways and Qantas. These carriers have therefore stepped in from time to time to exact royalty payments for sixth freedom traffic. British Airways had a royalty agreement with MAS until about 1980 under which MAS paid a royalty of nearly £50 for each passenger it carried between Australia and London. More recently, in 1983–4 Thai International had an agreement with British Airways whereby it was allowed to carry a certain limited number of sixth freedom passengers between London and Australia but had to pay a royalty of almost $120 for each passenger above this permitted number. The royalty was too high and Thai started to pull out of the sixth freedom market between the UK and Australia.

While royalty agreements covering sixth and more especially fifth freedom traffic have been fairly common for many years, a more recent phenomenon is the payment of royalties for third and fourth freedom traffic. This may occur when one of the two designated carriers on a route decides not to operate. It then argues that the other country's designated carrier will carry all the traffic including that which would have been carried by the airline which is not operating. The non-operating airline wants to be compensated for giving up its traffic share and may be able to push the other carrier into a royalty agreement. For many years, SIA was forced to pay royalties to Korean Airlines (KAL) for traffic carried between Singapore and Seoul because KAL was not operating on the route. This was done even though SIA was enjoying rights granted under the terms of a bilateral air services agreement. When KAL began flying the Seoul–Singapore route in 1983 the royalties were discontinued. In its turn KAL was paying royalties to Kuwait Airways and Saudia on its services from Seoul to the Middle East as long as these airlines were not using their reciprocal third and fourth freedom rights into Seoul.

Royalty payments, sometimes referred to as revenue compensation, are becoming more widespread. The royalty may be expressed as a percentage of the revenue generated, as in the case of the SIA–Olympic agreement previously mentioned, or it may be a fixed amount per passenger uplifted as in the British Airways–MAS agreements. Occasionally it may be a fixed annual sum not related to the amount of traffic carried. In some cases royalty payments may enable airlines to buy traffic rights that they do not have under the terms of existing bilateral agreements. In this way, they may improve the viability of certain routes. But if the airlines are forced to pay royalties for third and fourth freedom traffic, whose rights they already have under the bilaterals, then the result is merely to push up costs.

2.6   The role of IATA

IATA was founded in Havana in 1945, as a successor to the prewar association which had been largely European. Its primary purpose was to represent the interests of airlines and to act as a counter-weight to ICAO, which was an inter-governmental agency primarily concerned with government interests in aviation. Through its various committees and subcommittees, which bring together airline experts for a few days each year, IATA has been able to coordinate and standardize many aspects of airline operations. Thus the Financial Committee has harmonized methods of rendering, verifying and settling accounts between airlines, while the Traffic Committee has standardized aircraft containers and other unit load devices as well as many other aspects of passenger or cargo handling. IATA also represents the airlines in negotiations with airport authorities, governments or ICAO on matters as diverse as airport charges or anti-hijacking measures.

One of IATA's most important functions is to operate the clearing house for inter-airline debts arising from interline traffic, that is the carriage by one airline of passengers (or freight) holding tickets issued by other airlines. The sums involved are enormous. In 1982 the ninety-five IATA and fifteen non-IATA airlines using the clearing house submitted for clearance claims amounting to $13.1 billion. The clearing house settles inter-airline accounts in both dollars and sterling by off-setting members' counter claims against each other. In 1982 87 per cent of all claims could be off-set without the need for any cash transaction. The clearing house speeds up and simplifies the process of clearing inter-airline debts. Airlines that do not use the clearing house must negotiate individually with each airline whose ticket stubs they might hold. This is slow and laborious and may involve long delays before debts are cleared.

Undoubtedly IATA's most important function has been to set airline fares and cargo rates. Up to 1979 the process for establishing fares was rather rigid (IATA, 1974). It involved the so-called 'traffic conferences'; one covering North and South America, the second covering Europe, the Middle East and Africa, and the third the Pacific region and Australasia. Airlines operating in or through these areas belonged to the relevant conference. The conferences, meeting in secret and usually about 4–6 months in advance, established the tariff structure which would be operative for a specified period, usually of one year. The conferences also agreed on fares between the conference regions. About 200,000 separate passenger fares and over 100,000 cargo rates were negotiated together with complex conditions of service associated with each fare. The conditions would cover such aspects as seat pitch, number of meals to be served, charges for headphones and so on. Once each conference had agreed on its own tariffs then the three conferences came together in joint session for the tariffs proposed to be voted on. They had to be agreed unanimously. In other words, any airline, no matter how small, could veto the proposed tariffs and force further renegotiation. The tariffs process was lengthy and time-consuming.

From the airlines' point of view the traffic conference system had clear advantages: it produced a coherent and worldwide structure of inter-related passenger fares and cargo rates, together with tariff-related rules and regulations. The traffic conferences were also instrumental in developing standard documents and contracts of air carriage – tickets, waybills, baggage checks etc.

The IATA tariffs were accepted worldwide because in so many bilateral air services agreements governments had explicitly agreed that they would approve fares negotiated through the IATA process. This was the case even with some governments whose airlines were not IATA members. To give added force to its tariff agreements, IATA had compliance inspectors checking that member airlines were not illegally discounting on the IATA tariffs. If caught selling tickets or cargo space at discounted rates, the IATA airlines faced heavy financial penalties. Since no IATA airlines were allowed to deviate from the IATA tariffs, no price competition was possible.

There can be little doubt that IATA was effectively a suppliers' cartel, whose object was to maximize its members' profits by mutually fixing the prices at which they sold their services. But it was often argued that three features of the IATA traffic conference system safeguarded the interests of the public and the consumers and prevented the airlines' cartel from abusing its power. These were: first, a *de facto* ban on any kind of capacity regulation; second, the 'unanimity rule' mentioned above; and third, the fact that the IATA fare agreements had to be approved by the respective governments.

In theory, since IATA was not in a position to restrict capacity or control entry, it would be difficult for the airlines to extract monopoly profits by fixing both fares and output at the appropriate levels. In practice, as has been noted above, government and airline agreements outside IATA effectively upset the competitive element in the rate-making machinery. The entry of a new airline into a route is impossible unless its national government is willing and able to negotiate the necessary traffic rights. On many routes capacity is controlled either through the bilaterals or through airline agreements such as revenue pools. Often on routes such as London to Paris the fares were so disproportionately high that one had to suspect that monopoly profits were being extracted.

It was also argued that the unanimity rule favoured those airlines which were pressing for lower fares, since airlines wishing to maintain a higher fare structure would prefer some agreement to none, fearing that in the absence of any agreement free competition would push fares to even lower levels. At the same time it was clear that the unanimity rule did not work simply as a strong downward pressure on fares: first, because airlines knew that if no agreement was reached the respective governments would step in and fix the fares themselves; secondly, because the unanimity rule also resulted in higher fares in certain areas as a *quid pro quo* to the airlines in those areas for their agreement to lower fares elsewhere; thirdly, because several low-fare proposals (such as the advance purchase fares on the North Atlantic route) were held up for a number of years before unanimous agreement could be reached. The unanimity rule was most effective in preventing an upward movement of fares. It was less effective in ensuring that fares fell to levels proposed by the more efficient airlines.

All governments concerned must approve the tariff agreements made through IATA. Many governments did in fact intervene, notably the United States government through the CAB, which consistently tried to reduce the pace of fare increases. Other governments also intervened from time to time, but usually on relatively minor points affecting particular tariffs to their own countries. On the whole, the majority of governments have insufficient information on which to base valid arguments to influence their own airlines and the IATA machinery. Consequently, there has been a strong tendency among governments to approve the IATA fares more or less automatically. This is certainly what IATA preferred them to do, and it consistently pressed for a minimum of government interference.

Overall the apparent safeguards against IATA working as a producers' cartel were not very effective. But if IATA was a cartel it was failing to achieve the prime objective of any cartel, namely high profits for its members. Our earlier analysis has shown an industry characterized by poor financial results (see Sec. 1.5). Nevertheless, the travelling public and consumer groups remained unconvinced of the benefits of the IATA tariff machinery. During the 1970s pressure began to build up on governments in Europe and North America to allow greater pricing freedom.

At the same time the IATA tariffs procedures began to prove too rigid and inflexible to deal with two new developments. The first of these, which had started more than a decade earlier, was the growth of non-scheduled or charter air services. Attempts by IATA and many governments to stem their growth had failed. As a result, charter airlines were making serious inroads into scheduled markets in Europe and on the North Atlantic route. The second development was the emergence of new dynamic airlines belonging to newly independent states, especially in South East Asia. Airlines such as Thai International, SIA and KAL began to make an impact on regional and long-haul markets. As non-IATA carriers they captured market share either by offering much higher levels of in-flight service than was permitted under IATA's 'conditions of service' or, less frequently, through greater flexibility in their tariffs. To counter competition both from charters and from new non-IATA carriers the IATA airlines needed much greater pricing freedom than could be obtained within the cumbersome traffic conferences.

Faced with these external competitive pressures, IATA airlines found it increasingly difficult to achieve unanimity on the tariffs policies to be adopted at the traffic conferences. Several conferences broke up without agreement on tariffs in particular markets. Governments stepped in to fix the fares where the airlines could not agree. At the same time, more and more IATA airlines began to offer illegally discounted fares in very competitive markets or to flout the strict controls on in-flight service standards. Several governments, particularly that of the United States, began to push for a system which allowed consumers to benefit from greater pricing freedom. (Section 3.8 examines US moves against IATA.) Openly disregarded by its own members and under pressure from a number of governments, IATA's tariff machinery began to disintegrate.

In 1975 IATA began a review of its traffic conference system and other aspects of its activities. At the 1978 Annual General Meeting airlines approved a number of key changes in the conditions of membership and in tariff co-ordination, which was the new name for tariff setting. The changes were implemented in 1979. The most significant are:

(a)   Airlines can now join IATA as a trade association without participating in the passenger or cargo tariff co-ordinating conferences. In 1984 there were about 20 member airlines that did not take part in tariff co-ordination. Trade association members are not obliged to implement the IATA tariffs.

(b)   The primary interests of third and fourth freedom carriers in setting tariffs are now recognized by the fact that it has become possible within the traffic co-ordinating conference to reach limited agreements (covering travel between two countries) or sub-area agreements (covering a small geographical area) without the involvement of the full conference area. (As previously, the world is divided into three main conference areas.) In other words, the unanimity rule has been abandoned.

(c)   Third and fourth freedom carriers may introduce innovative fares between their two countries, without prior conference approval but subject to the agreement of the governments concerned.

(d)   Airlines participating in tariff co-ordinating have been encouraged to dispense with regulations on conditions of service relating to meals, bar service, free gifts, entertainment, and so on. This has been done in many sub-areas by the airlines concerned and with government approval. As a result, competition in the quality of in-flight service has become widespread.

(e)   The secretive and confidential traffic conferences of earlier days have been replaced by the much more open and public co-ordinating conferences. Observers from governments and international organizations may attend and third parties may make written or oral presentations to the conferences.

Under external pressure to reduce tariff controls, IATA has also had to adopt more flexible tariff structures. (See Ch. 9 on pricing.) The restructuring of IATA and the introduction of more flexible and open tariff-setting procedures have enabled IATA to survive despite the considerable pressures towards deregulation. IATA tariffs remain the government-approved tariffs for the majority of international air routes, even on routes where discounting is prevalent.

2.7 Limited regulation of non-scheduled air services

Unlike scheduled rights, non-scheduled traffic rights have not been regulated by bilateral air services agreements. At the time of the 1944 Chicago Convention non-scheduled air services were not expected to be of any significance, and a more liberal attitude was therefore adopted. Whereas under Article 6 of the convention scheduled air services specifically required 'special permission or other authorisation' from the destination countries, Article 5 left authorization for non-scheduled services at the discretion of individual states (ICAO, 1980).

In practice most countries have insisted on giving prior authorization to incoming non-scheduled flights, but attitudes towards authorization vary significantly. Some countries, such as India, have been restrictionist in their approach and have refused to authorize charter flights unless they are operated by their own national carrier or unless it can be shown that no scheduled traffic will be diverted. Others may insist, before authorizing an incoming charter, that one of their own airlines should be allowed to tender for the charter contract. In contrast, many other countries, particularly tourist destinations such as Spain, Morocco or Tunisia, have followed a more liberal 'open skies' policy and have readily authorized non-scheduled services.

In 1956, the member states of the European Civil Aviation Conference agreed to mutually waive the requirement for any prior authorization from the destination country for a wide range of non-scheduled flights (HMSO, 1956). This agreement has greatly facilitated the development of charter services, particularly inclusive tour charters, within Europe.

Some countries, notably the United States through the CAB, and the United Kingdom through the Air Transport Licensing Board and later the CAA, brought non-scheduled operations within some form of national regulatory control. Such regulation was aimed at clearly delineating the area and scope of non-scheduled operations so as to protect scheduled operations, while giving non-scheduled operators considerable freedom of action within their defined area (CAB, 1969).

British airlines have had to obtain an 'air transport licence' from the CAA for all commercial operations. An airline wishing to operate a charter inclusive tour for a particular tour operator applies for a Class 3 licence. The application may be for a large number of frequent flights to one or more destinations over a stated period of time. Today Class 3 licence applications are granted more or less automatically.

Initially IATA tried to regulate the non-scheduled activities of its own members by trying to fix minimum charter rates as a function of the scheduled fare and by other rules governing who could have access to charter flights. In the 1960s many governments, under pressure from IATA and to protect their own scheduled airlines, imposed arbitrary and often restrictive regulations on charter services. But as the tide of public opinion in many Western countries swung strongly in favour of cheap charter flights governments were forced gradually to dismantle the various controls on charters. This process was given added impetus by the moves in the United States to deregulate both domestic and international air transport. In particular, the United States has tried to remove all price and other controls on charters while at the same time making non-scheduled traffic rights explicit within bilateral air services agreements.

The non-scheduled airlines have been relatively free of international regulation but subject to national controls on licensing, tariffs to be charged and so on. In many countries these national controls have also withered away. In the two largest markets for passenger charters, in the Europe–Mediterranean area and more recently on the North Atlantic route, charter operators have been free for some time of both international and national controls on route access, capacity or fares. But uncertainty remains. Since charter rights are only explicitly included in a very few United States bilaterals charter services they are at the mercy of the destination countries which may give or refuse landing authorization. Many countries, particularly in the Middle East and other parts of the Third World, still refuse to authorize incoming charters.

2.8   Economic consequences of international regulation

2.8.1   OPERATIONAL CONSTRAINTS IMPOSED ON SCHEDULED AIRLINES

The three-pronged structure of international regulation based on the bilaterals, the inter-airline agreements and IATA has constrained the freedom of action of individual scheduled airlines in a number of ways.

First, their markets are often restricted. Airlines cannot enter any market at will, but are dependent on government action and support: firstly in making bilateral agreements to open up air routes and obtain the necessary traffic rights; and secondly, in negotiating the points which should be served on these routes. This is not always straightforward, particularly if an existing bilateral has to be renegotiated. The other country may refuse to negotiate or may want to exact a high price for accepting changes to routes or traffic rights granted under the existing bilateral. SIA has long wanted to operate from Singapore to Kota Kinabalu in Eastern Malaysia (Sabah) but the Malaysia– Singapore bilateral only grants traffic rights to the Malaysian designated carrier (MAS). The Malaysians have not been prepared to renegotiate on this so SIA is excluded from a potentially lucrative route. To obtain fifth freedom rights some airlines have had to pay royalties to other carriers. Some have even had to pay royalties to exercise third and fourth freedom rights granted to them under air services agreements.

Secondly, the level of output or production of each airline is not entirely at its own discretion. Its production may be limited through bilateral agreements on capacity control or on equal sharing of capacity, or through inter-airline agreements on revenue sharing and capacity. An airline wishing to increase its capacity and output on routes where there is some form of bilateral or inter-airline capacity control may well find that the other airline in the duopoly may be unable or unwilling to increase its own capacity, and therefore may veto the expansion plans. In 1982 MAS replaced their DC-10 aircraft on their services between Kuala Lumpur and London by larger Boeing 747 aircraft which they had bought from British Airways. The British government, under pressure from British Airways and in accordance with the capacity clauses in the UK–Malaysia bilateral, objected to this increase in capacity. As a result MAS have only been able to sell as many seats on their Boeing 747 aircraft as would be equivalent to the capacity of a DC-10. In practice this was modified to a maximum of 310 passengers per flight into or out of London, even though the Boeing's capacity is 392 seats. This limit continued through 1984. Capacity limitations are widespread but have not existed in all markets. On many routes to or from the United States there was little effective capacity control even before deregulation.

Finally, airlines' pricing freedom is also limited. This is partly because most tariffs have traditionally been set by the IATA tariffs conferences in which the influence of any individual airline was limited and partly because governments must ultimately approve all tariffs. Thus, even on routes where IATA tariffs do not apply or where

IATA now allows innovatory tariffs by the third and fourth freedom carriers concerned, the government at either end of the route may prevent a new fare being introduced. When in 1980, British Caledonian tried to introduce its very low 'Miniprix' fares on routes between London and Paris or Amsterdam its proposal was torpedoed by the French government. Even non-IATA airlines are required by governments to apply IATA tariffs on most of their international routes. Pricing freedom has only existed in markets where at times there has been widespread discounting of IATA tariffs or in markets where with the connivance of governments the IATA tariffs process has been abandoned. This has been the case on most of the North Atlantic and trans-Pacific routes to and from the United States since about 1978. With these major exceptions airline managers have not been free to choose and set their own tariffs at will. Tariffs have had to be approved by IATA or by the two governments concerned. In practice such approvals have depended on the agreement of the other airline(s) on the route in question. Pricing freedom was further restricted if airlines were in revenue pools with the other carriers.

The cumulative effect of all the above constraints has been that scheduled airline managers have been constrained in their ability to compete with other carriers, especially if their own airlines were IATA members. With some exceptions, there has been little scope for pricing competition. Until 1979 IATA airlines could not even compete in terms of in-flight services for their nature and quality were strictly controlled on a route by route basis. On many routes there was little scope for competition in terms of frequencies either because of capacity limitation clauses in the bilateral or because of inter-airline revenue pools. The latter also precluded competition through aggressive scheduling of departures.

2.8.2   TARIFFS NOT RELATED TO LOWEST COSTS

In markets where there is price competition, tariffs are more likely to be pushed down to the levels at which the more efficient carriers can operate profitably. Tariffs arrived at through inter-airline negotiations must inevitably be a compromise between the pricing policies of the high cost and those of the low cost airlines. This is what has happened within IATA. As a result the IATA tariffs appear to have been based less on the costs of the more efficient carriers and more on the concept of charging what the traffic will bear and on the projected costs of the higher cost operators.

Prior to 1979, the unanimity rule at IATA tariff conferences resulted in horse trading between participants in order to achieve unanimity among airlines with very diverse cost levels. This resulted in very different fares and cargo rates per kilometre for routes with similar cost characteristics. This was so even after 1979 when the unanimity rule was effectively abandoned. On many routes factors such as surface competition, or competition from charters, may have a more profound effect on tariffs than traffic density, sector length or other cost factors. (The relationship of tariffs to costs is examined in Ch. 9.)

The very high variation in IATA fare rates on routes which are outwardly similar suggests that there is considerable cross-subsidization between routes, and even between different classes of passengers on the same route. Cross-subsidization raises questions of welfare distribution which are too complex to go into here. But one significant effect on consumer interests in general is that it holds back the development of air services in growth markets because they may be burdened with unusually high fares.

The absence of effective price competition in most airline markets has had two adverse effects. It has meant higher tariffs for passengers and freight shippers than would otherwise have been the case. But, for many airlines, it has also meant higher costs than would have been the case in a more competitive environment because it has reduced the incentive to cut costs. This has been particularly the case among higher cost operators. Higher tariffs have also encouraged the growth of low fare charters.

2.8.3 MONOPOLY PROFITS EARNED?

On routes where an effective duopoly exists and where the duopolists are operating in a revenue-sharing pool, or where capacity is controlled and equally shared on the basis of the air services agreement, the carriers involved have been in a position to extract monopoly profits. They have done this by effectively controlling the provision of capacity and by controlling fare levels through the IATA traffic conference or inter-airline agreements. In practice, this has meant unusually high fare levels and high load factors. A particularly good example is the London–Paris route. This route has been operated in a revenue pool by British Airways and Air France for many years, though British Caledonian also carried about 12 per cent of the total traffic. The route has a cost disadvantage because it is relatively short, only 215 statute miles. The traffic, however, has been the busiest in Europe with 2.1 million passengers in 1983 and both Air France and British Airways have operated high frequencies with large aircraft. Therefore costs per passenger should be relatively low, particularly when compared with other European routes of similar stage length. At the same time the route generates a high proportion of business traffic and most of this travels at the full economy or more recently club class fare. So there is relatively less fare dilution than on more tourist oriented routes. Load factors on the route have also tended to be well above average. Lower costs, high yields and above average load factors should have resulted in fare levels 10–20 per cent below the European average. Yet the London–Paris fare, when expressed as a fare per kilometre, has always been one of the highest in Europe. This suggests that high profits have been earned. On some European routes such as London–Paris, on several routes in the Middle East and one or two routes in South East Asia the regulatory system has failed to protect the public from monopoly pricing.

3
Deregulation and its Impact on the Industry

3.1 The case for and against regulation

Traditionally, economists have justified the regulation of both international and domestic air services on one or more of three grounds. In the United States the Civil Aeronautics Act of 1938 was introduced to regulate and control competition between US domestic carriers because the unregulated competition which had prevailed up to then had led to chaotic economic conditions, little security for investors and low safety margins. For many years the American view was that while air transport is not a natural monopoly, regulation is required because 'unregulated competitive market forces may have adverse consequences for the public at large' (Richmond 1971). The same philosophy has been widely adopted to justify the regulation of international air transport as well. It has been argued that, whereas there are strong oligopolistic tendencies in air transport, absence of any regulation would inevitably lead to wasteful competition. This is because the industry has a non-differentiated product and a relative ease of entry. At the same time economies of scale are not very marked. New entrants into a particular market would try to establish themselves by undercutting existing fares, and a price war would result with adverse consequences for all participants (Wheatcroft, 1964).

The second economic argument favouring regulation has been based on the concept that air transport is a public utility, or at least a quasi-public utility. It has been argued that the external benefits arising from civil aviation are such that the industry needs to be regulated in order to ensure that these benefits are not jeopardized. These benefits are assumed to be not only economic but also strategic, social and political. The public utility nature of air transport has, rightly or wrongly, been considered so important that most countries have concentrated on developing one major scheduled operator, usually with direct government participation. The same carrier often operates domestic services and acts as the designated foreign carrier. These countries have tried to avoid a conflict between private commercial needs and 'national interests' by having a monopolistic structure in air transport with a strong direct or indirect government influence on the national airline. It was and still is a natural extension of this point of view to believe that free and unregulated competition on international air routes would endanger national interests because it might adversely affect that national airline.

The third argument in support of the regulation of international air transport is linked to the rapid development of non-scheduled air traffic. The Committee of Inquiry which examined British air transport and reported in May 1969, came out strongly in favour of protecting scheduled services on most routes because they had 'public service' features which imposed certain costly obligations upon them and which made them particularly vulnerable to price competition (HMSO, 1969). Once an airline is committed to operate a series of scheduled services the marginal cost of any empty seats is virtually nil, since services cannot be withdrawn at short notice. A fare war would thus result in disastrously low fares and a marked financial instability among scheduled airlines.

The committee also argued that in the long run scheduled operations cannot compete with charter operations because the former satisfy a 'collective' demand which necessitates the ready availability of spare seats on particular routes at short notice. In order to satisfy that demand scheduled operators must inevitably operate at lower load factors than charter airlines. Ready availability is after all one aspect of 'public service'. Lower load factors in turn mean higher passenger-kilometre costs than those achieved by non-scheduled operations. Where states wish to have scheduled services providing regular and readily available capacity with the minimum of special conditions for the public at large, some form of protection against the encroachment of charter operators is required. This is particularly so where the scheduled traffic is relatively thin, for even a small loss of traffic might jeopardize the continuation of scheduled operations. This argument was broadened by IATA and others. They argued that even greater price competition between scheduled carriers themselves would lead to a collapse of profit margins. This in turn would lead to the abandonment of thin routes and reduction of frequencies on others as airlines tried to compensate for lower fares by pushing up load factors. As a result the travelling public would be worse off.

During the 1960s economists in the United States and elsewhere began to question the benefits of regulation and argued the advantages of freer competition in air transport (e.g. Straszheim, 1969). Existing international regulations limited pricing freedom and product differentiation, restricted capacity growth and excluded new entrants. If these regulations were relaxed a more competitive environment would provide considerable benefits to the consumer in lower fares, innovatory pricing and greater product differentiation. Lower tariffs would push airlines to re-examine their costs and would force them to improve their efficiency and productivity. Lower costs would facilitate further reductions in tariffs. Some inefficient airlines might be forced out of particular markets. But it was argued that the economics of the airline industry did not justify the fear that freer competition would lead to economic instability. The capacity of most large international airlines to fight tariff wars on a limited number of routes at a time, combined with a strong sense of self-preservation, would prevent the established carriers from going too far in a price war because of the dangers of getting 'locked in'. In other words, they would avoid successive fare reductions which would ultimately leave each airline with much the same share of the market but with very low and possibly unprofitable fare levels. Fear of new entrants would almost certainly push down fares to a level where only normal profits were being secured. Excess profits would attract new entrants. By the same token cross-subsidization, which was prevalent, would be largely eliminated, since it implied excess profits on particular routes. Where airlines did enter new markets or routes they were likely to be innovative in their pricing and in their products. Existing carriers, hitherto protected by the regulatory environment, would be shaken out of their complacency. This could only be good for consumers.

Similar arguments were put forward regarding the benefits which would arise from the deregulation of domestic air services in the United States (Eads 1975). The CAB had imposed rigid regulatory controls on market entry, on pricing and on other aspects of airline operations. No new trunk airline had been authorized since the Board was set up in 1938. The number of airlines on any single route was strictly controlled. Airlines were not even free to withdraw from certain routes as a matter of commercial judgement if they were the only carrier. The CAB also approved all tariffs. It generally rejected discount fares which were considered discriminatory. Since it was difficult for airlines to obtain new route authorizations they tried to expand through take-overs or mergers, but even these were subject to CAB approval. Airlines were in a straitjacket. Only those operating entirely within one state, such as California, were free of CAB controls. The arguments for deregulation could readily be applied to US domestic air transport and they found favour with the American public.

3.2 The regulatory system under pressure after 1972

During the early 1970s the European scheduled flag carriers, many of them wholly or partly owned by their respective governments, began to complain of the inroads which cheap and unregulated charter services were making into their potential traffic and into their profits and campaigned for stricter controls. But the public, various consumer groups and the tourist industry were pressing for some deregulation of the scheduled sector and for greater freedom for non-scheduled operators, so that all travellers could readily enjoy the cheaper fares which the latter made possible. As the economic fortunes of both scheduled and non-scheduled carriers worsened, especially after the fuel crisis of 1973, the pressures on the regulatory system increased. One manifestation of these pressures was the growing difficulty, previously mentioned, of reaching unanimity at the IATA traffic conferences. Another was the spread of the illegal discounting of scheduled tariffs in many markets. To mitigate the effects of the deteriorating economic fortunes of the industry, governments and airlines took a series of unconnected decisions which collectively and often imperceptably began to change the regulatory framework. These various decisions were often contradictory but one can discern in the various regulatory developments which took place between 1973 and 1977 certain trends.

First, the distinction between scheduled and non-scheduled services became increasingly blurred as controls on the latter were relaxed and new concepts introduced. In the United Kingdom, the CAA finally abolished minimum price control of summer charter inclusive tours in November 1972. In April 1973, Advanced Booking Charters (ABCs) were introduced on the North Atlantic route. The aim was to do away with the previous concept of 'affinity' which had limited access to trans-Atlantic charters to members of a club whose purpose was not solely to provide cheap travel. To prevent or reduce diversion from scheduled services the use of ABCs was limited to passengers booking at least three months in advance. ABCs gradually replaced affinity and other forms of group charters on the North Atlantic route. The advanced booking period was progressively reduced. The ABC concept was also introduced on a few other long-haul routes. In the meantime, the European scheduled airlines had also developed the concept of part-charters. Under part-charter rules scheduled carriers could sell off blocks of seats to travel agents or tour operators who then packaged the seats into inclusive tour holidays. Part-charters were first introduced between Britain and Spain in 1971 but within a few years they were available on many of the major tourist routes in Western Europe. In the United Kingdom, the CAA initially placed a limit (50 per cent of an aircraft's seating capacity or seventy seats, whichever is greater) on the number of seats which could be sold in this way. Part-charters on scheduled services were introduced not merely as a competitive reaction to charters but also because they offered a number of economic advantages to the scheduled carriers. By mixing normal traffic and charter traffic, the scheduled carriers are able to improve load factors by filling up seats which would otherwise be empty. In this way, airlines can sustain scheduled services on routes where the scheduled traffic would otherwise be insufficient to maintain adequate frequencies and load factors.

The relaxation of controls on charter services, the emergence of ABCs on many long-haul routes and of part-charters in Europe were clearly blurring the operational distinctions between scheduled and charter services.

The second development during this period was a trend towards introducing greater international regulation of non-scheduled services both by bringing them within bilateral agreements and by controlling charter fares. It was becoming increasingly clear that one could not continue to regulate the scheduled sector of the industry while leaving the fastest growing sector, that of the charters, outside the framework of regulations. The fact that scheduled and non-scheduled services were becoming increasingly difficult to differentiate reinforced the argument for regulation on an industry-wide basis. Attention was focused on a bilateral approach to non-scheduled regulation. As early as March 1972, Secor Browne, then Chairman of the CAB, stated that a multi-lateral approach to charter regulation was 'simply not feasible' and that bilateral treaties were the only way to control charters. Subsequently, a number of bilateral air service agreements which were renegotiated also included separate treaties covering non-scheduled services; for example, the 'Nonscheduled Services' Agreement between Canada and the United States, in May 1974 (Canada Treaty Series 1974, No. 16). Meanwhile, the introduction of new charter concepts, such as ABCs, had necessitated bilateral negotiations between governments. These resulted in a large number of bilateral agreements, mainly between the United States and Canada and several Western European countries, which were affected by exchange of notes or memoranda of understanding (US Government 1973). Such agreements, while covering only one type of charter service, did involve the acceptance by the signatory governments of the principle of bilateral negotiation as a means of regulating charter operations. Certain governments also became involved in regulating minimum prices for ABCs and other types of charters.

As scheduled airline losses mounted following the 1973 fuel crisis, many governments set out to protect their own scheduled carriers. This growing protectionism was another tendency in the period after 1972. There were many manifestations of this. A number of governments attempted to obtain a more equal share of the total traffic, in particular markets for their own carriers. In 1974 the CAB, later to be the champion of deregulation, began to pressurize a number of European and other governments on the grounds that the latter's airlines were capturing significantly more than 50 per cent of the traffic on routes to the United States, even though American citizens generated over half the traffic. The CAB's aim was to help restore Pan Am and Trans World Airlines (TWA) to profitability. In October 1974 the Dutch agreed to cut KLM's trans-Atlantic capacity by 25 per cent, but by early 1975 the CAB was trying to impose even greater cuts on the Dutch airline (*Flight International*, 27 February 1975). But in some markets the CAB found itself on the defensive. In June 1976, the British government gave 12 months' notice of the termination of the 'Bermuda Agreement' with the United States with the express purpose of obtaining a larger share of the traffic on the North Atlantic route for British Airways and of limiting American airlines' traffic rights and earnings on other major routes passing through British territories. The British felt that they were doing badly under the existing Bermuda bilateral and produced figures to prove it (Doganis, 1977).

At about the same time the Japanese were arguing that on the routes between Japan and the United States, two-thirds of the passengers were Japanese but JAL carried only one-third of the traffic (*Flight International*, 21 August 1976). They too wanted a more restrictive bilateral with the United States. Following its own review of international civil aviation policy the Australian government in 1979 tried to restrict the Asian scheduled airlines offering sixth freedom services between Australia and Europe in order to protect Qantas.

3.3 Moves towards deregulation

Collectively, the various and often disconnected developments described above marked a tendency towards an extension of international regulation rather than its diminution. But the pressures were not all in one direction. There were, during the 1970s, countervailing tendencies towards deregulation.

In the United States pressures for domestic deregulation became very vocal in late 1974 during the hearings of the Senate Judiciary Subcommittee on Administrative Practice and Procedures. These so-called Kennedy hearings focused attention on the need for reform of CAB procedures and controls. A few months later, the 'Report of the CAB Special Staff on Regulatory Reform' came out strongly in favour of the deregulation of United States domestic air services. It argued that the undesirable effects of the existing system included: (a) *de facto* exclusion of new airlines from long-haul trunkline markets; (b) protection of the relatively inefficient carriers; (c) unduly high labour costs and unduly high-cost type of service; and (d) lack of emphasis on price competition and on variations in the price to quality mix in response to consumer preference (CAB, 1975). As a result of this report and the discussions which it generated the United States government introduced a deregulation bill in the spring of 1976, though this did not become law. In February 1977 President Carter announced he would be introducing a new Bill to Congress to allow greater competition among United States domestic carriers. In view of the forthcoming legislation the CAB began to relax its controls. Early in 1977 it began to encourage price competition through its approval of Texas International's 'Peanuts' fares and American Airlines 'Super Savers' fares. At the same time controls on the entry of new carriers into existing markets were relaxed in a series of individual route hearings. On 24 October 1978 the Airline Deregulation Act was signed into law.

The Act provided for the complete elimination of the CAB by 1985, bringing an end to all controls over routes and fares. Other aspects of the Board's responsibilities would be taken over by other branches of the Federal government. The law instituted a gradual decontrol between 1978 and 1985 primarily by making new routes easier to obtain and unprofitable routes easier to give up. The CAB retained authority over maximum and minimum fares until 1982 when tariffs were to become completely deregulated. Charter rules were relaxed, as were limitations on the right of scheduled carriers to operate charters. In practice, the Board reduced its own regulatory controls even more quickly than envisaged by the Act. The significance of US domestic deregulation was that the pressures for change which were generated inevitably spilled over to international air transport.

In Europe there were similar winds of change. In the UK the CAA became increasingly liberal in its licensing decisions from 1975 onwards. One example of this was the virtual deregulation of international freight charters in 1976. The European Parliament in Strasbourg and the European Commission in Brussels all began to discuss various aspects of deregulation within Europe. The European Commission went one step further and actually produced, in October 1975, a draft proposal aimed at creating a single and rather liberal regulatory authority to control all air services between the nine member states (CEC, 1975). This was to be the first in a series of proposals or draft directives on the liberalization of air transport that were sent by the Commission to the Council of Ministers, though none was actually approved. It was not until 1983 that the first directive, for the deregulation of inter-regional air services between regional airports of the member states of the European Community, was approved (CEC, 1983). This directive, a watered-down version of earlier proposals, had little impact, though it marked the first step towards liberalization on a Community-wide basis.

3.4 Reversal of US aviation policy

In the international arena, the three-pronged structure of economic regulation which emerged following the 1944 Chicago Conference had resulted in an industry characterized by a high degree of regulation and a very limited scope for competition. Most markets were duopolies or oligopolies. The only real competition was in certain non-scheduled markets. The United States had acquiesced in this pattern of regulation for more than 30 years. Then late in 1977 US international aviation policy began to change dramatically. Far from accepting the existing regulatory framework, the United States suddenly appeared to be hell bent on deregulation, on reducing existing regulatory controls to a minimum. It was supported in this by several other governments, especially those of the Netherlands and Singapore, but it was the United States that was the prime generator of change.

The change in US policy was linked with the Carter Administration which took over at the White House in January 1977. Three key factors explain the moves towards a new policy. First, 'consumerism' had been a key element in Carter's election campaign. In international air transport this meant reducing fares, facilitating access to air services, and opening new direct links from US cities not previously served by international services. There was considerable public and congressional pressure for international deregulation and the Carter Administration was eager to harness such pressure in its own support. Secondly, the Carter Administration had a fundamental belief in the benefits of greater competition. The early stages of domestic deregulation in the United States appeared to be producing lower fares for consumers and higher airline profits without any marked instability for the industry. The protected position of Pan Am, TWA and other US international airlines could not be justified. If greater competition was proving beneficial domestically, it would also do so internationally. Finally, there was a need to increase US airlines' share of international air transport. The once dominant US position had been eroded. The regulatory system together with the lack of drive of the established American airlines had resulted in a declining market share for these airlines. By 1977 US airlines had only about 40 per cent of the market between the United States and Europe and on some routes, such as those to the Netherlands or Scandinavia, their market share was below 20 per cent. More liberal bilateral air services agreements and the entry of new US carriers would enable the US industry to increase its market share. Here one can discern an element of self-interest behind the pressures for deregulation.

In October 1977 the White House produced guidelines on international aviation policy. These were further developed by the Department of Transportation and published in May 1978. Following public hearings in the summer of 1978 a statement on 'International Air Transport Negotiations' was signed by President Carter on 21 August 1978 (Presidential Documents, 1978). This stated that the United

States' aim was 'to provide greatest possible benefit to travellers and shippers' and that 'maximum consumer benefits can best be achieved through the preservation and extension of competition between airlines in a fair market place'. This broad aim was to be achieved through the negotiation or renegotiation of bilateral agreements. In such negotiations, the US would henceforth have the following objectives:

(a) 'Creation of new and greater opportunities for innovative and competitive pricing that will encourage and permit the use of new price and service options to meet the needs of different travellers and shippers'.

This would be achieved by ensuring that tariffs were determined by airlines on the basis of competitive considerations. Government involvement should be the minimum necessary to prevent predatory or discriminatory pricing, to prevent monopolistic practices and to protect competitors from prices that are artificially low as a result of government subsidies.

(b) 'Liberalization of charter rules and the elimination of restrictions on charter operations'
(c) 'Expansion of scheduled services through the elimination of restrictions on capacity, frequency and route operating rights'
(d) 'Elimination of discrimination and unfair competitive practices faced by US airlines in international transportation'

In particular, charges for providing *en-route* and airport facilities should be related to the costs created by airline operations and should not discriminate against US airlines.

(e) 'Flexibility to designate multiple US airlines in international air markets'
(f) 'Encouragement of maximum traveller and shipper access to international markets by authorizing more US cities for non-stop or direct service, and by improving the integration of domestic and international airline services'
(g) 'Flexibility to permit the development and facilitation of competitive air cargo services'.

The United States set out to achieve these objectives in a series of crucial bilateral negotiations which took place in the period 1977–80. The major objective of US policy was generalized deregulation. This made sense given the free enterprise and competitive aviation ment in the United States. But in most of the countries with

United States was negotiating there was only one airline or only one large scheduled airline which was usually state-owned and was the 'chosen instrument' of each country's aviation policy. As a result most countries negotiating with the United States had quite different objectives to those outlined above:

(a)   They generally wanted some capacity control and, in several cases, they wanted a reduction in US scheduled capacity rather than any increase. Italy and Japan were among countries that wanted some capacity controls.
(b)   Several countries, including the United Kingdom and France, wanted to limit existing US fifth freedom rights which had been liberally granted under the early Bermuda-type bilaterals.
(c)   Most countries did not favour 'multiple designation'. Since many of them only had one major international airline the concept was of little value. It was seen as little more than an American attempt to swamp the market with US airlines and capacity.

On the decontrol of tariffs, the liberalization of charters and air cargo, the position of several countries was more flexible and closer to that of the United States. The one common objective of most countries was to obtain rights to serve more gateway cities in the United States. This coincided with one of the President's own policies: increased access to the US market was the carrot used by American negotiators in order to obtain their own objectives.

3.5   New concepts in international regulation

In the process of renegotiating many of its key bilaterals between 1977 and 1980 the United States introduced some new concepts into international regulation and gave greater importance to others that, hitherto, had been of limited significance.

On traffic rights the most significant development was that of unlimited or *multiple designation*, that is the right of each party to a bilateral to designate as many airlines as it wishes to operate its own agreed routes. A few bilaterals, Bermuda 1 among them, had previously accepted multiple designation but they were the exception. In addition, many of the new US bilaterals include *break of gauge* rights. This is the right to change from a larger to a smaller aircraft in the other country's territory on a through service that is going beyond the other country, usually, but not necessarily, with fifth freedom rights. In order to use its break of gauge rights an airline would need to station smaller aircraft at the airport where the change of gauge takes place. A few of the bilaterals also grant *combination rights.* This allows an airline to carry two sets of third and fourth freedom traffics on a single stopping service. In other words, an American carrier may combine a service from New York to London with one between New York and Copenhagen by stopping in London but without traffic rights between London and Copenhagen. None of the above are entirely new concepts but they have now become much more widespread in US bilaterals.

During the 1970s there had been a number of bilateral memoranda or exchanges of letters covering aspects of non-scheduled services. But charter rights had not generally been covered by the bilateral air services agreements. In the new US bilaterals, *charter rights are explicitly covered by the bilaterals* and the general articles of each bilateral are deemed to refer to both charter and scheduled services and airlines. Hitherto it had been usual to try and ensure that rules regarding passenger access and other aspects of charter services (such as inclusive tour conditions if any) were more or less similar for traffic originating in each of the two countries involved. In order to be able to liberalize such charter conditions, the United States introduced the concept of *country of origin* rules. This gives each country the right to establish whatever conditions it requires for charter services originating on its own territory while leaving the other country in the bilateral free to do the same for its own originating charter traffic.

In a few bilaterals the country of origin concept was also introduced for scheduled tariffs. The idea here is that each country can only approve or disapprove tariffs for traffic originating in its own territory. It can not prevent the implementation of fares approved by the other country for traffic originating in that country. Clearly the country of origin rule for tariffs does not exclude the possibility that the two aeronautical authorities might decide to implement similar fares at both ends of the route, as has sometimes happened. But the country of origin concept allows an individual country to be more liberal in its tariffs policy than its partners might wish. The second new concept on tariffs is that of *double disapproval.* Under traditional air services agreements tariffs could not become operative unless approved by both governments. In other words either government on its own could block a particular tariff proposal. If double disapproval is introduced into a bilateral agreement a tariff can only be refused if both governments reject it.

It can be argued that the above concepts effectively change the previous bilateral philosophy of fair and equal opportunity for the airlines of both signatory states and of an equal balance of rights to a philosophy which strongly favours the larger aviation power. Multiple designation, break of gauge, country of origin rules for charters, or double disapproval for tariffs all favour the countries which have several large airlines and which are major traffic generators. They are concepts of limited value to countries which have only one airline, especially if it is not a large international carrier, and which are not themselves generators of substantial volumes of scheduled or charter traffic. In the case of the US bilaterals this imbalance was heightened by the unequal exchange of traffic rights. Whereas the US designated airlines are given rights from 'any point in the United States' to the major city or cities of the other country, the foreign designated carriers are given only a very few gateway points in the United States. Thus a single foreign airline flying to two or three US points may have to face the challenge of several US carriers able to operate from anywhere in the United States and with any tariff structure so long as it is not predatory.

3.6 Bermuda 2: The United States–United Kingdom bilateral

Picking off a country at a time, the United States gave away one or two new gateway points to the foreign carrier in exchange for minimum fare controls, multiple designation, elimination of capacity controls and the liberalization of charter rules. The British were fortunate in having opened negotiations in 1976, before the various objectives of the new US aviation policy had been clarified. As a result, in the new United States–United Kingdom bilateral signed in July 1977, and known as the 'Bermuda 2' agreement, the British got more and gave away less than their European counterparts did a year or so later (HMSO, 1977).

On traffic rights the United Kingdom achieved important gains. It increased its named gateway points in the United States from nine to fourteen, with the addition of San Francisco, Seattle, Houston, Atlanta and Dallas/Fort Worth. United States fifth freedom rights through London and Hong Kong were reduced. At the same time a new right was granted to both sides for the combination of services. The right of 'break of gauge' was clarified and extended. Finally there was a wide exchange of rights for all-cargo services.

Capacity control was one of the most difficult issues, though a compromise was eventually agreed for the North Atlantic route. Airlines were to be required to submit their forecasts and advance schedules to the two governments, who would consult with each other if they disagreed. If no agreement was reached airlines could operate the amount of capacity equivalent to the average of their forecasts. This limited but important safeguard on capacity did not appear in some of the bilaterals signed later.

The UK accepted the principle of multiple designation between the two countries but tried to secure single designation on each point to point route segment. In the middle of the negotiations, however, the

Court of Appeal ruled that the UK government had no right to de-designate Laker Airways, which had previously been designated to operate a London–New York Skytrain service. The Court of Appeal decision undermined the British negotiating position but a compromise was reached. Double designation, that is, two airlines from each country, was agreed for two routes only, New York–London and Los Angeles–London. Elsewhere single designation would prevail until the traffic on a route exceeded 600,000 one-way passengers a year.

It was agreed that tariffs would be subject to approval by both governments. If agreement could not be reached, the existing tariffs would continue to be operative. To prevent last-minute tariff changes and uncertainty the bilateral laid down a detailed timetable for the submission and approval of fare filings. This was a new departure.

Finally, charter rights were expressly included within the bilateral and the general articles pertaining to scheduled services were deemed to be applicable to charter services as well.

On several issues the Bermuda 2 agreement was much less liberal than the bilaterals that followed. Within a year it was being attacked in the United States as being too protectionist compared to subsequent US bilaterals. In March 1980 amendments were negotiated. They allowed for double designation on two more routes (Boston and Miami) and for up to twelve new gateway points to be opened in stages up to 1984. New US carriers were also required to fly to Gatwick rather than Heathrow. But the United States failed to achieve any significant concessions on tariffs liberalization or an increase in its fifth freedom rights. There have been subsequent amendments but the essential features of the 1977 agreement remain intact.

3.7 Deregulation through bilateral renegotiation

The Bermuda 2 agreement was the first major breach in the traditional pattern of bilateral agreements. But it was the United States–Netherlands agreement, signed in March 1978, which was to become the trendsetter for subsequent US bilaterals. During the negotiations the Dutch set out to ensure that Bermuda 2 did not become the basis for the international regulation of air transport (Wassenbergh, 1978). It was too restrictive, whereas the Dutch wanted to maximize competitive opportunities for their own airline, KLM, and they also viewed with alarm the diversion of trans-Atlantic traffic via London as a result of Laker's cheap Skytrain services and the low scheduled fares, both of which had followed quickly on the conclusion of Bermuda 2. Since the Dutch were starting from a viewpoint very similar to that of the United States it was inevitable that the

US–Netherlands bilateral agreement would be a particularly liberal one. Both sides set out to reduce the role of the government in matters of capacity, frequency, tariffs and in the setting of market conditions. The key terms of the agreement can be summarized as follows:

(a) Agreement covers both scheduled and charter services
(b) Multiple designation accepted (within two years the US Government had designated eight scheduled and thirteen charter airlines, though most did not operate; the corresponding Dutch figures were one and two (Raben, 1980)
(c) US airlines given unlimited authority from any points in USA via intermediate points to Amsterdam and points beyond with full traffic rights (i.e. fifth freedom rights)
(d) Dutch airlines given points in the Netherlands to New York, Chicago, Houston, Los Angeles and one additional US point, as well as a Netherlands–Montreal–Houston route (i.e. Dutch only given limited number of US gateways and some doubt whether they have fifth freedom rights beyond USA)
(e) No capacity or frequency restrictions
(f) No restrictions on sixth freedom traffic
(g) Unlimited charter rights between any points in either territory with country of origin rules
(h) Country of origin rules for scheduled tariffs, but government intervention should be limited to prevention of predatory or discriminatory pricing; tariffs should be set by each airline on the basis of commercial considerations.

The protocol for the US–Netherlands agreement was signed in March 1978 at a time when negotiations had already been opened between the United States and Belgium and Germany for a revision of their bilaterals. Because of the geographical proximity of these two countries to the Netherlands they could not afford to be less liberal either on scheduled or charter rights than the Dutch had been, otherwise considerable trans-Atlantic air traffic would be diverted to Amsterdam and then move by road the short distances to Belgium or Germany. As a result the US–Germany and the US–Belgium bilaterals concluded at the end of 1978 were very similar to the earlier US–Netherlands agreement. There were variations but the pattern was set. Other countries in the European area were under pressure to follow suit in their own negotiations with the United States. The US–Israel agreement went one step further because it included a double disapproval article on tariffs. One or two of the larger European aviation powers, notably the French and the Italians, held out against the trend towards deregulation, though they too had to compromise on some issues.

Deregulation through bilateral renegotiation was also being pursued by the United States in other international markets. The most important after the North Atlantic route for American airlines was perhaps the North and Mid-Pacific market. Here the United States negotiated several key bilaterals between 1978 and 1980 with Singapore, Thailand, Korea and the Philippines. These bilaterals follow the same pattern as those in Europe. The United States offered these countries a handful of gateway points in the United States, usually less than five, in exchange for most if not all of the US objectives previously outlined. One of the first renegotiated bilaterals was that between the United States and Singapore. The main features of the US–Singapore air services agreement of March 1978 as amended by a memorandum of understanding agreed in June 1979 are as follows:

(a) Multiple designation
(b) No unilateral control of frequency, capacity, scheduling or on type of aircraft used, though capacity should be related to traffic requirements
(c) No control of tariffs (except if predatory or discriminatory) unless both governments disapprove a particular tariff proposal (i.e. double disapproval)
(d) US airlines granted traffic rights 'from the United States via intermediate points to Singapore and beyond'
(e) Singapore's designated airline granted rights from Singapore via intermediate points to Guam, Honolulu, San Francisco and three additional points to be selected by Singapore
(f) Break of gauge permitted
(g) Unlimited charter rights for airlines of both countries with country of origin rules.

The other bilaterals between South East Asian countries and the United States generally incorporated the above features. Even the Philippines, one of the strongest opponents of deregulation, eventually succumbed and in October 1980 signed a new bilateral agreement with the United States, though it was not as liberal as the Singapore bilateral described above. The only country of significance to stand out against the trend was Japan. The Japanese wanted to maintain some control over capacity and preferred the IATA tariffs system to any general deregulation of tariffs. They also wanted fifth freedom rights between the United States and South America, which the Americans were loath to grant. It was not until June 1982 that an interim three-year agreement was signed. The United States obtained rights for United Airlines between Seattle and Tokyo and the Japanese obtained a Tokyo–Seattle–Chicago route and fifth freedom rights between Los Angeles and Brazil. Each country also obtained an annual quota of 300 charter flights. But there was no agreement on fares policy, multiple designation or wider fifth freedom rights.

Through the process of renegotiating its bilateral agreements the United States has managed to introduce a measure of deregulation on routes to and from the United States. International or bilateral controls on new airline entrants, on capacity or frequency, on tariffs and on charter services have been reduced or eliminated. This is particularly so on the North Atlantic and the Pacific routes and to an extent on the routes between North and South America. US pressures for deregulation have had an impact on other countries, such as Canada and the United Kingdom, and have induced them to be more liberal in their own aviation policies. For example, the new bilateral between Canada and the Federal Republic of Germany signed early in 1982 removed frequency and capacity limitation on the airlines operating between the two countries. But since no other country set about systematically renegotiating its own bilaterals on more liberal terms, deregulation in non-US markets has been fairly limited. Often it was achieved through unilateral rather than bilateral action. In the Netherlands, the United Kingdom, Singapore and elsewhere, governments, aviation authorities and airlines turned a blind eye to illegal discounting of government approved fares. In this way *de facto* liberalization of tariffs was introduced on many international routes. At the same time there are large parts of the world, such as Africa, where deregulation has had little impact and the traditional regulatory framework remains intact.

3.8 The Show Cause Order and the declining influence of IATA

The US policy objectives, outlined in the Presidential statement of August 1978, were pursued not only through the renegotiation of bilaterals but also through a direct attack on the tariff-setting activities of IATA. In June 1978 the American CAB issued an order requiring IATA and other interested parties to show cause why the Board should not withdraw its approval of, and consequently the anti-trust exemption for, IATA's traffic conferences and other related agreements. If exemption from anti-trust legislation was withdrawn then no airlines flying to the United States would be able to be parties to IATA tariff agreements without risk of being taken to court in the United States. Over 40 per cent of IATA member airlines' international traffic was and still is to and from the United States, so the potential threat to IATA was considerable. The Show Cause Order stirred up a hornet's nest of protests from IATA, from many governments around the world, from regional organizations such as the Arab

Civil Aviation Council and so on. Even the US Department of State, citing foreign government protests, urged caution.

Following the hearing on the Show Cause Order the CAB in a new order in April 1980 concluded that IATA tariff agreements substantially reduced competition. Nevertheless, they should be approved by the United States for a period of two years for reasons of diplomacy and to allow for some experimentation in pricing. But the order excluded US airlines from participating in IATA pricing on the North Atlantic route. In May 1981 a new CAB decision largely reconfirmed the decisions reached on its 1980 order. Subsequently the whole process of the Show Cause Order was wound up by President Reagan.

The Show Cause Order and the controversy which surrounded it undoubtedly undermined IATA's influence. Its immediate short-term effect was the withdrawal of all US airlines from IATA membership. When in 1979 IATA changed its constitution to allow airlines to participate in trade association activities without participating in tariff agreements, some of these carriers crept back as trade association members only. Following the abandonment of the Show Cause Order some US airlines began to participate again in the tariffs process. By June 1984 FlyingTigers, Pan Am, Eastern, TWA and United were full members of IATA again, while American was only a member of the trade association. Other US international airlines remain outside IATA.

A CAB order of April 1980 had required a non-IATA tariff experiment to be pursued on the North Atlantic route. In practice this meant either bilateral agreements on tariffs on some routes or an open rate situation on others. A major breakthrough came in May 1982 when discussions between the United States and the 10 key members of the European Civil Aviation Conference (ECAC) led to an agreement to set up fares zones – the so-called 'zones of reasonableness' – on most North Atlantic air routes (see Sec. 9.6). The fare zones agreement between the United States and ECAC was doubly significant. It introduced a new concept into international airline pricing but also it was a multilateral government agreement on tariffs completely outside the auspices of IATA. As such it undermined the tariff-fixing role of IATA. Subsequent IATA tariffs on the North Atlantic route have been fixed within the agreed fare zones or bands. Further evidence of IATA's declining influence can be found in the tariffs clauses of some recent bilaterals. Whereas traditionally most tariffs clauses had mentioned the use of IATA procedures where possible (see Sec. 2.3 above), reference to IATA has become less frequent. Even ICAO, in a 1978 document proposing standard bilateral tariff clauses, no longer mentions IATA. Instead there is an ambiguous article which suggests that tariffs agreements 'shall, wherever possible, be reached by the use of the appropriate international rate fixing mechanism' (ICAO, 1978).

3.9   The impact of international deregulation on airline operations

The impact of deregulation has been felt most acutely on routes to and from the United States, though, as previously mentioned, there have been spill-over effects on non-US routes as well. It is interesting to consider how airlines have reacted to deregulation by assessing developments in two major markets, the North Atlantic and the North Pacific routes in the period 1978–83.

3.9.1   NEW CARRIERS AND EXPANDED CAPACITY

The most immediate effect of the renegotiation of US bilaterals was a dramatic expansion in the number of airlines operating in deregulated markets and in the total scheduled capacity offered in those markets. Such expansion came about as a result of the multiple designation of United States airlines and of the opening of routes to new gateway points in the United States. In addition, several South East Asian airlines started services to the United States for the first time.

Before the Bermuda 2 agreement in 1977 there were only three US carriers on the North Atlantic, Pan Am, TWA and National, though the latter operated only from Miami. During the next two years or so they were joined by established scheduled carriers such as Delta, Braniff and Northwest Orient and by former charter airlines that moved into scheduled services such as World Airways, Transamerica, or Capitol. By the summer of 1984 there were about a dozen United States carriers flying scheduled services on the North Atlantic route. At the same time the number of US points served by European carriers had increased significantly as more gateway points were made available to them under the new bilaterals.

On the international routes across the North Pacific the jump in the number of carriers and of capacity offered was also marked. Prior to 1978 there had been only six airlines on these routes – Canadian Pacific, Pan American and Northwest Orient from North America, together with China Airlines, KAL and JAL from the Asian side. By 1981 three entirely new Asian entrants had joined the market, SIA, Philippine Airlines and Thai International, and between them they were offering twenty-two Boeing 747 flights each week on services to the United States. Later they were joined by China's CAAC. In April 1983 Cathay Pacific started flying from Hong Kong to Vancouver. It may well be that the entry of so many new Asian carriers into the North Pacific held back US airlines from entering the market. While many airlines showed a keen interest when multiple designation became possible, only Braniff went in in a big way in 1979 and subsequently collapsed. Other US airlines flirted with North Pacific services for a short time. By the end of 1983 United Airlines was the only new US entrant still operating in this market. Overall multiple designation has had less impact on the trans-Pacific routes than on the North Atlantic routes.

3.9.2 DOWNWARD PRESSURE ON TARIFFS AND YIELDS

Two aspects of deregulation created a strong downward pressure on fares. First, the abandonment of the IATA tariffs procedures on routes to the United States together with country of origin or double disapproval tariffs clauses in many bilaterals gave airlines considerable pricing freedom should they wish to use it. Secondly, new carriers entering existing markets had a strong incentive to undercut the established airlines in order to capture an appropriate market share. Laker Airways did this when launching their London to New York Skytrain services in 1978 and on their Los Angeles and Miami routes later on. As the market share of new entrants increased, the established carriers were forced to match their lower tariffs in order not to lose their own market share.

The impact of new entrants on tariffs and more particularly on yields can be seen in Table 3.1, which shows the average revenue per passenger-mile of United States' carriers in three markets in 1979, the first full year of deregulation. It is quite clear that in each market the airline(s) with the lowest yield and therefore the lowest fares are always the ones which entered these markets for the first time in 1978 or 1979. Conversely, the old established carriers have much higher

Table 3.1 Impact of new entrants on average fares: average revenue (yield) US cents per passenger-mile US airlines in 1979.

Airline	Atlantic	Route groups Latin America	Pacific
Braniff	5·65*	9·30	4·61**
Delta	5·74	6·87	
Continental			8·18
National	6·12	6·84**	
Northwest	5·65**		6·99
Pan Am	8·27	10·06	7·79
TWA	7·14		

NB: Year of entry of new entrants: * = 1978; ** = 1979. Underline indicates the lowest yield in each route group.
Source: Civil Aeronautics Board.

yields. The case of Braniff illustrates the point. On US to Latin America routes Braniff was an established carrier with a very high yield of 9.30 cents per passenger-mile. With deregulation Braniff expanded in a big way on the Pacific and to a lesser extent on the Atlantic. To capture market share it went into both markets with very low fares. So low, in fact, that both on the Atlantic and the Pacific Braniff had the lowest yield of any US airline. More surprisingly, Braniff's Pacific yield was less than half the yield on Braniff's own Latin American routes.

Further evidence of the falling yields can be found in the mix of traffic by fare type. On the IATA airlines' North Atlantic scheduled services in 1976 there were no ultra-low budget or standby fares and capacity-controlled advance purchase fares (APEX) accounted for only 11.1 per cent of the total passenger traffic. Two years later, in 1978, APEX-type fares had risen to 27.4 per cent of the market and budget and standby to 6.0 per cent. In 1979 36.6 per cent of passengers travelled on APEX-type fares and 6.0 per cent on standbys. Each year since 1980 around 45 per cent of the market has used these two low fare types compared to the 11.1 per cent in 1976 (IATA, 1984a).

The downward pressure on tariffs resulting from the liberalization of tariffs and from the marketing strategy of new entrants was compounded by over-capacity problems arising from the diminution of capacity controls. New entrants poured a great deal of extra capacity on to the markets while existing airlines did little to cut back their own capacity, especially as the lower fares at first generated new traffic and pushed up load factors.

3.9.3 HIGHER LOAD FACTORS

In 1978, the first full year in which the impact of fare and entry liberalization began to be felt, scheduled passenger traffic on the North Atlantic route jumped by 23.4 per cent and the following year it went up by a further 15.5 per cent (IATA 1982b). This dramatic growth resulted in a marked jump in the passenger load factor by 6–7 points in 1978 and 1979 compared to 1977 (Table 3.2). These were exceptionally high passenger load factors when one bears in mind that between 1960 and 1975 the average load factor on the North Atlantic route never once reached 60 per cent. Comparable figures for the North Pacific route are not available.

The increase in load factors resulting from the rapid growth in traffic became a commercial necessity as average fare levels declined. Airlines became locked into a situation where they had to try and fill their aircraft to compensate for the lower yields per passenger that they were obtaining. This was particularly so after fuel costs rose sharply in 1978–79.

Table 3.2 Average passenger load factors on North and South Atlantic scheduled services 1975–1983.

Year	North Atlantic	South Atlantic
1975	57·5	63·3
1976	60·8	52·4
1977	60·7	56·7
1978	66·6	61·6
1979	67·4	63·3
1980	66·8	60·5
1981	69·3	56·3
1982	67·4	56·6
1983	69·8	58·5

Note: North Atlantic covers IATA and non-IATA airline traffic; Miami included after 1977. South Atalntic includes estimates for non-IATA carriers, but these are few.
Source: IATA World Air Transport Statistics.

The effect of deregulation on load factors can best be seen by comparing load factors on the North Atlantic route with those on the South Atlantic routes where deregulation has had little impact (Table 3.2). On both routes load factors increased in 1978 and 1979 as traffic grew rapidly. But whereas on the North Atlantic load factors have stayed at the higher levels of 66–69 per cent, on the South Atlantic they have dropped to *c.* 55 per cent, the sort of levels being achieved before 1978. As a result one now finds that load factors are more than 10 points higher in the deregulated market than in the more controlled South Atlantic market.

3.9.4 COLLAPSE OF CHARTER TRAFFIC

An unexpected by-product of the liberalization of scheduled services was the collapse of the charter market on the North Atlantic. The reduction of scheduled fares partly brought about by the intrusion into the scheduled market of an airline, Laker Airways, operating with charter economics, diverted charter traffic on to scheduled services. From a peak of 4·4 million charter passengers in 1977, large successive drops in traffic reduced the number of North Atlantic charter passengers to 1·8 million in 1981. Since 1981 charter traffic has picked up somewhat, but is still only about half its peak level. The declining role of charters on the North Atlantic has been illustrated earlier in Chapter 1 and Table 1.3.

3.9.5   NO INCREASE IN US AIRLINES' MARKET SHARE

One of the objectives of the change of United States aviation policy in favour of deregulation had been to increase the market share of United States airlines (Sec. 3.4 above). This has not happened, as can be seen from the data in Table 3.3. US airlines' share of the passenger traffic to Europe has increased slightly between 1978 and 1983 but it is still well below half. The improvement on European routes has been largely on the US–UK services following the collapse of Laker Airways early in 1982. In most other country markets US airlines' share of traffic is declining. On the US–Netherlands routes several US airlines entered the market briefly and then withdrew. By 1983 US market share was only 2.9 per cent of the traffic. In the two other major international markets, US to Central America and Mexico and US to the Far East, the US airlines have lost market share during the period following deregulation.

3.9.6   PRESSURE TO REDUCE COSTS

The impact of new low-cost operators such as Laker Airways, together with the downward trend in fares, put tremendous pressure on the existing international airlines to reduce their costs, particularly following the hefty increase in the price of oil in 1978. Newer airlines, both US and non-US, with lower wage rates, fewer staff and an absence of costly work practices, were able to achieve labour costs one-half of those of some established carriers (Tillinghast, 1983). Since labour costs often represent about one-third of total operating

Table 3.3   Share of total passenger traffic (scheduled and charter) carried by United States airlines 1978–1982

Market area*	Percentage of Traffic carried by US airlines (%)				
	1978	1979	1980	1981	1982
US–Europe	43·9	44·6	42·9	41·0	44·9
US–Central	56·1	56·0	54·3	55·8	52·6
US–Far East	41·7	44·4	42·0	39·0	39·3

*These three markets represent about 75 per cent of international air travel to or from the USA.

Source: US Department of Transportation, US International Air Travel Statistics (Cambridge, Mass. Transportation Systems Centre).

costs, a 50 per cent saving represents a cost advantage of about one-sixth of total costs. Established airlines were forced to closely re-examine all their costs, but the most important changes came on the labour side through staff reductions and changes in work practices. TWA cut its staff from almost 40,000 in 1979 to about 29,000 by mid-1982, a drop of 27·5 per cent. British Airways cut its own staff from a peak of 56,000 in 1979 to about 37,000 by the end of 1983, a drop of almost one-third, while its total output was reduced by less than 10 per cent. In addition, many of the US airlines, such as Pan American, persuaded their reduced staff to accept wage freezes or even wage cuts as well as revised work practices. Competitive and financial pressures forced many airlines to cut costs and revise work practices in all areas of activity, not just those most directly affected by competition.

3.9.7 SPIRALLING OPERATING LOSSES?

The deepening financial crisis of the world's airlines from 1979 onwards has been discussed in Section 1.5. It is difficult, however, to establish the degree to which spiralling losses can be attributed to the general economic recession and to the dramatic fuel price increase of 1978 rather than to the impact of deregulation. Certainly on the North Atlantic route there is a close correlation between worsening financial results and the advent of deregulation in 1978 and 1979 (Table 3.4), though this does not necessarily indicate causality. While Table 3.4 shows the deteriorating position of US carriers, losses among non-US airlines on the North Atlantic route have also been substantial.

Table 3.4 United States airlines' operating results on Atlantic services

| Airline | Profit or loss before interest (millions US$) | | | | |
	1978	1979	1980	1981	1982
American					− 3·0
Air Florida					− 12·1
Braniff	+ 4·2	− 16·5	− 37·5	− 11·9	− 0·1
Delta	+ 2·3	+ 5·4	− 0·4	+ 0·3	+ 10·1
National	+ 9·8	− 7·7			
Northwest		− 21·1	− 29·3	− 19·5	− 11·0
Pan Am	+ 14·7	+ 19·2	− 52·4	− 89·7	− 27·7
TWA	+ 46·6	+ 4·4	+ 5·5	+ 58·7	+ 104·5
Western				− 17·5	n.a.
Total	+ 77·6	− 16·3	− 114·1	− 79·6	+ 60·7

Elsewhere, Singapore Airlines blamed the arrival of Braniff with its ultra-low fares policy for the low yields and losses on the North Pacific routes in the three or four years following deregulation.

While any causal relationship between deregulation and worsening financial performance cannot be established it is clear that the absence of effective capacity and/or tariff controls makes it particularly difficult for airlines to climb out of a crisis. With no multilateral agreement on tariffs no single airline is prepared to increase its tariffs unilaterally in order to reduce its losses or to compensate for cost increases for fear of losing traffic. If one airline actually reduces its tariffs the others feel they have to match them. The evidence on the North Atlantic route after 1979 suggests that while liberalization of tariffs makes it easy to reduce fares it makes it very difficult to push them up again if losses are incurred. Equally, unless capacity control is imposed on all carriers in a market, a single carrier is loath to reduce his own capacity or frequencies for fear of losing market share. While the airline crisis of recent years cannot be attributed to deregulation, there is some evidence to suggest that deregulation deepened and prolonged the crisis. This raises an important theoretical question. Have deregulated airline markets behaved as expected?

3.10   Competition in international air transport in theory and practice

The economic theory of perfectly competitive markets requires that the product should be homogeneous and that there should be ease of entry for new suppliers to enter the market and operate without price or capacity controls. The theory also requires that consumers should be fully aware of the prices being offered by the different suppliers. To obtain the benefits of competition in the airline industry United States' and other policy makers had to ensure that the above conditions prevailed within the industry. Airline products are fairly homogeneous so this was not a problem. Multiple designation, more US gateway points and relaxation of charter rules ensured freedom of entry. Absence of marked economies arising from large scale operations within the airline industry facilitated new entrants. Reduction of government intervention in pricing through country of origin rules, double disapproval or zones of reasonableness, together with the rejection of IATA tariffs procedures enabled airlines to have considerable pricing freedom. By removing capacity or frequency controls through the bilaterals and by banning inter-airline pooling agreements as illegal under anti-trust legislation, airlines operating to the USA were freed of any output limitations.

Having created conditions of free competition in markets such as the North Atlantic, then economic theory predicts what should happen. Airlines compete primarily in terms of price but also in terms of frequencies, departure times, in-flight service, points served and so on. Those airlines that are inefficient either because they are unable to capture sufficient market share or because their costs are too high in relation to the prevailing tariffs, make losses and withdraw from the market. The more efficient, low-cost airlines remain in the market operating at tariffs that are lower than in the pre-competition days but are nevertheless profitable. Even if only one or two airlines remain they will be inhibited from increasing tariffs to obtain excessive profits for fear of new entrants coming on to the routes. In this competitive environment, consumers would be better off. They would enjoy lower tariffs and a wider range of services and product features. In brief, this was the theoretical argument put forward by the protagonists of deregulation.

When applied to international air transport there is a flaw in the theory which has been overlooked. The theory of competition requires not only freedom and ease of entry but also freedom of exit so that loss-makers leave the market to the more efficient carriers. In practice, on international air routes the loss-makers tend not to leave the market but continue to operate despite their losses. This is because many will be state-owned airlines and may receive direct subsidies or government guarantees to enable them to raise further loans, as British Airways has done. Paradoxically, in this way deregulation and increased competition may increase protectionism and subsidies. Even if privately owned, unprofitable airlines stay in business by selling off non-airline assets. Some years ago Pan Am sold the Pan Am building in New York and in 1981 when it lost $341 million it was able to cover the loss by disposing of the Inter Continental Hotel chain. In the United Kingdom, British Caledonian sold off and leased back its new headquarters building. In the last analysis loss-making airlines may be able to continue operating for longer than would otherwise be the case because of their ability to reschedule their debts, as Braniff did for a time before its collapse in May 1982. Many airlines in recent years have had particularly poor debt : equity ratios since they have been dependent on huge loans to finance their aircraft purchases. The banks and other creditors have preferred to see these large debts rescheduled rather than to see the airlines collapse and then be left with aircraft that they can not easily sell.

The ability of airlines to continue to operate on routes on which they are incurring substantial losses, as has happened on the North Atlantic and North Pacific markets, clearly undermined the economic theory. It resulted in over-capacity and in subsidized or cross-subsidized competition which forced tariffs of all operators down to uneconomic levels. Airlines became locked in to a situation where tariffs were too low in relation to the costs of even the more efficient operators but where it was impossible to raise the tariffs or reduce capacity because of competitive pressures from loss-making airlines. All airlines ended up making losses year after year and no-one seemed able to break out of this mould. Despite appearances the international airline industry cannot be freely competitive as the airline industry within the United States may be.

By 1983 several governments were having second thoughts about free and unregulated competition. In April the US and UK governments agreed to a two-year moratorium on the designation of new airlines between their two countries as a way of slowing down capacity growth. A few months later Israel was backtracking on an earlier agreement to allow four United States airlines to fly to Israel. The implication of these and other similar actions suggests that international aviation cannot operate entirely free of both capacity and tariff regulation. Some limited bilateral or multilateral control of one or the other is needed to prevent self-destructive competition between airlines.

What about the consumer viewpoint on all this? There can be little doubt that both on the North Atlantic and the North Pacific routes the consumer has benefited. First, he has had a wider range of airlines and airline products to choose from. On the other hand there has been some instability in the industry. In the first two or three years of deregulation on the North Atlantic route, schedules changed frequently, flights were often cancelled and some carriers dropped out altogether (Raben 1980). It seems that a few carriers underestimated the cost and effort of breaking into new markets. Secondly, the passenger benefited from much lower fares. The very low walk-on fares introduced on Laker Airways' Skytrain services generated a host of new low-fare types on the North Atlantic such as budget fares, stand-by fares and so on, as well as the illegal discounting of fares. More recently, the low cost operators People Express and Virgin Atlantic have maintained the pressure for low fares on the North Atlantic. On the North Pacific route it was Braniff, through its ultra-low budget and APEX fares, which was the leader in inducing other carriers to lower or discount their fares. On the London–Hong Kong route the entry in 1980 of Cathay Pacific and British Caledonian on a route previously reserved for British Airways produced a stand-by fare of £99 (at that time about $230) for a 15-hour flight. Passengers welcomed lower airline costs and higher load factors in so far as these were passed on in the form of lower tariffs. Finally, the consumer has benefited from an increase in the number of direct point-to-point air services between new US gateways and destinations (or origins) in Europe and Asia. The above benefits have also accrued to the cargo shipper. Overall, deregulation has been good for consumers – at least in the short term; in the longer term, if airline losses on deregulated routes continue, one may question whether a loss-making industry is in the consumer's interest.

3.11 Focus switches to Western Europe

While in the early 1980s the pressure for international liberalisation and change emanated from the United States and primarily affected air services to and from North America, in the second half of the decade the focus of deregulation is likely to switch to Europe. There is mounting pressure both from within the European Parliament and from the Commission of the European Communities for major changes to the structure of regulations affecting air services between the member countries of the Common Market. The Commission's long-term civil aviation policy objectives were outlined in the so-called 'Memorandum No. 2' published in March 1984 (CEC, 1984).

The Commission, while accepting that American-style deregulation would not work in the present European context, nevertheless wishes to introduce important changes to the regulation of intra-Community air services. The aim is to make such services more flexible and more competitive so as to increase airline efficiency, to allow efficient and innovative airlines to flourish and to better meet consumer needs. In order to achieve these objectives the Commission outlined in its memorandum a number of changes it would like to see adopted by the member states of the Community.

At the government level it would like to see capacity controls within bilateral air services agreements weakened. To do this it suggested that no government should intervene unless its airlines' share in a particular market fell below 25% or some other agreed but low level. This is the so-called safety net principle. On fares and tariffs the Commission put forward proposals reducing government control on fares so as to allow airlines greater pricing flexibility. One way of allowing this would be to introduce zones of tariff flexibility within Europe. (See Section 9.6.)

At the airline level, the Commission proposed to accept for a limited period inter-airline agreements on capacity sharing provided airlines are free to opt out of them. Where such agreements include revenue pooling there must be a very tight transfer limit so that competition between carriers is not blunted. Airline consultations on tariffs would also be accepted provided that dissenting airlines had a right to propose and implement tariffs independently of other airlines, but subject to government approval.

Under a strict interpretation of the Treaty of Rome state aid, that is subsidies, to airlines are illegal unless approved by the Commission.

But rules governing state aid have not yet been applied to the airline industry. In its 1984 memorandum, the Commission decided that it would complement its action on competition by reviewing the state aids given to airlines in the light of certain guidelines outlined in the memorandum. This was necessary to ensure that greater airline competition within Europe did not merely lead to a subsidy race between governments.

As can be seen, the Commission's 1984 policy objectives and proposals were far-reaching and, if implemented, would dramatically change the regulatory environment for intra-Community air transport. In practice, the need to achieve unanimity on Community directives means that changes will only come about slowly. While the Commission has indicated the way things should go, it is individual governments that have accelerated the pace of liberalization. A major breakthrough came in June 1984 with a new agreement between the Netherlands and the UK which effectively deregulated air services between them. Free entry of new carriers, no capacity controls and country of origin rules for tariffs were among the features introduced. The latter provision means that tariffs no longer require approval of both governments but only of the government of the country where the journey begins. This agreement was followed by a similar, though not quite as liberal agreement between Germany and the UK signed in December 1984. These liberal bilateral agreements are likely to be followed by others within Europe during the second half of the 1980s.

4

The Structure of Airline Costs

4.1 The need for costing

The cost of supplying airline services are an essential input to many decisions taken by airline managers. The way that an airline's costs are broken down and categorized will depend on the purpose for which they are being used. In airline planning cost information is required for three key purposes. First, airlines require an overall breakdown of their total expenditure into different cost categories as a general management and accounting tool. They need a general breakdown of costs to show cost trends over time, to measure the cost efficiency of particular functional areas such as flight operations or passenger services, and ultimately to enable them to measure their operating and non-operating profit or loss. Secondly, an assessment of costs is essential in any evaluation of investments either in new aircraft or in new routes or services. Finally, cost identification is crucial in the development of pricing policies and pricing decisions.

No single cost categorization is capable of satisfying all of these three management requirements simultaneously. A cost breakdown developed for general management purposes may be useless as a guide to pricing strategy. As a result, most airlines break down their costs in two or more different ways in order to use them for different aspects of management. While the approach to cost categorization used by each airline is strongly influenced by accounting practices in its home country, it is also influenced by the cost classification adopted by ICAO. The ICAO cost classification was in any case based fairly closely on prevailing cost practices in the United States and among several European airlines. Thus worldwide throughout the airline industry there tends to be a fairly standard approach to the categorization of costs for general management use.

4.2 The traditional approach to airline costs

4.2.1 OPERATING AND NON-OPERATING ITEMS

It is normal practice to divide airline accounts into operating and non-operating categories. The aim is to identify and separate out as non-operating items all those costs and revenues not directly associated with the operation of an airline's own air services. ICAO, the United States' CAB and most airlines have adopted this practice.

ICAO identifies five *non-operating items*. The first of these are the gains or losses arising from the retirement of property or equipment, both aeronautical and non-aeronautical. Such gains or losses arise when there is a difference between the depreciated book value of a particular item and the value that is realised when that item is retired or sold off. The second non-operating item is interest paid on loans, as well as any interest received from bank or other deposits. Thirdly, all profits or losses arising from an airline's affiliated companies, some of which may themselves be directly involved in air transport, are also considered as a non-operating item. In some cases this item may be of some importance in the overall financial performance of an airline. British Airways, for example, has over a dozen subsidiaries and more than twenty-five associated companies (airlines, hotels, telecommunication companies), as well as trade investment in another thirty or so companies. A fourth non-operating category encompasses an assortment of other items which do not fall into the previous three categories, such as losses or gains arising from foreign exchange transactions or from sales of shares or securities. In recent years airlines have from time to time made large losses or profits as a result of sudden marked fluctuations in exchange rates. These are clearly a non-operating item. The final item which should appear in the non-operating part of an airline's accounts is that of direct government subsidies or other government payments. In the case of some airlines subsidies are very substantial. Thus in 1983 Air France received a government subsidy of approximately $52 million, though it still made a profit of only $11 million. Such subsidies would appear as non-operating items.

For some airlines non-operating items may have a major impact on their financial results. Thus in the financial year 1983–4 Singapore Airlines produced an overall profit before tax of $60 million. But of this only $32 million was from airline operations. The remainder came from non-operating items. $18 million was dividends from subsidiary companies while there was a surplus on the sale of aircraft and other assets of $10 million. Non-operating items are not necessarily profits or surpluses. They may well be losses or costs. In 1981–2 British Airways turned an airline operating surplus of £13 million into a deficit of about £540 million before taxation by the inclusion of three large non-operating costs – a £199 million provision for staff severance pay; interest charges of £111 million; an accelerated depreciation of certain aircraft and buildings of £208 million and some smaller items such as currency losses amounting to £35 million. Since the nature of each airline's non-operating costs and revenues is probably unique, in that many non-operating items are influenced by circumstances which are very particular to each airline, inter-airline comparisons of total non-operating costs are of little value.

On the operating side, airline accounts are divided into operating revenues and *operating costs*. The latter can be further subdivided into direct operating and indirect operating costs. In theory, the distinction between these two cost categories is fairly clear. Direct operating costs should include all those costs which are associated with and dependent on the type of aircraft being operated and which would change if the aircraft type was changed. Broadly speaking, such costs should include all flying expenses (such as flight crew salaries, fuel and oil), all maintenance and overhaul costs and all aircraft depreciation costs. Non-operating costs are all those costs which will remain unaffected by a change of aircraft type because they are not directly dependent on aircraft operations. They include areas of expenditure which are passenger related rather than aircraft related (such as passenger service costs, costs of ticketing and sales, and station and ground costs) as well as general administrative costs. In practice, however, the distinction between direct and indirect operating costs is not always clear cut. There are certain cost items, such as maintenance administration or costs of cabin staff, which are categorized as direct costs by some airlines and as indirect costs by others.

The main categories of airline operating costs are shown in Table 4.1. The cost categories shown are those currently accepted and used, with some modification by the ICAO, by the British CAA and by the American CAB while it was still in the business of collecting airline financial data (CAB, 1976). Similar cost categories are used by the majority of airlines round the world.

4.2.2 DIRECT OPERATING COSTS

(a) Cost of flight operations This is undoubtedly the largest single element of operating costs. It includes, in the first place, all costs associated with *flight crew*. Such costs cover not only direct salaries and travelling and stopover expenses but also allowances, pensions, insurance and any other social welfare payments. Flight crew costs can be directly calculated on a route-by-route basis or, more usually, they are expressed as an hourly cost per aircraft type. In the latter case the total flight crew costs for a particular route or service can be calculated by multiplying the hourly flight crew costs of the aircraft type being operated on that route by the block time for the route.

The second major cost element of flight operations is *fuel*. Fuel consumption varies considerably from route to route in relation to the sector lengths, the aircraft weight, wind conditions, the cruise altitude

Table 4.1   Structure of operating costs

DIRECT OPERATING COSTS (DOC)
1 *Flight operations*
   Flight crew salaries and expenses
   Fuel and oil
   Airport and *en-route* charges*
   Insurance
   Rental of flight equipment and/or crews†
2 *Maintenance and overhaul*
3 *Depreciation and amortization*
   Flight equipment
   Group equipment and property (could be IOC)
   Extra depreciation (in excess of costs)
   Amortization of development costs and crew training

INDIRECT OPERATING COSTS (IOC)
4 *Station and ground expenses*
5 *Passenger services*
   Cabin crew salaries and expenses (could be DOC)
   Other passenger service costs
6 *Ticketing, sales and promotion*
7 *General and administrative*
8 *Other operating costs*

---

*ICAO classifies airport and *en-route* charges as an indirect operating cost under 'Station and Ground Expenses'.
†The Civil Aeronautics Board (CAB) classified rentals under depreciation.

and so on. Thus an hourly fuel cost tends to be even more of an approximation than an hourly flight crew cost and it is normal to consider fuel consumption on a route-by-route basis. In addition to aviation fuel, aircraft also use up *oil*. But the oil consumption is negligible and rather than try to calculate it directly for each route, the normal practice is to have an hourly figure for oil consumption for each type of engine. The oil consumption on a particular route is then calculated on the number of engines on the aircraft flying the route multiplied by the hourly oil consumption for that engine and by the block time. For some turbo-prop aircraft there is additional expenditure on water methanol which is used to boost engine power at take-off. This is a very small cost element which can be directly related to the number of take-offs per route. Fuel and oil costs include all relevant taxes and duties, such as taxes on fuel or oil, levied by governments, or fuel throughput charges levied by some airport authorities on the volume of fuel uplifted.

Another significant element of flight operation costs is made up of *airport and* en-route *charges*. Airport charges normally have two elements: a landing fee related to the weight of the aircraft and a passenger charge levied on the number of passengers boarded at that airport (occasionally it is calculated on the number of disembarked passengers). Many Third World airports do not charge the airlines for the number of passengers embarked but collect a fee directly from each passenger on departure. This does not appear as an airline cost. Additionally, if an aircraft stays at an airport beyond a stated time period it will have to pay parking or hangarage fees. These are relatively small compared to the basic landing and passenger charges.

Since about the mid-1960s, airlines have increasingly had to pay *en-route* navigation charges to cover the cost of *en-route* and aerodrome navigation facilities. The actual level of the navigation charge is related to the weight of the aircraft and the distance flown over a country's airspace. As a result both airport charges, where they are not passenger related, and navigation services charges will vary with the type of aircraft used and are therefore considered as a direct operating cost. On the other hand, passenger-related charges do not vary with aircraft type. This may partly explain why ICAO insists on treating landing and *en-route* charges as an indirect cost, though few airlines follow this lead. Since landing and *en-route* charges vary by individual airport and country they must be separately calculated for each flight or route.

A relatively smaller cost in flight operations is that of the *insurance of the flight equipment*. The insurance premium paid by an airline for each aircraft is calculated as a percentage of the full purchase price. The annual premium may be between $1\frac{1}{2}$ and 3 per cent depending on the airline, the number of aircraft it has insured, and the geographical areas in which its aircraft operate. If the airline wants full war risk cover, if it wants to be covered against terrorist action or if it is operating in or through an area where there is armed conflict an additional premium of up to 2 per cent may need to be paid. The annual premium is converted into an hourly insurance cost by dividing it by the projected annual aircraft utilization, that is, by the total number of block hours that each aircraft is expected to fly during the year.

Finally, there may be some costs related to flight operations which do not fall into any of the above three categories. Such additional costs may include costs of *flight crew training*, or of *route development*. However, if training costs are amortized over two or three years then they are grouped together with depreciation. Some airlines may, in addition, have to meet *rental charges* for the hiring or leasing of aircraft or crews from other airlines. These are usually considered as part of flight operation costs. Several of the smaller national airlines of newly independent countries have been launched on the basis of leased aircraft. In such cases, one finds that rental charges are high, pushing up that airline's total flight operations costs to abnormally high levels. This is because the rental charges for aircraft leased on a year-round basis effectively cover both the depreciation and the interest charges for the leased aircraft. Conversely, airlines heavily dependent on leased equipment tend to have very low depreciation charges, since they pay for depreciation indirectly through the rental charge. It is because rentals include a large element of depreciation that the American practice is to categorize rental charges under the heading of depreciation rather than to treat them as a cost of flight operations.

(b)   Maintenance and overhaul costs   Total maintenance costs cover a whole series of separate costs, related to different aspects of maintenance and overhaul, which ideally ought to be treated separately. In practice there are so many joint costs in the separate maintenance areas that it is difficult if not impossible for many airlines to break down total maintenance costs into separate cost categories. As a consequence both ICAO and the CAA, which closely follows ICAO practice, group all maintenance and overhaul expenditure into a single undivided cost item. This item covers not only routine maintenance and maintenance checks but also periodic overhauls and repairs. It encompasses labour costs and expenses related to all grades of staff involved directly or indirectly in maintenance work. Where possible costs of maintenance staff at outstations should be separated out from station costs and included under maintenance. The costs of components and spare parts consumed are also included, as are the costs of workshops, maintenance hangars and offices. Finally, if an airline is subcontracting out any of the maintenance done on its own aircraft then the charges it pays for any such work should be allocated to the maintenance and overhaul category.

In the United States, the CAB required airlines to split their flight equipment maintenance costs into three categories: direct maintenance on the airframe; direct maintenance on the engines; and a maintenance burden. The maintenance burden is essentially the administrative and overhead costs associated with the maintenance function which cannot be attributed directly to a particular airframe or engine but are allocated on a fairly arbitrary basis. The American airlines were obliged to furnish the CAB with these three categories of maintenance costs separately for each aircraft type that they operated. This data was then published periodically by the CAB and provided an excellent basis for the comparison of the maintenance costs between airlines but also between different aircraft types and engines (CAB, 1982).

Outside the United States, airlines also try to apportion their maintenance costs between different aircraft types but there is no standard way of doing this so inter-airline comparisons would not be valid even if such data was publicly available. Individual airlines, having estimated the total maintenance costs for one particular aircraft type, may then convert these costs into an hourly maintenance cost by dividing them by the total number of block hours flown by all the aircraft of that particular type operated by the airline.

(c) Depreciation and amortization Depreciation of flight equipment is the third component of direct operating costs. Airlines tend to use straight line depreciation over a given number of years with a residual value of zero to 15 per cent. Up to the early 1970s depreciation periods were generally 12 years or less. The introduction of wide-bodied jets led to a lengthening of the depreciation period, first, because the capital cost of such aircraft was very much higher than that of the previous generation of aircraft; second, because air transport technology appeared to have reached a plateau. It became much more difficult then it had been previously to predict that further developments in technology might adversely affect and shorten the economic life of the wide-bodied jets. Their economic life was dependent on the strength and technical life of their various components and was unlikely to be affected by any new leaps forward in aircraft technology which might make them obsolescent. In response to these two factors and to their worsening financial performance, airlines throughout the world have tended to lengthen the depreciation period of their large wide-bodied jets to 14–16 years with a residual value of around 10 per cent. For smaller short-haul aircraft depreciation periods are shorter, generally 8–10 years.

The annual depreciation charge or cost of a particular aircraft in an airline's fleet depends on the depreciation period adopted and the residual value assumed. An airline buying a Boeing 747-200 early in 1984 might have paid $75 million for the aircraft and another $5 million for a spares holding, making a total of $80 million. Assuming it depreciated the aircraft over 15 years to a 10 per cent residual value, then the annual depreciation charge could be calculated as follows:

$$\frac{\text{Annual}}{\text{depreciation}} = \frac{\text{price of aircraft and spares (\$80m.)} - \text{residual value (10\%)}}{\text{depreciation period (15 years)}}$$

$$= \frac{\$80m. - \$8m.}{15} = \frac{\$72m.}{15} = \$4 \cdot 8m.$$

The hourly depreciation cost of each aircraft in any one year can be established by dividing its annual depreciation cost by the aircraft's annual utilization, that is the number of block hours flown in that year. Thus, if the Boeing 747-200 above achieved 3,600 block hours in a year its hourly depreciation cost would be $1,333 ($4·8 million divided by 3,600. It is evident that any changes in the depreciation period, in the residual value or the annual utilization will all affect the hourly depreciation cost.

It is ICAO practice to include depreciation of ground property and equipment as a further item of direct operating costs. This practice is questionable in that such depreciation charges are not directly related to the operation of aircraft and, except where they relate to ground equipment which is specific and unique to a particular aircraft type, they will remain unaffected if an airline changes its fleet.

Many airlines amortize the costs of flight crew training as well as any developmental and pre-operating costs related to the development of new routes or the introduction of new aircraft. In essence this means that such costs, instead of being debited in total to the year in which they occur, are spread out over a number of years. Such amortiziation costs are grouped together with depreciation.

4.2.3 INDIRECT OPERATING COSTS

(a) Station and ground expenses Station and ground costs are all those costs incurred in providing an airline's services at an airport other than the cost of landing fees and other airport charges. Such costs include the salaries and expenses of all airline staff located at the airport and engaged in the handling and servicing of aircraft, passengers or freight. In addition there will be the cost of ground handling equipment, of ground transport, of buildings and offices and associated facilities such as telex machines, telephones and so on. There will also be a cost arising from the maintenance and insurance of each station's buildings and equipment. Rents may have to be paid for some of the properties used. By far the largest expenditure on station and ground staff and facilities inevitably occurs at an airline's home base. At some of the smaller airports it serves an airline may decide to contract out some or all of its check-in and handling needs. Handling fees charged by third parties should appear as a station expense.

Some aircraft maintenance may be done at an airline's outstations and the costs arising from such maintenance work should ideally be included as a direct operating cost under the 'maintenance and overhaul' category. But maintenance expenditures are frequently difficult to disentangle from other station costs and are in many cases left as part of 'station and ground' costs.

(b) Costs of passenger services The largest single element of costs arising from passenger services is the pay, allowances and other expenses directly related to aircraft cabin staff and other passenger service personnel. Such expenses would include hotel and other costs associated with overnight stops as well as the training costs of cabin

staff, where these are not amortized. As the number and grading of cabin staff may vary by aircraft type, some airlines consider cabin staff costs as an element of flight operations costs; that is, as a direct operating cost.

A second group of passenger service costs are those directly related to the passengers. They include the costs of in-flight catering, the costs of accommodation provided for transit passengers, the costs of meals and other facilities provided on the ground for the comfort of passengers and expenses incurred as a result of delayed or cancelled flights.

Finally, premiums paid by the airline for passenger liability insurance and passenger accident insurance should also be included here.

(c) Ticketing, sales and promotion costs Such costs include all expenditure, pay, allowances, etc., related to staff engaged in ticketing, sales and promotion activities as well as all office and accommodation costs arising through these activities. The costs of retail ticket offices or shops, whether at home or abroad, would be included. Problems of cost allocation arise. It is frequently difficult, especially at foreign stations, to decide whether particular expenses should be categorized as 'station and ground expenses' or 'ticketing, sales and promotion'. For instance, where should an airline allocate the costs of ticketing staff manning a ticket desk at a foreign airport who may also get involved in assisting with the ground handling of passengers? The same difficulty arises with the costs of an airline's 'country manager' in a foreign country who may have overall charge for sales as well as the handling at the airport.

The costs of advertising and of any other form of promotion also fall under this heading. Finally, commissions or fees paid to agencies for ticket sales would normally be included here.

(d) General and administrative costs General and administrative costs are usually a relatively small element of an airline's total operating costs. This is because, where overhead costs can be related directly to a particular function or activity within an airline, such as maintenance or sales, then they should be allocated to that activity. Thus, strictly speaking, general and administrative costs should include only those cost elements which are truly general to the airline or which cannot readily be allocated to a particular activity. Inter-airline comparison of these general costs is of little value since airlines follow different accounting practices. While some airlines try to allocate their central costs to different cost centres as much as possible, other airlines do not do so either as a matter of policy or because their accounting procedures are not sophisticated enough to enable them to do so.

Where airlines cannot legitimately include a particular expense under one of the cost categories discussed above, they may include it as a separate item under 'other operating expenses'.

4.3 Trends in airline costs

The distribution of total operating costs between the various cost elements discussed above can be seen in Table 4.2. It is apparent that for the world's scheduled airlines as a whole well over half or about 58 per cent of total operating costs now arise from direct costs and just 42 per cent from indirect costs. While this is a useful generalization, it hides the fact that there may be differences between airlines in their cost structure. A number of factors cause variations in airline cost structures, but direct operating costs are generally between 50 and 70 per cent of total operating costs. It is only in non-scheduled operations that direct costs generally surpass 70 per cent of total operating costs and may reach as high as 80 or 85 per cent.

It has previously been pointed out (Fig. 1.1) that as a result of rapid

Table 4.2 Distribution of operating costs: scheduled airlines of ICAO 1972–1982

	1972	1977	1982
Direct operating costs			
Flight operations	29·8	36·4	41·7
Flight crew salaries/expenses	(10·1)	(8·6)	(7·3)
Fuel and oil	(11·0)	(19·2)	(27·2)
Airport and *en-route* fees	(3·7)	(5·0)	(4·7)
Insurance and aircraft rentals	(5·0)	(3·6)	(2·5)
Maintenance and overhaul	13·8	12·4	9·8
Depreciation and amortization	10·6	7·7	6·8
Total DOC	54·2	56·5	58·4
Indirect operating costs			
Station to ground	14·0	12·5	10·8
Passenger services	10·1	9·7	9·1
Ticketing, sales and promotion	15·1	14·8	15·5
General and administration	6·6	6·6	6·1
Total IOC	45·8	43·6	41·6
Total operating costs	100·0	100·0	100·0

Source: ICAO (1983c). CAO (1984d).

technological developments since the Second World War, the unit operating costs of air transport declined steadily in real terms in the 1950s and 1960s. This downward trend ended in 1970 and since then the unit operating costs have remained fairly steady in real terms despite two hiccups in 1974 and 1979/80. In current terms the unit operating costs of the world's scheduled airlines more than doubled in the decade 1970–80. They rose from 16·2 cents per available tonne-kilometre in 1970 to 42·5 cents in 1981 and they have fallen slightly since then (Fig. 1.1).

The escalation of costs since 1970 has not been uniform in all cost categories. The cost of *flight operations* has risen more dramatically than any other single cost element (Fig. 4.1). Between 1970 and 1982 the unit cost of flight operations rose by almost 400 per cent. This very rapid escalation of flying costs was due in large measure to the rapid and unprecedented rise in fuel prices following the Arab–Israeli war in the autumn of 1973 and subsequent increases in 1979–80. IATA studies show that international aviation fuel prices stabilized during 1974, averaging 40·6 cents per US gallon in July of that year. Yet this price represented a 225 per cent increase over the fuel price of some 12·5 cents in early 1973 (Hammarskjold, 1975). After 1974 aviation fuel prices in effect declined in real terms since this was a period of high inflation. This decline was deceptive for much worse was to come. Towards the end of 1978 and early in 1979 political instability in Iran and the ensuing war with Iraq created a sudden shortage of crude oil. This, together with the pricing policies of OPEC, led to an escalation of fuel prices even more dramatic than that of 1974. In the last quarter of 1978 the IATA airlines were paying an average of about 45 cents per US gallon. By the end of 1979 the price of aviation fuel had doubled, and during 1980 it rose to between $1.15 and $1.25 but was as high as $1.50 in some markets. Fuel prices stabilized in 1981–2 and then began to decline slowly in dollar terms in the latter part of 1982. The decline continued in 1983 but was more than offset by the increasing strength of the dollar *vis-à-vis* most currencies. Since aviation fuel is priced in dollars, the real cost of fuel for many airlines in their own currency actually increased in 1983. This was certainly the case in the United Kingdom.

The two successive oil crises of 1973 and 1979–80 have dramatically altered the structure of airline costs. Whereas in 1972 fuel and oil had on average represented about 10–11 per cent of ICAO airlines' total operating costs, by 1977 this figure had gone up to about 19 per cent. Five years later, in 1982, fuel and oil accounted for close to 29 per cent or nearly one-third of airline costs. Airline total costs are now very susceptible to even small changes in the price of fuel. The change in the relative importance of fuel costs has provided a very distinct incentive for airlines to reduce their fuel bill by holding down or even

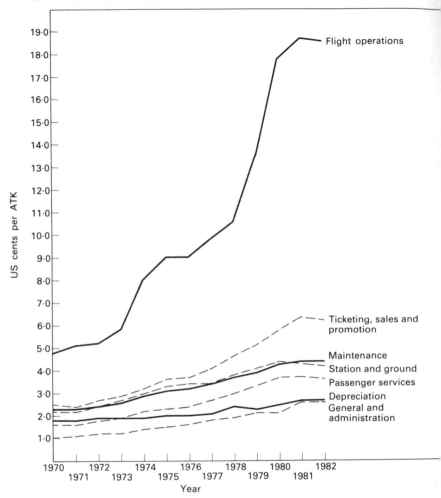

Figure 4.1 Trends in unit costs 1972–1982 scheduled airlines of ICAO. ———, direct operating costs; -----, indirect operating costs.

reducing their frequencies, while accelerating the introduction of larger aircraft which are more fuel efficient.

Other aspects of flight operations costs such as flight crew salaries and airport charges have also been increasing and have aggravated the impact of fuel prices on costs. But it is largely as a result of the escalation of fuel prices that flight operations costs have gone up from just under 30 per cent of total costs in 1972 to a figure of 40–42 per cent (Table 4.2).

The two other elements of direct operating costs, maintenance costs and depreciation, were not as adversely affected by the general inflation of costs as were flight operations. The unit costs of *maintenance and overhaul* rose by about 90 per cent between 1970 and 1982, while the unit cost of *depreciation* rose by only 50 per cent in the same period. Both these cost elements, but particularly depreciation, were helped by the introduction of the wide-bodied jets during the 1970s which were technically more proficient and had lower maintenance requirements. At the same time their annual productivity was such that despite their high purchase price their unit cost of depreciation was actually lower in real terms than that of the aircraft they were replacing. As a result, the share of both maintenance and depreciation in total costs has declined significantly. This has been more than compensated for by the increasing importance of flight operations costs. The net effect has been that direct operating costs as a whole have risen from about 55 per cent of total operating costs to around 60 percent (Table 4.2).

Indirect operating costs have grown more rapidly in absolute and relative terms than both maintenance and depreciation costs though much less rapidly than fuel costs. The most marked increases occurred in ticketing, sales and promotion costs. The unit cost per available tonne-kilometre of ticketing sales and promotion more than trebled between 1970 and 1982. Ticketing, sales and promotion is today the most significant indirect cost accounting for about 15 per cent of total costs (Table 4.2).

The unit costs of the various categories of indirect cost rose as follows between 1970 and 1982:

station and ground	+ 90 per cent
passenger services	+ 125 per cent
ticketing, sales and promotion	+ 260 per cent
general and administrative	+ 250 per cent.

All these cost categories are relatively labour intensive and were affected by the general rate of inflation, especially in wages and salaries.

4.4   The concept of 'escapability'

The traditional classification of costs described above is essentially a functional one. Costs are allocated to particular functional areas within the airline, such as flight operations or maintenance, and are then grouped together in one of two categories, either as direct operating costs (DOC) or indirect operating costs (IOC). This cost breakdown is of considerable value for accounting and general management purposes. This is particularly so where the organizational structure within an airline corresponds fairly closely to the same functional areas as may be used for costing purposes. In other words, where an airline has a flight operations division, an engineering (maintenance) division, a sales division, and so on. A functional classification of costs is useful for monitoring an airline's performance over time and also for inter-airline comparisons. Costs can be broken down relatively easily to produce disaggregate costs within particular functional areas. For instance, one could analyse separately labour costs in the maintenance area as opposed to the labour costs in station and ground operations.

In addition, the broad division into direct and indirect costs is especially useful when dealing with aircraft evaluation. The IOCs of a particular network or operation can be assumed to remain constant since they are unaffected by the type of aircraft used. An evaluation of a new aircraft type or a comparison between several aircraft can then be based purely on an assessment of the DOCs. This simplifies the process of evaluation.

The great disadvantage of the traditional approach to cost classification is its simplicity and the fact that in allocating costs by functional area it avoids many of the problems associated with trying to allocate joint or common costs. For instance, station and ground costs to particular flights or services. But the simplicity of this cost classification is also its major drawback. It is only of limited use for an economic evaluation of particular services or routes, or for pricing decisions, or for showing how costs may vary with changes in the pattern of operations on a particular route.

To aid decision-making in these and other related areas the concept of 'escapability' of costs needs to be introduced. Clearly some costs may be immediately escapable, as a result of a particular management decision, while others may not be avoided except in the very long run. The concept of escapability involves a temporal dimension. Different costs will require different periods before they can be avoided but ultimately all costs are escapable. There is also a technical dimension to the concept, in that the degree of escapability varies with time, but also with the size and nature of the airline service or activity being considered. Thus, if all services on a particular route were to be cut the nature of the escapable costs would be different than if only one flight on a particular day of the week were cancelled on this same route. The former course of action might involve not only a saving of flight operation costs but also the closure of a complete station or a reduction in the number of crews or even the number of aircraft in the fleet. Cancellation of only one flight a week may involve a reduction in some flight operation costs but little else. This is because many costs are joint or common costs and will go on being incurred if only one flight a week is cancelled. The interaction of the temporal and technical aspects of escapability must be constantly borne in mind by airline managers.

Airlines vary in the way they introduce the concept of escapability into their costing procedures. The most usual way is by adopting the traditional accounting distinction of fixed and variable costs. Airlines do this by taking those elements of cost generally accepted as being direct operating costs and further subdividing them into 'fixed' and 'variable' costs. There are several ways in which this can be done because of the temporal and technical considerations outlined above. The larger and more sophisticated airlines may use one breakdown of costs for, say, pricing decisions and a different one for evaluating particular services. One possible approach is discussed below.

4.4.1 FIXED AND VARIABLE DIRECT OPERATING COSTS

Fixed or standing costs are those DOCs which in the short run do not vary with particular flights or even a series of flights. They are costs which in the short or medium term are not escapable. They are certainly not escapable within one scheduling period. That is to say, having planned its schedules for a particular programme period and adjusted its fleet, its staff and its maintenance requirements to meet that particular schedules programme, an airline cannot easily cut back its schedules and services, because of public reaction and its own obligations towards the public, until the next schedules programme is introduced. New schedules would normally be introduced twice a year. If the airline decided to cut back its frequencies when the next schedules programme was introduced, it could reduce its fleet by selling some aircraft, and it could reduce its staff numbers and cut its maintenance and other overheads. Thus fixed or standing DOCs may be escapable but only after a year or two depending on how quickly the airline could actually change its schedules and cut back on aircraft, staff and so on.

Variable or flying costs are costs which are escapable in the short run. They are those costs which would be avoided if a flight or a series of flights was cancelled. They are immediately escapable costs, such as fuel, flight crew overtime and other crew expenses arising in flying particular services, landing charges, the costs of passenger meals, and so on. These are fairly self-evident. Less self-evident are the engineering or maintenance costs which should be classified as variable. Certain maintenance checks of different parts of the aircraft, involving both labour costs and the replacement of spare parts, are scheduled to take place after so many hours of flying or after a prescribed number of flight cycles. A flight cycle is one take-off and

Table 4.3 Cost structure based on fixed and variable direct operating costs

Variable direct operating costs	*Fixed or standing direct operating costs*	*Indirect operating costs*

1 *Fuel costs*
  Fuel
  Oil consumed
  Water methanol (if any)
	7 *Aircraft standing charges*
	  Depreciation or rental
	  Insurance
		11 *Station and ground expenses*

2 *Variable flight crew costs*
  Flight crew subsistence and
  bonuses
	8 *Annual flight crew costs*
	  Fixed salaries and other
	  expenses unrelated to amount
	  of flying done
	  Flight crew administration
		12 *Passenger services*
		  Passenger service staff
		  Passenger insurance

3 *Variable cabin crew costs*
  Cabin crew subsistence and
  bonuses
	9 *Annual cabin crew costs*
	  Fixed salaries and other
	  expenses unrelated to amount
	  of flying done
	  Cabin crew administration
		13 *Ticketing, sales and promotion*

4 *Direct engineering costs*
  Related to number of flight cycles
  Related to number of flying hours
	10 *Engineering overheads*
	  Fixed engineering staff costs
	  unrelated to aircraft
	  utilization
	  Maintenance administration and
	  other overheads
		14 *General and administrative*

5 *Airport and en-route charges*
  Landing fees and other
  airport charges
  En-route navigation charges		

6 *Passenger service costs* Passenger meals/hotel expenses		

Note: Cabin crew costs and passenger meals/expenses here classified as direct costs whereas in Table 4.2 they were part of indirect costs.

landing. Cancelling a service will immediately reduce the hours flown and the flight cycles and will save some engineering expenditure, notably on the consumption of spare parts, and some labour costs.

One possible division of direct operating costs between fixed and variable costs is shown in Table 4.3. Using published operating cost data for the financial year 1982 (CAA, 1984) it proved possible to break down British airline costs in the way suggested in Table 4.3. This analysis showed that for the British airline industry as a whole (that is on a weighted average basis) costs in 1982 were made up as follows:

direct operating costs	
variable	50%
fixed or standing	24%
indirect operating costs	26%
	100%

In other words, about half of the total operating costs are immediately escapable. The same exercise conducted a few years earlier, that is, before the fuel price increases of 1974, would have shown that variable costs were only about 30 per cent or less of total costs. The phenomenal increases in the price of fuel and, to a lesser extent, in airport and *en-route* charges during the 1970s have totally altered the structure of airline costs. They have increased the variable element of airline costs from 25–30 per cent to a figure that is around 50 per cent, though it will vary from airline to airline and from route to route. The change on a particular route can be gauged from the costs on British Caledonian's North Atlantic operations. In 1972 immediately variable costs including fuel on this route were only 24 per cent. In 1978 they were up to 33 per cent and by 1981 they had risen to 48 per cent.

The high proportion of variable costs has important implications for airline operations planning and for pricing. It shows that significant savings can be achieved in the short term by cancelling a flight or a series of flights. The potential savings have risen as the relative proportion of variable costs has increased.

Variable costs are those that are immediately escapable. In the medium term, that is, within a period of a year or so, many costs previously considered fixed start to become variable. Aircraft can be sold, cutting depreciation costs; staff numbers can be run down or staff redeployed; sales offices shut; headquarters buildings sold off. Elements of both fixed direct costs and indirect costs are escapable in the medium term. Ultimately all costs are escapable. What is perhaps more significant and often forgotten is that as much as 90 per cent of total costs can be varied in the medium term either by discontinuing all operations or by a partial withdrawal of certain operations. Airlines can disinvest or dramatically cut their operations more easily than most forms of public transport because they do not have fixed investments in navigational aids, runways or terminals (with some exceptions in North and South America).

4.5   The significance of labour costs

None of the preceding discussion deals explicitly with a major input cost, that of labour. Labour costs are disaggregated and appear as parts of different cost categories such as flight operations, maintenance or ticketing and sales. In so far as most airlines do identify staff costs as a separate cost within each of these cost categories it is possible to assess the total labour costs of each airline.

It is generally assumed within the airline industry that total labour costs, that is, the gross wage costs of all groups of workers together with bonuses, travel expenses and other allowances, amount to about one-third of any scheduled airline's total operating costs. However, closer examination of a sample of the six largest international airlines in each of three regions shows that not only are there very wide variations in the impact of labour costs between airlines but also between regions (Table 4.4). It is true that the major North American international carriers as a group have labour costs which are about one-third of their total costs, though Northwest Orient with a figure of 27 per cent is well below the average. For the larger European airlines labour costs are lower at between 25 and 33 per cent of total operating expenditure.

In contrast to North American and European airlines one finds that among many Third World airlines labour costs represent a very much smaller proportion of total costs. This is certainly the case with the

Table 4.4   Labour costs as a proportion of total operating costs 1982

North America	%	Europe	%	Asia/Australasia	%
American	39	Swissair*	33	Qantas	27
Eastern Airlines	38	Lufthansa	32	JAL	24
TWA	38	Alitalia (1981)	31	SIA*	15
Air Canada*	36	KLM	29	Air India	10
Pan Am	33	Air France	26	Thai International	10
Northwest Orient	27	British Airways*	25	Korean Airlines (1981)	9
Average:	35	Average:	29	Average:	16

Source: ICAO Digest of Statistics or * Airline Annual Reports.

South East Asian airlines illustrated in Table 4.4. On average, labour costs for these airlines are well below 15 per cent of their total costs. For Thai International and Korean they are only around 10 per cent. These figures are remarkable, even though they may be suppressed by a few percentage points as a result of contracting out certain activities such as engine overhaul (e.g. in SIA). They show that these airlines enjoy a major cost advantage compared to their non-Asian competitors. This may partly explain the competitive strength of these relatively young airlines over the last ten years and their very high growth rates (Table 1.2). As long as these airlines continue to enjoy this labour cost advantage, the European and American carriers will find it difficult to compete with them and may continue to lose market share.

5
Determinants of Airline Costs

5.1 Management control of costs

Variable operating costs, which may represent up to 50 per cent of total operating costs, can be escaped in the short term by cancellation or withdrawal of services. In the medium term perhaps as much as 90 per cent of costs can be saved by disposal of aircraft, reduction of staff, closing of offices and so on. Through their ability to increase or reduce their scale and pattern of operations airline managements can directly affect their total costs. In this sense management control over costs may be absolute and constrained only by the desires of shareholders, whether governments or private individuals or firms. Clearly overall costs are broadly determined by the level of supply, that is the volume of output, decided upon by the management. But once a level of output has been decided upon and is being planned for, what factors then determine the precise level of costs that will be incurred?

Airline managers' prime objective is to match the supply of air services, which they control, with the demand, over which they have much less control, in such a way as to be both competitive and profitable. Having decided upon the appropriate level of supply for particular routes or markets they must then ensure that their operating costs are as low as possible. In deregulated markets with little or no tariff or entry control costs per passenger-kilometre or tonne-kilometre must be at least as low as those of other competing airlines. If not, the airline may be unable to compete effectively and be profitable at the same time. Even in regulated markets unit costs must be kept low, not so much for competitive reasons but in order to ensure high or at least adequate profits at the prevailing tariffs.

Unit cost levels among international airlines vary widely. The accompanying Table 5.1 shows the unit costs for the six largest international carriers (in terms of international tonne-kilometres performed) in each of three regions of the world. Together these eighteen airlines carried 57 per cent of the world's international tonne-kilometres in 1982. The unit costs are for their total operations. (Subsequent tables also refer to these eighteen airlines.) The table amply illustrates both the wide range in cost levels between airlines and the existence of marked regional variations. High cost airlines

Table 5.1 Unit operating costs of selected international airlines 1982 (US cents per tonne-kilometre available)

Rank	North American		European		Asia/Australia	
1	Northwest	28·0				
2					Thai International	31·2
3					Korean*	31·8*
4					SIA	33·1
5	Air Canada	34·4				
6	Pan Am	34·9				
7					Air India	35·4
8					JAL	35·5
9					Qantas	38·9
10			KLM	39·7		
11	American	39·9				
12	TWA	41·0				
13			Air France	42·5		
14			British Airways	43·4		
15			Lufthansa	45·0		
16	Eastern	47·1				
17			Swissair	52·7		
18			Alitalia	55·2		

*Figures presented are for 1981.
Source: ICAO (1984c).

such as Alitalia or Swissair have unit costs twice as high as low cost Northwest Orient or Korean Airlines. The range is even wider if one includes some African or South American carriers such as Air Zimbabwe (65·6 cents per ATK) or Aerolineas Argentinas (75·0 cents in 1981). Asia/Australasia is the region which stands out as having low cost airlines. Six of the nine lowest cost operators are from this region. In contrast, the six European carriers tend to be at the bottom of the list, indicating relatively high costs. The North American carriers are scattered in the rankings indicating a diversity of cost levels.

The numerous factors which affect airline operating costs can be grouped into three broad categories according to the degree to which they can be influenced by management. First, one can identify a number of external economic factors over which airlines have little control. Such factors include the prevailing wage levels, fuel prices and airport and navigation user charges. An airline has to accept these as more or less given and can only marginally mitigate their impact through negotiations with unions or fuel suppliers. The levels and patterns of demand that an international airline is trying to satisfy are also largely externally determined by economic and geographical factors beyond its control. Secondly, there are two major determinants of costs over which airlines have somewhat greater but still limited control. These are the type of aircraft used and the pattern of operations for which the aircraft are used. While both of these might seem to be entirely at the discretion of airline management, in practice managements' hands are tied to some extent by factors beyond their control. The geographical location of an airline's home base, the bilateral air services agreements signed by its government, the traffic density on its routes and other such factors will strongly influence the type of aircraft required and the network operated. Management does not have an entirely free hand to do as it wishes. This is particularly so of national airlines in countries with only one flag carrier. The third category of cost determinants is that over which management have more or less total control. Marketing, product planning and financial policy fall into this category. In the final analysis one must also consider managerial efficiency as a cost determinant. It is crucial in that it determines the degree to which the impact of the other factors mentioned above, whether favourable or unfavourable, can be modified to the benefit of the airline concerned.

The analysis in this chapter of the effect of different variables on costs is qualitative rather than quantitative. Earlier studies have used various forms of multivariate analysis to establish the influence of a range of independent variables (for instance airline size, pilot wage levels or stage length) on a dependent variable such as unit costs or labour productivity. Straszheim (1969) used a multivariate approach in his examination of international airlines as did Pearson (1977) in his study of European carriers. In theory multivariate analysis should be able to establish the relative impact of the various independent variables on the unit costs of the airlines concerned. Certainly Pearson in his work was able to produce high coefficients of determination suggesting that a high proportion of the variations in the dependent variable could be explained by variations in the independent variables. Subsequent work by the CAA has questioned the value of multivariate analysis (CAA 1977a; Appendix B). The CAA carried out its own multivariate analysis of European airline performance. For instance, it examined labour productivity as a dependent variable. Using independent variables, different but comparable to those used by Pearson, it was able to produce equally high coefficients of determination. But one or two airlines that were labour efficient when analysed by Pearson were inefficient in their use of labour when assessed by the CAA model. Such discrepancies occurred in other areas too. Two models using the same technique and broadly comparable sets of explanatory variables should have produced consistent results. The fact that they did not raises serious doubts about the validity of multivariate analysis for comparative studies of international airlines. It is for this reason that a more qualitative approach has been adopted here.

5.2 Externally determined input costs

The cost of a number of key airline inputs or factors of production are determined by external economic variables and are largely outside the control of individual airline managements. Since the external variables vary between countries and regions the input prices of different airlines may also vary significantly. While airlines can try to reduce the prices of their inputs, in the case of some key inputs they can only do so to a limited extent. They have to accept the general level of these input prices as given and they have only limited scope to negotiate downwards from that given level. Another feature of these input prices is that they are subject to sudden and often marked fluctuations. Adjusting to sudden changes in the price of fuel or in the level of charges at a particular airport is a common headache among airline managers.

5.2.1 PREVAILING WAGE LEVELS

For most international airlines wage costs represent between 25 and 35 per cent of their total operating costs, though the figure is lower for many Third World airlines. Since wages represent a high proportion of total costs, variations in the average level of wages paid has a direct effect on an airline's total costs and may also lead to appreciable cost differences between airlines. But the salaries and wages paid by any airline depend primarily on prevailing salary levels and the labour market in its home country rather than on the negotiating skill of the airline's personnel department.

In a country with free wage bargaining it is the interplay of supply and demand for the categories of labour required by the airline(s) together with the strength of particular unions which will broadly determine the level of wages that an airline has to pay for its various categories of staff. In other countries wage levels may be set by national agreements between governments or employers' associations and the trade unions. In some cases governments themselves virtually determine the levels to be paid and impose them on employers and employees alike. In all cases the prevailing wage levels are related to the standard and cost of living in the country concerned. Airlines can negotiate with the unions representing their employees but usually only within a fairly narrow band whose level is pre-determined by the prevailing wage levels in the country concerned. An interesting by-product of deregulation in the United States was the way in which new largely non-unionized airlines undermined the power of the established airline unions, including the pilots' union (Air Line Pilots' Association: ALPA). The new carriers had no trouble in getting employees willing to work at much lower salaries and under stricter work conditions. The established carriers were forced either to induce their employees to accept wage cuts, which was done by several airlines, or they introduced a two-tier wage structure whereby any new employees were taken on at much lower salaries than existing ones (Nammack, 1984). American Airlines did the latter.

The significant variations which exist in wage levels for similar categories of staff between regions and between airlines in the same region are illustrated in Table 5.2. This shows the average annual remuneration or wage for three discrete types of airline employees for those airlines whose costs were given in Table 5.1, plus British Caledonian. Some variation in pilot salaries may be due to differences in flight equipment, since pilot salaries vary with type of aircraft flown, or with the age and seniority of the pilots. Nevertheless, allowing for this and other minor discrepancies, some interesting conclusions emerge.

United States airlines tend to pay higher wages for all categories of staff than other international airlines. This is particularly the case with maintenance and engineering staff. At the same time wages paid in the United States tend to be very similar for all carriers. In other words, it is the prevailing labour market conditions that set the levels and most airlines, with one or two particular exceptions, pay wages close to the norm. Conversely, when one examines European or Asian carriers one finds large differences in wage levels even between airlines in neighbouring states. Thus KLM or Swissair pilots are getting paid nearly three times as much as British pilots.

Finally, it is apparent that Asian carriers, with the exception of JAL, pay very low wages for all categories of staff when compared to most of their international competitors. This explains why wage costs are a relatively small proportion of their total costs (Table 4.5). It may also be one explanation for the low unit costs of Asian carriers shown in the previous table (Table 5.1). The extreme case is Air India, where wage rates are extremely low even by Asian standards. Significantly lower wage levels are a distinct cost advantage enjoyed by a number of Third World airlines. More surprisingly it is also an advantage enjoyed by British Airways and British Caledonian for airline wages in the United Kingdom have lagged behind similar wages in other European countries. The steady devaluation of sterling has reinforced this tendency.

Table 5.2 Average annual remuneration for different staff categories in selected airlines in 1982

Region/airline	Average annual remuneration (US$)		
	Pilots and co-pilots	Cabin attendants	Maintenance and overhaul staff
United States			
Pan Am	88,300	23,000	27,700
American	83,500	24,100	32,300
Eastern	83,500	22,700	23,800
Northwest	82,600*	23,800	30,900
TWA	79,800	28,900	38,500
Air Canada	52,300	19,900	23,700
Europe			
Swissair	100.900	26,500	n.a.
KLM	100,100	24,000	20,700
Air France	80,300	20,500	n.a.
Lufthansa	70,500*	25,100	26,000
Iberia	68,000	23,100	n.a.
British Caledonian	37,400	10,700	17,000
British Airways	35,800	14,000	14,600
Asia/Australasia			
Qantas	74,500	22,100	22,800
JAL	72,100*	22,900	n.a.
SIA	39,100	13,300	10,200
Korean airlines	33,200	8,400	3,900
Thai International	31,700*	6,300	13,200
Air India	11,000	2,500	3,000

*Figure includes flight engineers.
Source: International Civil Aviation Organisation Digest of Statistics, Series FP: Fleet Personnel 1982.

The ultimate cost of labour depends not only on the wage rates paid but also on the productivity of that labour. This partly depends on institutional factors such as working days in the week, length of annual holidays, basic hours worked per week, maximum duty periods for flying staff and so on, and partly on operational factors such as size of aircraft, stage length and frequencies operated. Within these constraints, management has a role to play in trying to achieve as high productivity as possible amongst its various groups of workers. In particular, airlines paying high wages can try and compensate for their high wage levels by achieving high productivity per employee. When comparing wage levels (Table 5.2) and employee productivity (Fig. 5.1), it is evident that several North American carriers, such as Pan Am, American and TWA, do this, as does Japan Airlines. The outstanding case is Northwest Orient, which achieves an exceptionally high labour productivity. European carriers are noticeable as a group for their generally low productivity even when, as is the case with KLM or Swissair, their wage levels are unusually

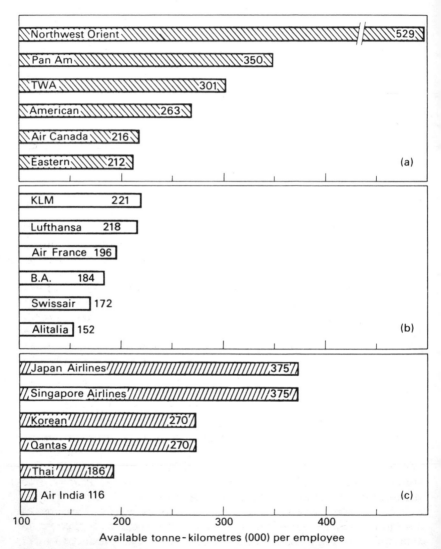

Figure 5.1 Labour productivity 1983: (a) North American; (b) European; (c) Asian/Australasian. *Source* ICAO (1984e) and (1984f).

high. Airlines which have both low wage levels and high or relatively high labour productivity are in a very strong competitive position. Korean and Singapore Airlines are in this position. Conversely a few very low wage airlines, such as Air India, are overstaffed and do not get the full cost advantage of their low wages.

Some Third World airlines face a particular labour problem which is the need to employ expatriate staff as flight crew and in engineering. Expatriate staff are very expensive both because they expect to receive salaries comparable to those in their own country and also because they receive accommodation and other allowances in order to move to the country of the airline employing them. Thai International, for example, was still employing many expatriate engineers in 1982 and this pushed up its average salary level for engineering staff to $13,200, which was high in comparison with neighbouring airlines where few expatriates were employed. Management in airlines using expatriate staff can significantly reduce their labour costs by encouraging and financing the training of their own nationals as pilots and aeronautical engineers.

5.2.2 PRICE OF AVIATION FUEL

The price of aviation fuel at any airport depends partly on the companies supplying the fuel and partly on the government of the country concerned. As far as the fuel companies are concerned, the price of crude and refinery costs are fairly similar worldwide. But distribution and handling costs vary considerably. While oil refineries are widely scattered around the world only a relatively small number refine jet fuel. The supply of fuel to some airports may involve lengthy and costly transportation, especially if the airport is well away from a port. Transportation costs also rise if the volume of fuel supplied to an airport is small. Handling costs vary in relation to the facilities used and the volume handled. Governments may influence the price of jet fuel in two ways. They may impose import duties or some other kind of tax, though many governments do neither of these things for fuel supplied to international flights. Philippine Airlines, for example, has for many years complained of the high prices it pays for jet fuel in its own country because of government taxes. Some governments may also try to control or fix the price of fuel as a matter of government policy. During the 1970s United States government regulations maintained domestic crude oil prices and the prices of refined products at well below world levels. US airlines thus enjoyed cheap fuel. It was not until April 1979 that President Carter introduced a programme of phased decontrol of crude oil prices that was to be completed by the end of September 1981. The Australian government, which had also followed a cheap oil policy, abandoned it in 1978. As a result in both countries the price of jet fuel is now closer to prices in other countries. But other governments, that of Brazil is one, continue to impose price controls on fuel.

The interplay of oil company costs and pricing strategies and individual government policies on taxation and fuel pricing determines the posted fuel prices at airports around the world. Inevitably considerable variations arise. In February 1984 the posted fuel price per US gallon exclusive of duties or taxes was 180 cents in Accra (Ghana), 130 cents in Paris and Oslo, 128·30 cents in Singapore and only 120 cents in Caracas, Lagos or Amsterdam (Aeroshell, 1984). Regional variations are also quite marked. African airlines seem particularly disadvantaged by the very high fuel prices at most African airports south of the Sahara except Lagos, while fuel prices in North America are the lowest (Table 5.3).

Few airlines pay the posted price. Regular users of an airport will negotiate their own contract price with the fuel suppliers. This will be at a discount on the posted price, the level of the discount depending on the total tonnage of fuel that an airline expects to uplift during the contract period. Thus early in 1984, when the posted price in London was 142 US cents per US gallon, a large British carrier was probably paying around 90 cents a gallon. Airlines with only a handful of flights a week would be paying much more. The discount will also be influenced by the number of fuel suppliers. If there is only one oil company providing fuel the scope for pushing down the price is clearly limited. At most airports round the world there are generally only a few aviation fuel companies. In the United States, on the other hand, the existence of a large number of small refineries and of common carrier pipelines open to use by any company has resulted in very large numbers of companies competing for fuel supply contracts. This has a strong downwards pressure on jet fuel prices.

The price of fuel is crucial for airlines since on any particular route it may represent as much as 40 per cent of operating costs, though

Table 5.3   Fuel prices on international scheduled services 1982

Route group	Average fuel or oil price paid (US cents per US gallon)	Index (North America = 100)
Africa	163·9	184
South America	127·2	142
Asia/Pacific	118·8	133
Europe	117·0	131
North America	89·3	100

Source: ICAO (1984b).

overall it accounts for 25–30 per cent of the total costs of many airlines. The cost of fuel for any airline will depend on the posted prices at its main operating airports and in particular its home base and on its ability to negotiate discounts on those posted prices.

Airlines can try to mitigate the impact of high fuel prices at certain airports by reducing their fuel uplift at those airports. Instead captains may be instructed to tanker as much fuel as possible at airports where fuel prices are low. Such a policy, however, needs careful monitoring since extra fuel will be burnt during the flight to carry the additional fuel loaded as fuel consumption rises with the total weight of the aircraft.

An added problem for airlines is that today fuel contracts are no longer at a fixed price for a fixed period of, say, six months or a year. Having got badly burned with fixed price contracts in 1974 and 1979 oil companies now generally insist on escalation clauses in fuel supply contracts. These allow the fuel price to move up or down in response to changes in the price of crude oil. In some contracts prices may also fluctuate in response to supply and demand considerations. Airlines cannot isolate themselves from external economic pressures through fixed price contracts.

The differential impact of fluctuating exchange rates may also adversely affect some airlines since fuel prices in most parts of the world are quoted in United States dollars. If the dollar exchange rate of a particular currency drops rapidly then the cost of fuel in that country in terms of its own currency will rise equally rapidly. This will hit hardest the country's own national airline, most of whose earnings are in local currency. This happened in many countries in recent years. Between 1981 and 1984 the dollar prices of jet fuel at first stabilized and then dropped slowly. But the value of the dollar during the same period rose sharply against many European and other currencies. For many airlines, such as those in Britain, the price of fuel when expressed in their own currency did not decline.

While unable to influence the basic price of fuel except marginally, airlines can lower their fuel costs by trying to reduce their fuel consumption. A number of options are open to them. They can try and reduce the weight of their various aircraft by using lighter equipment in the cabin, and less paint on the outside of their aircraft. They can also reduce weight by avoiding unnecessary 'tankering', that is carrying more fuel than is required to meet safety minima on a particular sector. Then they can save fuel by reducing the aircraft cruising speed. A 3–4 per cent reduction in the cruising speed of a jet aircraft on a sector of 1 hour or more may reduce fuel consumption by 6–7 per cent at the cost of a few minutes' extra flying. Computerized flight planning can also help. By choosing particular rates of climb or descent and particular cruise altitudes airlines may be able to further reduce the fuel consumed. But ultimately the biggest savings come from switching to newer, more fuel-efficient aircraft, especially where one can replace three- or four-engined jets by aircraft having fewer engines. When in 1981 Singapore Airlines changed from the three-engined Boeing 727 to a twin-engined Airbus A300 on the Singapore-Madras sector, they found that despite an 84 per cent increase in seating capacity, fuel burn rose only 40 per cent or so.

5.2.3 USER CHARGES

For the world's airlines as a whole user charges, that is, airport charges and *en-route* facility charges, account for nearly 5 per cent of their total costs. The proportion generally rises for international airlines operating relatively short sectors, where landings occur more frequently. In 1982 Aer Lingus and Austrian Airlines both found that airport and navigation user charges together represented well over 10 per cent of their total costs. For Austrian it was 11·5 per cent and for Aer Lingus 13·7 per cent. Yet for some airlines such as Air Canada the proportion dropped to about 3 per cent or less.

User charges, like wage levels and fuel prices, are largely externally determined. But in contrast, user charges give little room for manoeuvre. While the airlines as a whole, acting through IATA, may try to hold down increases in landing fees or *en-route* charges in a particular country, an individual airline has no scope for negotiating better rates for itself. All are in the same boat.

The level of airport charges will depend partly on the costs at the airports and partly on whether the airport or the government is trying to recover those costs fully or even make a profit. As a result, landing charges vary enormously between different airports (Table 5.4). Except in the United States, airport charges consist of two major elements: a landing fee based on the weight of the aircraft and a passenger fee levied on a per passenger basis. ICAO recommends that the passenger fees should be levied on the airlines and their cost recouped through the ticket. Most European and some Third World airports do this. Elsewhere the fee is levied directly on passengers on departure and therefore does not appear as an airline cost. Airlines based in or operating through airports where passenger charges are levied directly on passengers enjoy a cost advantage. This is reinforced if the aircraft landing fee is also low. Examination of Table 5.4 suggests that this might well be the case with South East Asian or South American airlines.

The position in the United States is unique. Passenger charges imposed by airports are forbidden and landing fees are generally low. On the other hand airlines at most airports build and run their own

Table 5.4 Representative airport charges 1982 (landing plus passenger fees)*

Airport	Boeing 747 (US$)	DC-9 (US$)
London (Heathrow) (peak)	8,956	1,575
Manchester	6,516	1,195
New York (JFK)	3,866	1,492
Tokyo (Narita)	3,679	515
Paris	3,580	533
Frankfurt	3,470	613
Amsterdam	3,467	703
London (Heathrow) (off-peak)	3,238	440
New Delhi/Bombay†	3,079	272
Buenos Aires†	2,312	272
Cairo	2,001	319
Rome/Milan	1,892	348
Singapore†	1,583	174
Kuala Lumpur†	1,359	142
Rio de Janeiro†	1,353	215
Caracas†	1,305	183
Nairobi†	1,121	123
San Francisco	1,072	188
Miami	446	78

*Based on 60 per cent load factors, i.e. DC-9: 56 passengers and Boeing 747: 212 passengers.
†Excluding passenger charge paid direct by passenger to airport.
Source: IATA (1982a).

terminals, which clearly increase their costs. Elsewhere in the world it is very unusual for airlines to operate their own passenger terminals, though they may have their own cargo complexes.

En-route navigation charges are imposed by civil aviation authorities on aircraft flying through their airspace to cover the cost of air traffic control and navigational and other aids provided. The charges are generally levied on the basis of the weight of the aircraft and the distance flown within each country's airspace. While there is some uniformity in the method of charging the level of charges varies enormously, as can be seen in Table 5.5. By far the highest charges are those in Japan and those imposed by Eurocontrol for use of the airspace in Western Europe. At the other extreme many countries have very low charges or none at all, like South Africa or the United States. In the States, navigational facilities are provided as a free public service without a direct charge to the airlines by the Federal

Table 5.5 Representative *en-route* charges for a 500 km overfly distance in 1982

	Boeing 747 (US$)	DC-9 (US$)
Japan	987	855
Eurocontrol	970	360
Germany	815	302
Argentina	695	64
Egypt	495	26
France	459	170
India	440	124
Venezuela	371	84
Kenya	347	49
Indonesia	125	35
Canada	84	84
Malaysia	36	24
Philippines	25	25
United States	none	none

Source: IATA (1982a).

Aviation Administration. Costs are recovered by a tax on airline tickets paid by passengers.

A few airlines have been able to persuade their governments or airport authorities to give them preferential treatment on airport or *en-route* navigation charges. They are either exempted from payment altogether or they may get a substantial discount. The Greek airline Olympic, for instance, has not been paying landing fees at Athens on its international flights for some years. Elsewhere, one finds some national airlines that are billed but do not pay their bills to the civil aviation authorities. Such cases are relatively few, however, because such preferential treatment runs counter to Article 15 of the Chicago Convention and to the principle of equal treatment of each other's airlines which is enshrined in bilateral air services agreements.

The costs of labour, fuel and airport and navigation facilities together represent between 55 and 70 per cent of most airlines' total expenditure. Therefore the prices that any airline pays for these inputs have a major effect on its cost levels. Moreover, differences in input prices may explain some of the variation in costs between airlines. Yet airlines can only marginally influence the level of these input prices. What they can do is to try and minimize the use of these inputs for any given level of output. In other words they must strive to be as efficient as they can in their use of inputs. A key determinant of efficiency in the use of inputs is the type of aircraft being used and the sector lengths over which it is being flown. But before considering the impact of aircraft type on costs one needs to consider the influence of demand.

5.3 The influence of demand on costs

It is generally understood and accepted that airline costs have a direct impact on the demand for air services since they influence the prices at which those services are sold. What is frequently forgotten, however, is that costs are not entirely independent of demand. They are themselves influenced by demand. There is a two-way relationship between supply (costs) and demand; each affects the other. There are two aspects of demand, in particular, which impact on costs, namely route traffic density and sector length.

The traffic density on a route and the sector length(s) on that route will influence the size and type of aircraft chosen for that route. Aircraft type, and more especially the size of the aircraft are key determinants of unit costs. Route traffic density also influences the frequencies which are needed and will thereby affect the annual utilization, that is the number of hours flown by each aircraft. The higher the utilization the lower the costs. Traffic density also affects the level of station costs per passenger or tonne of cargo. Since station costs do not go up in proportion to the traffic handled then more traffic going through a station means lower costs per unit of traffic. These relationships will become clearer in the following sections. There is one other aspect of demand which impacts on costs and that is the variations in demand over time. Marked seasonal peaks create a need for extra capacity in terms of aircraft, crew, ticketing and sales staff, catering facilities and so on which may be grossly under-utilized in off-peak periods. Carrying that extra capacity during the off-peak is costly. From a cost point of view airlines are better off if they are trying to satisfy a pattern of demand that is more or less constant throughout the year.

In a truly competitive environment airlines would be free to choose their own markets in terms of the length of routes and traffic densities that they wish to serve. This may be happening among United States domestic airlines and to a more limited extent among European charter airlines. But the vast majority of international airlines do not have an entirely free hand with regard to the demand that they set out to satisfy. The routes that they serve and the density of demand on those routes is largely determined by the interplay of geographical, political, economic and social factors outside the airlines' control. The starting point for any international airline is its home base. The geographical location of the home base, together with the level of business and tourist interaction between the home country and other nations, will influence the potential sector lengths and traffic densities that can be fruitfully operated. Australia and Malta represent the two extremes. The international airline of Australia must be a long-haul carrier because of its geographical location. Conversely the national airline of Malta, as a result of the island's location and size, is predetermined to be a short to medium haul airline with only a small number of relatively thin routes.

Where an airline is a country's only international airline, which is the case with most airlines, it may also be under political pressure to operate some routes which it would otherwise ignore. Conversely, where there are two or more international carriers, as in the United Kingdom or the United States, they may have much more choice as to the routes they can serve.

Though constrained by some of the above factors airlines do have some ability to influence the patterns of demand on the routes they serve or wish to serve. First, they can as a matter of policy concentrate on the denser traffic sectors. Second, they can try to increase the total traffic on their routes through their pricing policies and promotional activities. Third, a particular airline can try to improve its own traffic density by increasing its market share when it has competitors on the route. Many airlines place considerable emphasis on increasing their market share on their major routes. This is not merely because it increases their revenues but also because it can help them to reduce costs.

5.4 Aircraft type and characteristics

5.4.1 AIRCRAFT SIZE

Many technological aspects of each aircraft type have a direct effect on that aircraft's operating costs. The most important from an economic viewpoint are likely to be the size of the aircraft, its cruising speed and the range or distance which that aircraft can fly with a full payload. The significance of size, speed and range is reinforced in that, taken together, they determine an aircraft's hourly productivity, which in turn also affects costs.

As a general rule, though there are exceptions, the larger an aircraft the lower will be its direct operating costs per unit of output that is per tonne-kilometre available or per seat-kilometre. In other words, other things being equal, the direct operating costs of aircraft do not increase in proportion to their size or their payload capacity. The cost per hour of the larger aircraft will be higher than that of a smaller aircraft but when converted into a cost per seat-kilometre or per tonne-kilometre it is lower. For example, in 1981, in the United States (CAB, 1982) a Boeing 737-200 aircraft with, say, 113 seats would have incurred direct operating costs of about $2,400 per airborne hour. (Airborne rather than block-hour is used here to reduce impact of sector length on costs.) An Airbus A300 B2 aircraft with 240 seats would cost about $3,800 per airborne hour to fly. The larger aircraft's hourly costs were almost 60 per cent higher than those of the Boeing but its capacity in terms of seats was about 110 per cent more. The A300's greater capacity more than compensated for its higher hourly cost. As a result the cost per seat-kilometre of the A300 was significantly lower. Assuming the same average airborne speed of 620 km/h for both aircraft, the direct cost per seat-kilometre of the Boeing would have been 3·4 cents and of the A300 only 2·6 cents.

Aircraft size influences costs in two ways. In the first instance, there are certain aerodynamic benefits from increased size. Larger aircraft have proportionally lower drag and more payload per unit of weight. At the same time larger and more efficient engines can be used. Thus the Airbus A300 has a maximum take-off weight (MTOW) which is nearly three times as great as that of the Boeing 737, yet its hourly fuel consumption is only slightly more than twice as high (CAB, 1982). It is relatively easier and cheaper per unit of weight to push a large mass through the air than a smaller one. The same applies to mass in water. Hence the development of supertankers. Secondly, there are other economies of size related to the use of labour. Maintenance costs, a large part of which are the costs of labour, do not increase in proportion to increases in aircraft size. In the case of the two aircraft discussed above, the hourly maintenance costs in 1981 for the Airbus A300 were actually lower than those of the smaller Boeing aircraft. Eastern Airlines were incurring a maintenance cost of $345 per block hour on their Airbuses, while Boeing 737 operators' maintenance costs were around $380 per block hour. In addition large economies arise in flight crew costs. While the Boeing 737 can and is flown with a two-man flight crew, most jets in commercial airline services have required a three-man flight crew complement. As a result, larger aircraft have generally meant no increase in flight crew numbers, though the crew might be paid more for flying a larger aircraft.

Thus when in 1975 Cathay Pacific switched from Boeing 707s to Tristars, both with three-man crews, it found that crew costs went up by about 8 per cent but the larger aircraft offered 86 per cent more seats. Since 1982–3 three new large twin jet aircraft (the Boeing 757 and 767 and the Airbus A310) have started to come into service specifically designed for two-man operation, even on medium haul sectors. Developments in digital and cathode ray display technology have allowed redesign of the cockpit so as to eliminate the role of the flight engineer. Airlines now switching from some smaller aircraft such as Boeing 727s or Tridents to these newer and larger jets obtain a significant saving in flight crew costs as flight crew numbers are cut from three to two.

The close relationship between aircraft size and unit costs for the major aircraft types operated by United States trunk airlines can be seen in Figure 5.2. The relationship between increasing size or seating capacity and declining unit costs is clear though there are deviations. Such deviations relate either to new and improved versions of existing aircraft types, which explains the lower unit costs of the DC-9-80 compared to the Boeing 727, or to the latest generation of twin-engine aircraft, such as the Boeing 757, with unit costs lower than those of some

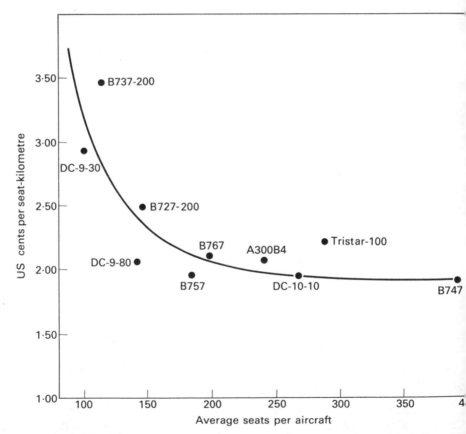

Figure 5.2 Direct operating costs against aircraft size – US trunk airlines (first quarter 1984). *Source*: Avmark Inc. quarterly aircraft operating costs and statistics, first quarter, 1984.

larger aircraft. It should always be borne in mind that the aircraft illustrated are in practice flown on different average sector lengths and this also influences the unit costs shown in the diagram.

Finally, it is important to emphasize that while larger aircraft generally produce lower seat-kilometre or tonne-kilometre costs than smaller aircraft when flown on the same sectors, their total round trip costs are in most cases higher. This is a basic conundrum of airline planning. Does an airline choose the aircraft with the lower seat-kilometre costs or the one with the lower trip costs?

5.4.2 AIRCRAFT SPEED

Apart from size, aircraft speed also affects unit costs. It does this through its effect on an aircraft's hourly productivity. Since hourly productivity is the product of the payload and the speed, the greater an aircraft's cruising speed the greater will be its output per hour. If an aircraft flies at an average speed of 800 km/h and has a 20-tonne payload, its hourly output is 16,000 t-km. An aircraft with a similar payload flying at 900 km/h would generate 18,000 t-km/h, or about 12·5 per cent more than the slower aircraft. Some elements of cost might be higher for a faster aircraft. Fuel consumption might be slightly higher unless the faster speed was due to improved aerodynamic design. But many costs, particularly those that are normally estimated on a per block hour basis, would be similar. Flight and cabin crew costs, maintenance costs, insurance, landing fees and depreciation would certainly be fairly similar. These similar hourly costs would be spread over 12·5 per cent more tonne-kilometres. Therefore assuming other things are equal, the cost per tonne-kilometre for the faster aircraft would be lower. In the earlier cost comparison between the Boeing 737-200 and the Airbus A300 it was assumed that both aircraft had an airborne speed of 620 km/h. This was in fact the average speed achieved in 1981 by the smaller aircraft. The Airbuses were actually faster and their average speed was around 735 km/h. At this speed the Airbus unit costs go down from the 2·6 cents per seat-kilometre previously calculated to 2·2 cents per seat-kilometre. This compares to the 3·4 cents per seat-kilometre of the smaller and slower Boeing 737. Since in practice the faster aircraft are frequently larger as well, the cost advantages of size and speed reinforce each other, producing the lowest seat-kilometre or tonne-kilometre costs.

5.4.3 TAKE-OFF PERFORMANCE AND RANGE

The lower unit costs of larger and faster aircraft does not mean that airlines should always choose to operate such aircraft in preference to smaller, slower aircraft. Airlines must resolve the conundrum previously mentioned. The larger aircraft with the lower tonne-kilometre costs will have higher trip costs than smaller aircraft. In making a choice between aircraft types other factors must also be considered, such as the level and pattern of demand on the routes for which aircraft are needed and the design characteristics of the aircraft in relation to those routes. Aircraft are designed to cater for particular traffic densities and stage lengths. As a result each aircraft type has different take-off and range characteristics and these in turn influence unit costs. An aircraft requiring particularly long runways or with engines adversely affected by high ambient temperatures at airports suffers cost penalties. In either case it can overcome its design handicap by reducing its payload so as to reduce its take-off weight. This would enable it to take off despite a runway or temperature limitation. But the reduced payload immediately results in higher costs per tonne-kilometre since the same costs need to be spread over fewer units of output.

An aircraft's range performance is illustrated in payload–range diagrams such as the one in Figure 5.3. Each aircraft is authorized to take off at a maximum take-off weight (MTOW.) This weight cannot

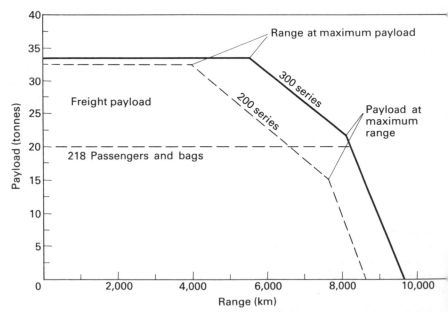

Figure 5.3   Payload range for two versions of the Airbus A310. (The 300 series is an extended version of the 200 series. The passenger payload is based on eighteen first class at 100·7 kg plus 200 economy at 90·7 kg.)

be exceeded for safety reasons. The MTOW is made up of the 'operating weight empty' of the aircraft, plus some combination of fuel and payload. With maximum payload the aircraft taking off at its MTOW will be able to fly up to a certain distance for which it has been designed. This is known as the 'range at maximum payload'. To fly beyond this distance the aircraft must substitute fuel for payload, always ensuring that it does not exceed its MTOW. Initially the reduction in payload may be in terms of belly-hold freight rather than passengers. The aircraft's range can be progressively increased by further uplift of fuel and a continuing reduction in payload. This process continues until the fuel tanks are full and no extra fuel can be uplifted. The amount of payload at this point is known as 'payload at maximum range'. This is the effective maximum range of the aircraft. In practice, an aircraft could fly further without more fuel by reducing its payload since a lighter aircraft consumes less fuel per hour. This is why the payload line at maximum range is not exactly vertical but very steep sloping. The shape of each aircraft's payload range line is different since aircraft have been designed to satisfy particular market needs.

Aircraft size, speed and range together determine an aircraft's productivity curve and hence its unit costs. The relationships are illustrated in Figure 5.4. Hourly productivity is the product of aircraft size and speed. As sector length increases average aircraft speed rises. This is because aircraft speed is calculated on the basis of the block time for a journey. Block time is from engines on to engines off. It therefore includes an amount of dead time on the ground. Ground time will vary with runway, taxiway and apron layout at each airport and with the number of aircraft movements during a given period. On departure at a very busy international airport such as London–Heathrow or Frankfurt, aircraft may spend up to 20 minutes from engine start-up to lift-off. This may be spent on being pulled out from the stand, disconnecting from the ground tractor unit; waiting further clearance from ground traffic control; taxiing to the end of the take-off runway, which may be some minutes from the stand; perhaps waiting in a queue of aircraft for clearance to taxi on to the runway and take-off. On landing the ground time is usually less, though at peak periods an aircraft may have to wait for a taxiway to be clear or even for a departing aircraft to vacate a stand. The total ground manoeuvre time at both ends of a flight may amount to 20–30 minutes at large and busy airports and will rarely be less than 15 minutes on any international air services. When airborne, the aircraft may have to circle the airport of departure and it will then climb to its cruise altitude. The climb and descent speeds are relatively slow, especially if based on the horizontal distance travelled. On short sectors an aircraft may spend most of its airborne time either in climb or descent,

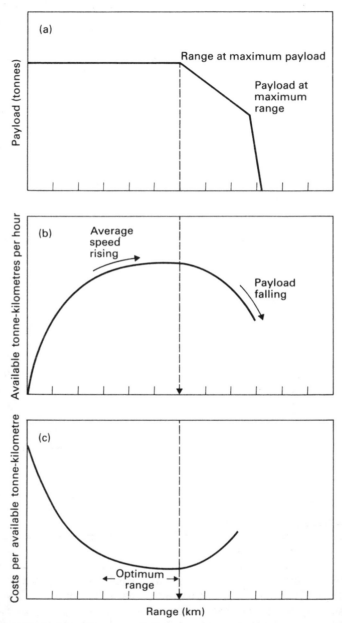

Figure 5.4 Productivity, cost and range relationships: (a) payload-range; (b) hourly productivity; (c) unit costs.

that is at slow speeds, and may only fly at its higher cruising speed and altitude for a few minutes. As the stage distance increases more and more time is spent at the cruising speed and ground manoeuvre and climb and descent times become a smaller proportion of block time. Average block speed therefore increases.

At first the payload capacity is constant. The increasing average speed ensures that hourly productivity rises (Fig. 5.4b). It continues to rise until the range at maximum payload is reached. For distances beyond this payload falls and though average speed may still be rising marginally the net effect is that hourly output falls.

Hourly productivity directly affects unit costs because all the costs which are constant in hourly terms, such as flight crew costs or depreciation, are spread over more units of output. Thus a unit cost curve can be derived from the productivity–range curve showing how unit costs decline as range and hourly productivity increase. Unit costs continue to decline until payload has to be sacrificed to fly further and hourly productivity begins to drop. (Fig. 5.4c) The unit cost curve is typically U-shaped. The precise level and shape of the cost curve will vary for each aircraft type depending on its size, speed and range characteristics. For each aircraft type it is possible to identify a range of distances over which its unit costs are uniformly low. This might be considered the optimum cost range for that aircraft. The preceding discussion has assumed that total costs per hour are constant irrespective of sector length. A later section on the effect of stage length on costs will indicate that costs decrease relatively with distance. This reinforces the effect of increasing hourly productivity. More of this later.

5.4.4 ENGINE PERFORMANCE

A key characteristic of any aircraft type is the engine it uses. Increasingly, the same engines or engines with similar thrust made by different manufacturers are being used by broadly similar types of aircraft. This is because there are only three major manufacturers of civil jet engines in the Western world and competition to get their engines into the same aircraft drives them to produce similar products. This should not obscure the fact that even similar engines may have different fuel consumptions. The earlier Boeing 747s were powered by the Pratt and Whitney JT9D-7A engines. Later versions of the same engine on the same aircraft were more fuel efficient. This is why late in 1979 Singapore Airlines (SIA), which had been operating Boeing 747s with the 7A engine, began the gradual introduction into its fleet of twelve Boeing 747s powered by the JT9D-7Q engine. These engines had lower maintenance costs than the 7As and were expected to offer a 2–3 per cent better fuel consumption. By 1981/2 SIA's fuel costs were 32 per cent of their total costs, thus a 3 per cent saving in fuel consumption would represent a saving of almost 1 per cent in total costs. At about the same time Qantas was introducing newer 747s into its own fleet but with Rolls Royce RB211 engines. It found that the Rolls Royce engines were saving 5–7 per cent on fuel compared to the older Pratt and Whitney engines, but there was a weight penalty because the new engines were heavier. It is clear from these two examples that the type of engines in an airline's fleet and in particular whether they are new or old versions of the engine type may influence operating costs. More recently Boeing have claimed that third generation engines such as the Pratt and Whitney JT9D-7R4 or the RB211-524G together with other refinements on their 747 aircraft will reduce fuel burn per seat by 26 per cent compared to early models of the same aircraft (*Flight International*, 15 October 1983). In assessing the costs of different airlines one needs to consider the impact not only of the aircraft type being used but also the version of engine which powers it.

There can be little doubt that the type of aircraft operated has a significant effect on cost levels. With this in mind the key question is how far does an airline have the freedom to choose any aircraft type it wishes or how far is the choice constrained by the sector lengths and the traffic densities on the routes concerned, or other factors. The choice of aircraft occurs in two stages and management influence is critical only in the second. The first stage is short-listing the possible aircraft types for a given operation. As previously emphasized an international airline's route structure and demand pattern is dependent on its geographical location and on economic and political factors largely beyond its control. The route structure, the airports used and the traffic density on those routes will broadly delimit the type of aircraft needed. For particular parts of its network, the sector lengths and traffic densities taken together will reduce the options open to the airline to perhaps only two or three aircraft types. In some cases only one type may fit the requirements. Until 1985 airlines operating across the Atlantic could not choose twin-engined aircraft because FAA regulations forbad such long cross-water sectors on only two engines. They had to fly three-or four-engined aircraft. If the traffic densities on a particular airline's trans-Atlantic routes were low, Boeing 747 aircraft might be precluded as being too large. It was then left with a choice between a DC-10 or a Lockheed Tristar. At another level, an airline planning to operate international charters into the Aegean islands of Greece, such as Myconos, can only use Boeing 737 or DC-9 aircraft because of runway limitations. In both the above examples it is a combination of external factors that produce the short-list of possible aircraft. It is only when one moves to the second stage, that of choosing between the short-listed aircraft, that the role of management becomes critical. Management has to make several key and related decisions. It must not only choose the aircraft which best meets its airline's needs and objectives, but it must also choose the number of aircraft and optimize the mix of aircraft in the fleet. Management must also decide on the engines which will power its aircraft, if more than one engine type is available. All these decisions will eventually affect the airline's cost levels.

Once an airline has made its choice and invested in particular aircraft types for various parts of its network then those aircraft types have to be considered as given. They cannot be changed from year to year. Because of investment in flight crew training, maintenance and ground facilities, aircraft types are unlikely to be changed except after several years. Once aircraft have been introduced into an airline's operation the most significant factor which will then affect their costs of operation, other than the level of input costs, is the route structure on which they will be operated.

5.5 Pattern of operations

5.5.1 STAGE LENGTH

Several aspects of an airline's operating pattern may influence its costs but the most critical are the stage lengths over which it is operating its aircraft. The average stage lengths will vary within an airline by aircraft type since it is likely that different aircraft will have been chosen for different types of routes within the total network. For each aircraft type, nevertheless, the longer the stage length which can be flown the lower will be the direct operating costs per unit. This is so until sectors get so long that payload has to be sacrificed. A study of the actual costs of Canadian airlines in 1977 showed that as a general rule increasing the sector length from 300 miles to 1,000 miles resulted in a drop of costs per seat-mile of about one-third. This appeared to be the case for all commercial jet aircraft then operated in Canada. If flown on 2,500 mile sectors the unit costs of wide body aircraft fell by a further 20–25 per cent (CTC, 1981).

The rapid decline of unit costs as stage distance increases is as true today as it was then. A number of factors help to explain this relationship. One of these, the effect of stage length on block speed, has already been discussed in the previous section. It was pointed out that ground manoeuvre time and the relatively slow climb and descent phases of a flight become a decreasing proportion of the total block time as stage length increases. Consequently, the average block speed increases. In turn, the hourly productivity in terms of tonne-kilometres or seat-kilometres also rises. Fixed costs, both direct and indirect, are spread over more units of output and therefore the total operating cost per unit goes down.

The same considerations which affect block speed also influence block fuel. During ground manoeuvre time on departure or arrival aircraft are burning fuel. In 20–30 minutes on the ground they can burn a considerable amount of it. During climb and to a lesser extent during the descent phase, fuel consumption is relatively high in relation to the horizontal distance travelled. Conversely, fuel consumption is least at higher altitudes and in the cruise mode. Ground manoeuvre and climb and descent fuel becomes a decreasing proportion of total fuel burn as stage distance increases. The net result is that fuel consumption does not increase in proportion to distance. Thus if an Airbus A310 or a Boeing 767 doubles its stage distance from, say, 500 km to 1,000 km the fuel burnt will not double. Depending on the particular circumstances of the route the fuel consumed will only increase by about 60–70 per cent. Looking at an actual example, in 1983 the A310 on London–Paris at a 65 per cent load factor would have consumed about 3,000 kg of fuel. Flying to Geneva, whose distance from London is 118 per cent greater, the Airbus would have burnt about 4,800 kg, an increase of only 60 per cent. As a result the fuel burned per kilometre and the fuel cost per kilometre would have dropped by 27 per cent (Fig. 5.5). This is a major saving, given that fuel may be a significant proportion of total costs. On longer sectors beyond 2,500 kms the fuel savings become marginal.

Stage length influences aircraft and crew utilization and this too impacts on costs. An aircraft is a very expensive piece of capital equipment. It is only earning revenue and paying back its high initial cost when it is flying. The more flying it does the lower become its hourly costs. This is because the standing annual charges, notably depreciation and insurance, can be spread over a greater number of productive hours. It is much easier to keep aircraft in the air if stage lengths are longer. On short sectors such as London–Paris or Singapore–Kuala Lumpur, where aircraft have to land after every 40–45 minutes of flight and then spend up to an hour on the ground, achieving more than 5 or 6 block hours per day with an aircraft becomes very difficult. Higher utilization requires either a reduction in the aircraft turn-round time so as to carry out more flights within the operating day, or an extension of the operating day by scheduling very early morning or late evening departures. Charter airlines in Europe achieve very high utilization on relatively short sectors by extending the operating day. Conversely, when one looks at longer sectors involving, say 5 block hours an aircraft can fly out and back and with just two flight sectors achieve a daily utilization of 10 block hours while spending only a couple of hours or so on the ground. The close relationship between stage length and aircraft utilization can be seen

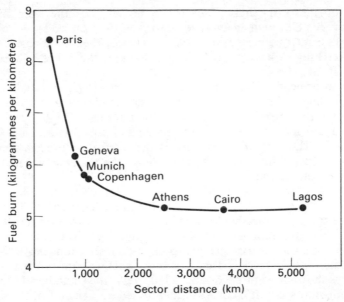

Figure 5.5 The impact of sector distance on fuel burn – Airbus A310 on routes from London. (Fuel burn is the average of outward and return trips based on a 65 per cent load factor.)

by examining British Airways' Tristars in 1983. The 200 series aircraft with an average stage length of 2,739 km achieved a daily utilization of 8·2 hours. Yet the 100 series aircraft being flown on sectors of 1,641 km could only achieve an average of 5·2 block hours per day equivalent to about 1,000 hours per year less than the 200 series aircraft. (CAA 1984a)

Flight and cabin crew like aircraft are a valuable and costly resource. A high proportion of crew costs are fixed and do not vary in the short term. The more flying that crews can actually do, the lower will be the crew costs per block hour. On short sectors crews spend relatively more of their time on the ground. On 1–1½ hour sectors, crews may actually only be flying for 4–6 hours during a 12–14 hour duty period. As stage lengths increase they should be able to spend more of their duty period actually flying.

A more obvious complication of short stages is that airport charges and station costs are incurred more frequently than on longer stages. Their impact on total costs is therefore greater. One can see this when examining the cost structure of short-haul airlines, whether inter-national or domestic. In 1982 landing and other airport charges represented about 3·5 per cent of scheduled airlines costs. For short-haul operators the figure was much higher. For the small British carrier, Air UK, with an average sector length of only 304 km, airport charges came to a staggering 16·0 per cent of their total costs. While for Aer Lingus, average stage length 742 km, the figure was 9·2 per cent (ICAO, 1984c).

Some elements of maintenance expenditure are also related to stage length. This is because certain maintenance checks and spare parts replacement schedules are related to the number of flight cycles, that is, take-offs and landings. These occur less frequently as stage length increases. The most obvious part of the aircraft whose maintenance is related to the number of flight cycles is the undercarriage, though there are others too.

All the above factors reinforce the cost–range relationship, based on aircraft productivity, discussed in the preceding section. Together, they result in a typically U-shaped cost curve for every aircraft type. Unit costs fall rapidly at first as stage length increases, then gradually flatten out until they rise sharply as payload restrictions begin to push up costs. A cost curve based on a route costing study of the Airbus A310 is shown in Figure 5.6. The A310 study, the Canadian Transport Commission study (CTC, 1981) mentioned earlier and other similar

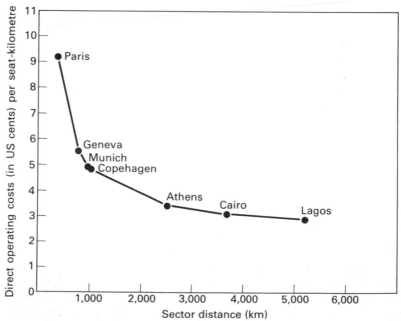

Figure 5.6 The impact of sector distance on unit costs for the Airbus A310 on routes from London.

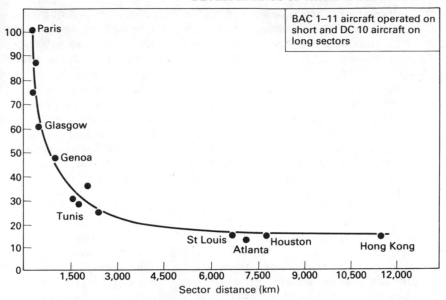

Figure 5.7 Impact of sector distance and aircraft size on unit cost, British Caledonian scheduled services from London 1982. *Source*: British Caledonian.

analyses indicate that the most significant economies with respect to distance occur by increasing stage lengths at the short to medium range. The implication for airlines is clear. They must avoid short sectors, because they impose much higher costs, and should try and operate each aircraft at or near the stage distances where costs are at their lowest.

In so far as larger aircraft tend to be used on longer stages the twin effects of aircraft size and stage length frequently reinforce each other. The result is that operating costs on long sectors flown by large wide-body aircraft may be as low as 20 per cent of the costs on short-haul sectors flown by small aircraft. This is vividly illustrated by the case of British Caledonian in Figure 5.7.

5.5.2 FREQUENCY OF SERVICES

High frequencies provide airlines with greater flexibility in schedules planning, thereby enabling them to increase aircraft and crew utilization. The availability of further schedules to be operated whenever an aircraft and crew return to base makes it much easier to keep them flying throughout the operating day. Airlines operating low frequencies face the problem of what to do with their aircraft when they have completed their first round trip. On long haul routes high frequencies also enable airlines to reduce the length and cost of crew stop-overs. Conversely, low frequencies prove costly. Malaysian Airlines' European services early in 1984 provide a good example. Of the four weekly flights between Kuala Lumpur and Europe, two stopped in Kuwait and two in Dubai. Crews were changed in both places both on outward and return flights. The split operations in the Middle East meant that at both Kuwait and Dubai there were at all times two crews stopping over for three or four nights waiting to take over the next flight. In October 1984 all the four flights were scheduled through Dubai and the Kuwait station was closed. As a result the airline saved about $1·5 million per annum. Among other economies it was able to cut its cabin crew numbers by about fifty.

An international airline's stage lengths are broadly influenced by its geographical location and the patterns of demand it is trying to meet. Demand patterns together with bilateral air services agreements or inter-airline agreements influence or even determine the frequencies to be operated. In those countries such as the United States, Canada, the United Kingdom or France, where more than one national carrier operates international services, the countries own licensing or regulatory controls may influence the sectors on which their airlines operate. While a number of external factors influence both stage lengths and often frequencies an airline has some scope to try and reduce or cut out its short sectors and to try and increase its frequencies by changes in operating pattern or route structure. Because changes in stage lengths or frequencies tend to be piecemeal and gradual it takes time before they have an effect on an airline's overall cost. Nevertheless there is some scope here for management action.

5.5.3   LENGTH OF PASSENGER HAUL

Many costs associated with sales, ticketing and the handling of passengers are related to the number of passengers rather than to the distance that each passenger travels with the airline on a particular journey. This is true with costs of reservation, of ticketing and of the handling of both passengers and their baggage. It is also frequently true of airport passenger charges when paid by airlines. In other words, a passenger who buys a single ticket and travels 3,000 km on an airline network will cost less to the airline than three separate passengers each travelling 1,000 km. In the latter case each of the three will impose his own ticketing and handling costs and the airline may have to pay a separate airport charge for each. From the cost point of view an airline is better off carrying fewer passengers travelling long distances rather than many more passengers on short journeys. However, the shorter haul passengers may produce higher yields and generate more income because of the way fares are structured (see Ch. 9). But purely in cost terms the long-haul passenger is to be preferred. What is surprising is how the average length of passenger haul varies between airlines operating what outwardly appear to be very similar types of networks. This point is illustrated by reference to four airlines Qantas, JAL, SIA and Thai International, whose international operations have common features. These are a strong regional network covering East Asia and Australasia, one or more routes to Europe and in most cases a trans-Pacific route as well. Yet in 1983 the average length of haul for international passengers varied widely from 6,870 km for Qantas and 5,300 km for JAL down to 4,080 km for SIA and 3,530 Thai International. Qantas is in a particularly favoured position.

5.5.4 AIRLINE AND FLEET SIZE

Early studies of airline economics, particularly in relation to US airlines, had suggested that there might be significant economies of scale, particularly at the lower end of the size scale (Wheatcroft 1956). Such economies were expected to arise through the ability of larger carriers to gain the benefits of bulk buying and of spreading contingency provisions over more units of output. Large carriers would also benefit from their ability to themselves undertake discrete activities such as certain maintenance checks or computerized reservations systems, for which a minimum scale of operations was necessary. Increasingly the view that there are economies of scale in airline operations began to be questioned. In 1969 the Edwards Committee (HMSO, 1969) concluded that an analysis of United States domestic airline results suggested that the advantages of scale as such might be exaggerated. Quality of management, the committee believed, might be more significant in determining airline costs than factors related to size of output. An American study by Straszheim (1969) came broadly to the same conclusions. It found that direct operating costs declined sharply as airline size increased but this was not due to any scale effect. Smaller firms reported higher direct costs because they flew thinner routes using smaller aircraft over short stage lengths. Subsequent studies both in the United States (Reid and Mohrfeld 1973; White, 1979) and elsewhere have also failed to establish any economies of scale in airline operations. These findings were confirmed in practice following United States domestic deregulation and liberalization on the North Atlantic. From 1978 onwards many small carriers entered new markets and were able to be price competitive against very much larger and well established airlines.

The airline industry appears to be characterized by constant returns to scale. In other words, there are no marked economies of scale. Such a conclusion has important implications on regulatory policy. It means that in the absence of entry or capacity controls new small carriers will always be in a position to enter existing markets and be cost competitive with established carriers. The economics of the airline industry indicate a natural tendency towards competition or oligopolistic competition rather than monopoly. In practice in international air transport, that tendency is distorted by bilateral agreements, by state involvement in aviation and by other constraints discussed in earlier chapters on regulation.

If there are no economies of scale, what about the related question of fleet size? The Edwards Committee was impressed by the evidence that there are economies from increasing the scale of operations of a standard fleet of the same aircraft type. The committee estimated that if one operated five aircraft of one type the hourly direct operating costs would be about 5 per cent higher than those of an airline operating fifteen of the same aircraft type (HMSO, 1969). Varied stage lengths and differing traffic densities impose the need on many airlines to have quite mixed fleets. This in turn means that some airlines, especially smaller Third World airlines, like Zambia Airways or Air Tanzania, may only operate two or three aircraft of one type. When the number of aircraft in a fleet of one type is so small there are likely to be higher costs. The cost of spares holding will be higher since the spares holding expressed as a proportion of the purchase price of the aircraft goes up as the number of aircraft purchased drops below a certain level. Flight crew training and engineering training costs have to be spread over fewer aircraft and are therefore higher. Maintenance costs would be particularly high for small fleets if engines or aircraft have to be sent elsewhere for major overhauls. The small numbers may preclude the installation of more advanced local maintenance facilities. Sets of flight crews per aircraft may be higher for very small mixed fleets because of the inability in emergencies to switch crews between aircraft if they are of different types. Pilots are certified for only one aircraft type at a time. All the above considerations mean that an airline, such as Kenya Airways, with a small but mixed fleet, has a cost disadvantage. In 1983, Kenya Airways operated six aircraft of four different types on international services. In contrast Qantas operated twenty-four aircraft, all Boeing 747s. Though they were different variants, in some cases with different engines, the degree of commonality of spare parts, maintenance procedures and flight crews must have produced significant economies.

5.6 Marketing Policy

5.6.1 PRODUCT QUALITY

Airlines have to decide on the nature and quality of the product they are going to offer in the various freight and passenger markets that they serve. They do not have an entirely free hand. For commercial and competitive reasons they may have to conform to certain minimum standards of product quality. This is particularly so if they are IATA members and operating on routes where IATA conditions of service still apply, though such routes are declining in number. They must also conform to a variety of international or national safety and technical regulations. These affect many aspects of the cabin layout such as the seat pitch next to emergency exits, or the minimum number of cabin staff, and so on. Within these constraints airlines enjoy considerable freedom to decide on the quality of the product they are going to offer and on the costs they are prepared to incur. The product standards may be different for the various markets served by the airline and will be related to the stage length, to the timings of the services and above all to the degree and nature of competition from other carriers. On routes where a revenue pool exists product competition will inevitably be less acute than on routes where airlines are involved in head-on competition.

The range of seating densities among international airlines in three aircraft types is illustrated in Table 5.6. The cost implications are serious. For example, the seat-kilometre costs of the Portuguese airline TAP with 370 seats in its Boeing 747s are 39 per cent higher than they would be if it adopted JAL's 449-seat layout. The impact

Table 5.6   Seating densities of selected international airlines in 1982 (i.e. standard numbers of seats for plane types and airlines given)

Airbus A300 B4		DC-10-30		Boeing 747-200B	
		Scheduled Airlines			
Air France	292	Laker*	345	JAL	449
Lufthansa	265	Pan Am	386	Air India	394
Olympic	262	UTA	275	Olympic	393
Alitalia	251	Alitalia	271	Cathay Pacific	385
SIA	246	KLM	264	El Al	385
Thai International	246	Continental	259	Saudia	384
Air India	238	Swissair	235	TAP	370
Varig	234	Varig	235	South African	322
		Charter Airlines			
Hapag–Lloyd	315	World	380	Wardair	452
		Martinair	376		
		Condor	373		
		Balair	345		

*Also used for charters.
Source: ICAO (1984c).

of different seating densities on costs is normally less marked than that and involve unit cost variations of up to 15 per cent. The economics of charter operations, as discussed in the following chapter, require high seating densities. It is for this reason that the charter airlines shown in Table 5.6 push their seating densities way above those found acceptable for scheduled services with a concommitant reduction of seat-kilometre costs.

A second aspect of cabin service standards which has important cost implications is the number of cabin crew used. Safety regulations impose a minimum number for each aircraft type. It is up to each airline to decide how many more than the minimum it wishes to use. On short- to medium-haul sectors where there is less time for meals and other in-flight services cabin crew numbers may be close to the minimum. On long-haul sectors airlines have more scope to try and differentiate their product through their in-flight services and one aspect of this may be more cabin staff. In 1983 Singapore Airlines were flying their Boeing 747s with eighteen cabin crew when the minimum required was eleven. Other South East Asian airlines had fewer cabin crew on their 747s. Cathay Pacific and Malaysian had seventeen, Philippine Airlines fifteen, while Thai and Garuda had fewer, at only fourteen. When cabin crew wages are low by international standards then the cost of improving the in-flight product by having more cabin staff is not high. This is the case with these Asian carriers (Table 5.1 above). Conversely it is costly for high wage airlines to compete in terms of cabin staff numbers.

The third key element of cabin service standards is that of catering. As more and more airlines have abandoned the IATA conditions of service pertaining to particular routes and fare classes, so the scope for management initiative has increased. Competitive pressures, however, have pushed most carriers to more or less match what their competitors are doing. For this reason, while catering costs may vary between airlines, they are unlikely to be important in explaining differences in total unit costs between those airlines. The same is also true of the minor elements of cabin service such as newspapers and journals, free give-aways, head sets, the showing of films and so on.

There is also scope for product differentiation on the ground. Airlines can operate and pay for more check-in desks to speed up check-in and they may also decide to provide more ground staff for passenger handling and assistance in general. Some international airlines go further and provide sometimes quite luxurious and costly first or even businesss class lounges at airports, while their competitors may provide neither.

It is difficult to assess the impact of product quality decisions of different airlines on their comparative costs because of the paucity of reliable data. One way of doing this, however, is to establish the expenditure on passenger services per 100 passenger-kilometres of traffic carried. Passenger services expenditure, according to the ICAO statistics, covers the costs of cabin crews and passenger service personnel as well as passenger-related costs such as in-flight catering and hotel accommodation. By expressing such expenditure per 100 passenger-kilometres rather than per passenger one can partially adjust for the fact that there will be quite different passenger hauls on the airlines selected. The relative passenger services expenditure levels for our selected carriers are shown in Table 5.7. With the exception of three United States carriers, all the airlines listed generate more than 50 per cent of their output on international services. The implication of Table 5.7 is that European airlines spend more on product quality than their North American or Asian counterparts, in many cases 20–30 per cent more; yet Asian carriers, because of their lower wage rates, may be providing more cabin crew and ultimately a better cabin service.

5.6.2 SALES AND PROMOTION ACTIVITY

Airlines enjoy considerable discretion in the way they organize and run their sales and promotion activities. They decide on the extent to which they should sell their services through their own sales outlets rather than through other airlines or agents. Such decisions have cost

Table 5.7 Passenger services expenditure 1982 (US cents per 100 passenger-kilometres)

Rank	American		European		Asian/Australasian	
1			Swissair	120·6		
2			Lufthansa	116·9		
3			Air France	113·0		
4			Alitalia*	109·7*		
5			British Airways	99·6		
6	Air Canada	96·5				
7	TWA	90·7				
8					JAL	88·4
9	Pan Am	87·5				
10			KLM	84·5		
11	Eastern	83·5				
12	American	80·3				
13					Qantas	78·2
14					SIA	77·1
15					Air India	76·5
16	Northwest	63·2				
17					Thai International	61·2
18					Korean*	52·2*

*1981 data.
Source: ICAO (1984c).

implications. While setting up and operating its own sales outlets costs money, the airline saves the commissions it would otherwise have to pay agents. An important decision in this respect is whether an international airline should set up off-line sales outlets, that is, outlets in cities or countries to which it does not fly. Equally crucial may be the decision on whether it should itself staff and operate sales offices at some of its less important overseas destinations or whether to appoint a general sales agent, who may or may not be another airline.

Having taken these decisions on whether to provide its own sales outlets, an airline has to decide on their location and size within each city. If opening a sales outlet in London, does it insist on its being with many of the other airlines in a small area bordered by Bond Street, Piccadilly or Regent Street, one of the most expensive shop locations in the world, or does it follow Philippine Airlines and Air Algerie and choose a less expensive location in central London but somewhat away from the other airlines?

It is open to airlines to decide themselves how much to spend on advertising and promoting their services and how to spend it. Numerous promotion channels are open to them from television, radio or national press advertising aimed at large numbers of potential customers at one end to promotional activities or trade press advertising involving relatively small numbers of freight and travel agents or travel journalists at the other.

Ticketing, sales and promotion represents about 15 per cent of total operating costs of scheduled airlines of ICAO member states, or 16·5 per cent if one considers just international services (ICAO 1983c). As such, it is clearly a major item of expenditure, yet one which very much depends on the policies adopted by individual airlines. While most international airlines spend around 15–18 per cent of their total expenditure on ticketing, sales and promotion, some spend much more (Table 5.8). SIA and Qantas both spend over 20 per cent of their expenditure in this area. While European airlines also have relatively high expenditures on sales and promotion, North American carriers appear to spend much less. In the case of Eastern or American, it may well be due to the fact that the bulk of their operations are domestic. It is clear that both product quality and sales and promotion activity are key elements of airline marketing policy where management decisions have a direct impact on costs.

Table 5.8 Ticketing, sales and promotion expenditure as a percentage of total operating costs 1982

Rank	North American		European		Asian/Austalasian	
1					Qantas	23·5
2					SIA	22·7
3			Alitalia	20·7		
4			KLM	19·7		
5					Korean*	19·4*
6			Swissair	19·4		
7			Lufthansa	18·5		
8					Thai International	16·9
9					Air India	16·6
10			British Airways	16·1		
11	Northwest	15·7				
12	American	15·5				
13	TWA	15·4				
14	Air Canada	15·2				
15			Air France	15·1		
16	Pan Am	15.0				
17					JAL	14.8
18	Eastern	14.4				

*1981 data.
Source: ICAO (1984c).

5.7 Financial policies

5.7.1 DEPRECIATION POLICY

The hourly depreciation cost of an aircraft at a given price depends on the length of the depreciation period, the residual value of the aircraft at the end of that period and the annual utilization of the aircraft. The annual utilization, that is, the block hours flown during the year, is dependent on the pattern of operations, on the stage lengths flown and on the scheduling efficiency of an airline's management. The depreciation period adopted and the residual value assumed are determined by an airline's financial policy. In many countries legislation or accounting convention may require the adoption of a particular depreciation policy or may impose certain minimum requirements. Most international airlines, however, have some flexibility in deciding on the effective commercial life of their aircraft and their residual value at the end of that life. This flexibility is important. If an airline can adopt the practice of depreciating its new wide-body aircraft over 16 years to a zero residual value, its hourly depreciation costs (assuming the same annual utilization) will be less than half what they would have been had it used a seven-year life for the aircraft with a 10 per cent residual value.

Both these depreciation policies are currently in use by different airlines and they show the significant variations in depreciation costs that can result from the adoption of different policies. Since, on average, depreciation charges represent around 6 per cent of airlines' total operating costs, then the depreciation policy adopted can influence total costs by as much as 2–3 per cent.

Having adopted a particular depreciation policy, airlines may subsequently change it in order to increase or reduce their costs. For many years Singapore Airlines had adopted a policy of using depreciation periods which were exceptionally short by international airline standards. They estimated the life of their aircraft to be between 5 and 6 years with zero residual value. The purpose appears to have been to build up reserves from the depreciation charges to finance the rapid renewal of the fleet and also to mask the large operating profits that were being made. When in 1979 the fortunes of the airline industry were hit by the rise in the price of fuel, Singapore Airlines promptly lengthened the life of its aircraft to reduce its costs and thereby still managed to show a profit. The process is clearly documented in Singapore Airlines' annual report for 1979/80. It shows that in that year the airline made a profit on its airline operations of Singapore $15·7 million. But the operational life of the airline's aircraft was estimated to be 5–8 years with appropriate residual values. In the previous years aircraft lives had been 5–6 years with nil residual values. The report states: 'As a result of the change in the estimated useful lives of the aircraft fleet the depreciation charge for the year is reduced by Singapore $44·37 million.' In other words, had the airline continued to use the depreciation policy adopted in previous years its costs would have been Singapore $44·37 million higher and the airline profit of S$15·7 million would have been converted into a loss of S$28·7 million! Singapore Airlines has continued to use a 5–8 year life for its aircraft with appropriate residual values. This is still very short compared to most international airlines. It explains why Singapore Airlines' depreciation costs per tonne-kilometre available are amongst the highest when compared to international airlines with roughly similar average stage lengths.

Other airlines have also changed their depreciation policies from time to time. Cathay Pacific, which had been depreciating its Boeing 747 aircraft over 8 years, switched to a 15-year period after 1980 and almost halved its depreciation cost. In its 1981/2 accounts, British Airways threw in a massive provision of £208 million for accelerated depreciation of some of its aircraft and other assets. The result was substantially lower depreciation costs in subsequent years and a marked improvement in profitability.

5.7.2 CURRENT OR HISTORIC COST ACCOUNTING

The theoretical justification for depreciation is that money set aside each year as depreciation charges should be used to build up a reserve fund, from which new aircraft or equipment can be bought to replace existing aircraft when the latter are retired or sold off. A failure to cover depreciation charges out of revenue means that an airline is not generating enough revenue to renew its assets. Inevitably, however, new aircraft costs more than the aircraft being replaced, so there is normally a shortfall between the funds set aside through depreciation based on the historic cost of the aircraft and the capital required to finance the new purchases. At times of relatively low inflation this shortfall was of manageable proportions and could be covered by raising loans. But the annual rates of inflation in many industrialized countries began to accelerate in the early 1970s and reached abnormally high levels in the second half of the decade. As a result, the difference between the historic cost of aircraft and their replacement cost became excessively large. A number of airlines began to consider whether they should depreciate their aircraft and other assets on the basis of their current cost rather than on the basis of their historic cost.

Different methods can be used to calculate the current cost of an asset or aircraft purchased some years ago, but they all involve inflating the historic cost through some price index such as the index of manufacturing costs or aircraft prices. By inflating the cost of assets to be used for depreciation purposes, one of the effects of current cost accounting is to increase depreciation charges and thereby an airline's operating costs. In the financial year 1982/3 British Airways' depreciation costs went up from £126 million on a historic cost basis to £209 million in current cost terms. Few airlines have yet embraced current cost accounting. The adoption or otherwise of current cost accounting is another aspect of financial policy which influences airline costs. Some airlines have adopted a compromise position of charging extra depreciation in addition to historic cost depreciation without formally adopting current cost accounting. This is done on an *ad hoc* and arbitrary basis. It could also be argued that using relatively short asset lives, as Singapore Airlines does, has the same result as current cost accounting. It accelerates the accumulation of reserves needed to finance new aircraft purchases.

5.7.3   METHODS OF FINANCE

Interest charges on loans are considered within the airline industry as a non-operating item. As such they do not affect operating costs or the operating results. However, they do affect each airline's overall profit or loss after inclusion of interest and other non-operating items. The bulk of interest charges relates to loans raised to finance aircraft acquisitions, though some airlines may also be paying interest on bank overdrafts arising from cash flow problems or from the need to finance losses incurred in previous years. An airline can reduce or avoid interest charges by financing part or all of its aircraft purchases internally from self-generated funds. Self-financing is clearly cheaper than borrowing, especially at a time when interest charges are high, as they have been since the mid-1970s. In the five years up to March 1980 British Airways was able to self-finance 72 per cent of its capital expenditure. As a result its interest charges on capital borrowings were generally below £25 million a year, though in 1979/80 they rose to £38 million, which was still a containable figure. But from 1979 onwards, British Airways' financial performance worsened dramatically as a result of the increase in fuel prices and stagnating demand. The airline did not generate sufficient reserves to finance its capital requirements. In 1980/1 its self-financing ratio fell to zero, which meant it had to borrow to meet all its capital requirements and its interest on capital loans almost doubled to £73 million. This interest charge accounted for half the total loss of £145 million. The following year, 1981/2, there were again no cash reserves to finance capital acquisitions and interest charges shot up to £111 million. Thus British Airways' failure to self-finance its aircraft purchases virtually trebled its annual interest costs in two years from £38 million to £111 million.

High rates of interest, which in recent years have averaged around 10–12 per cent but have been as high as 16 per cent or more, have pushed annual interest charges to very high levels. This is so even for airlines that have been able to self-finance part of their capital expenditure. Carriers such as Singapore Airlines who, as a result of a policy of rapid depreciation previously referred to and high profits, built up sufficient reserves to be more than 70 per cent self-financing in most years, are relatively few.

Most airlines would prefer to be self-financing but may be unable to generate sufficient reserves from their depreciation charges and retained profits to do so except to a limited extent. Their remaining capital requirements can be met in one of two ways. First, there may be an injection of equity capital into the airline. The advantage of equity finance is that airlines only pay interest on it in the form of dividends if they make a profit. Most international airlines outside the United States are government-owned but governments have been loath to put in more capital to finance aircraft purchases, especially as the sums involved are very large. Private shareholders have also been hesitant because of the poor financial performance of the airline industry. If equity finance is unavailable, airlines must borrow in one form or another from commercial or government banks. Several different forms of loan finance are available, but either directly or indirectly they all involve interest charges.

The growing reliance of national airlines on external finance rather than self-financing or equity capital has pushed them into having very high debt : equity ratios. In other words, too much of their capital is financed by loan capital and too little by equity. Many airlines are now under-capitalized and need an injection of capital if the interest burden is to be kept within manageable proportions, and if they are to be in a position to order new aircraft without bankrupting themselves. Even Singapore Airlines, which has been able to self-finance so much of its investment, had a major injection of equity capital in 1981/2 of Singapore $404 million (US$190 million) from its major shareholder, the Singapore government. As a result, in the following year 1982/3, Singapore Airlines' debt : equity ratio was 46 : 54. It is generally believed that a debt : equity ratio of 25 : 75 is desirable and that a ratio of up to 50 : 50 is acceptable. Given the very high cost of new aircraft, airlines can only stay within acceptable limits by injections of new capital. Most governments have been loath to follow the example of Singapore and their airlines' debt : equity ratios have deteriorated to 70 : 30, as with British Airways in 1981/2, or worse. Many airlines around the world, especially in developing countries, need an injection of equity capital in order to reduce their interest charges and to be able to finance new aircraft.

Early in 1984 Malaysian Airlines was finalizing its five-year development plan. This required substantial investment in new aircraft. In the absence of additional equity capital from the Malaysian government, the airline would have to raise commercial loans. But it was already heavily in debt and interest charges were likely to be high, so it had to try and self-finance part of its capital needs. The management estimated that to do this it needed to generate a profit of about $30 million per annum. In 1982/3 its profit was only $3.4 million and though in 1983/4 it was about $40 million the $30 million target could not be met every year. Without it the airline's development programme would be in jeopardy. This was why in 1984 it was decided to inject new capital into the airline by privatizing it.

5.8   The quality of management

The analysis so far indicates that the most important variables affecting airline costs are the level of input prices, the type and size of aircraft used and the stage lengths operated. In so far as the last two of these variables are themselves influenced by the pattern and levels of demand that an airline is trying to satisfy, then demand may also be considered an important variable. Other, though less important, variables have been discussed. Many of the latter are particularly prone to management decision and choice. But there is a further dimension of management whose importance may be absolutely crucial in establishing an airline's unit cost levels, but which may be difficult to define or measure. One might broadly define it as the quality of management and it permeates through to most areas of an airline's activities.

The quality of management affects the efficiency with which the management of an airline brings together the various factors of production at its disposal in order to meet different levels and types of demand in different markets. In theory it is management ability, or the lack of it, which should explain cost differences between airlines which cannot be attributed to variations in input costs, aircraft types operated, stage lengths or any of the other cost variables. Northwest Orient best illustrates the importance of management. Northwest is clearly the lowest cost operator of the airlines sampled, and its unit costs are markedly lower than those of other North American airlines (Table 5.1). Yet it appears to have no apparent advantage in terms of the key cost variables. Its input costs are broadly similar to those of other North American carriers. The wages it pays are similar (Table 5.2) and it is likely to be paying the same prices for fuel. Its average aircraft size is smaller than that of several other carriers and its average stage length is shorter than most. Yet Northwest appears to be very efficient in its use of labour. Its output per employee is by far the highest in the sample (Fig. 5.1). This efficiency in the use of resources probably permeates other areas of activity too. Northwest has also made marketing policy decisions which ensure that its passenger service costs per 100 passenger-kilometres are among the lowest (Table 5.7) and that it spends a relatively low proportion of its total costs on ticketing, sales and promotion (Table 5.8). It is policy decisions in this and other areas, together with the quality of its management, which enables Northwest to produce at lower unit costs than the other airlines sampled.

In practice no airline management is likely to be equally efficient or inefficient in all areas of management. It may well be efficient in one area, such as flight crew scheduling, but relatively inefficient in the organization of maintenance procedures. Thus the total unit cost of an airline may mask wide variations of performance in discrete areas of activity such as flight operations or maintenance management. Ideally, inter-airline comparisons should be on a disaggregate basis, looking at such discrete areas separately.

6

The Economics of Passenger Charters

6.1 The nature of non-scheduled passenger services

One of the enigmas of international air transport is the ability of charter airlines to sell seats at one-half or even one-third of the price of their scheduled airline competitors and still make a profit. The fare advantage offered by charters can be gauged by examining the London–Athens route during the peak summer months of 1983 (Table 6.1). The cost of a charter round trip per passenger was only one-third of the scheduled excursion fare and around half of the advanced purchase fare. The charter fare advantage was much less in comparison with the consolidation or group fares on scheduled services which could be bought by travel agents. But it should be borne in mind that the number of seats on any scheduled flight

Table 6.1 Scheduled and charter fares: London–Athens summer peak (July to September) 1983.

	Return Fare (£)	Index (Excursion = 100)
Scheduled – Publicly available		
Club/business class	560	168
Eurobudget	442	132
Excursion	334	100
Advanced purchase	228	68
Scheduled – Available to agents		
Individual inclusive tour or 'consolidation'	184	55
Group inclusive tour	164	49
*Charter – Cost per passenger**		
Friday day flight	125	37
Friday night flight	120	36
Tuesday night flight	110	33

*Charter cost assumes 85 per cent load factor on Boeing 757 and includes meals and airport taxes.

available for consolidation or group fares was limited, especially during periods of peak demand when scheduled carriers had little difficulty in filling seats at the higher fares. It is the charter airlines' ability to offer such low seat costs which has enabled them to capture around 55 per cent of the international passenger market (in terms of passenger–kilometres) within the Europe–Mediterranean area. Their penetration of the North Atlantic market is lower at around 10–12 per cent, but it has been as high as 29 per cent in 1977 (Table 1.3). Passenger charters are important in these two major international markets. Their impact in other markets has been more limited though charters are significant on a few individual but smaller routes such as Canada to the Caribbean.

The regulatory constraints on charter services, their early history and subsequent development have been described earlier (Secs 1.4, 2.7 and 3.2). The present chapter examines how passenger charter airlines can achieve such low costs and fares while continuing to operate profitably. But first one needs to consider the nature of non-scheduled operations.

The Chicago Convention in 1944 had asserted that non-scheduled flights were those 'not engaged in scheduled international air services'. But no attempt was made to define 'scheduled' until 1962 when the Council of ICAO agreed that a scheduled international air service is one '... operated so as to serve traffic between the same two or more points either: (i) in accordance with a published timetable, or (ii) with flights so regular or frequent that they constitute a recognizable systematic series'. Within a few years of this definition being drafted it was meaningless as the basis for any real distinction between scheduled and non-scheduled services. Many inclusive tour and affinity group charters were being operated as a 'recognizable systematic series' of flights and though the timetables were not published by the charter airlines they were to all intents and purposes published by the tour operators and travel agents. The formal distinction between the two types of services became increasingly blurred.

Today, within the Europe–Mediterranean area, the vast majority of passengers charter flights are inclusive tour charters (ITCs). These are where the whole of an aircraft is chartered by one or more tour operators who combine the round trip seats with hotel or other accommodation into 'package' holidays. The passenger buys the holiday package from a travel agent or tour operator at a single price and is unaware of the cost of travel within that total price. Some charter packages may involve minimal accommodation or may include car hire, boat hire or something else in lieu of accommodation. Apart from ITCs there are some affinity group and student charters within Europe, and in one or two markets, such as UK–Switzerland, advance booking charters (ABCs) are operated. But these other forms of charters are relatively limited compared to ITCs, which dominate the market. On the North Atlantic routes the reverse is the case. ABCs account for around 80 per cent of the total charter traffic, though the figure varies from route to route. ABC rules require the prepurchase of tickets a minimum number of days prior to departure and that such tickets must be bought from licensed travel agents, not the airlines themselves. On UK–United States charters in 1984 the pre-booking period was 21 days at both ends of the market. Following deregulation the United States had espoused the concept of 'public charters' with such minimal controls on seat access for charter passengers that such charters would be difficult to differentiate from scheduled services. Most European countries have not wished to go so far. Apart from ABCs, most of the remaining charters on the North Atlantic are inclusive tour charters that operate very much as they do in Europe. Charter flows in other smaller markets such as Europe to East Africa or to Sri Lanka and from Canada to the Caribbean generally involve inclusive tours.

ITCs are distinctive in that a passenger cannot, in theory, buy only a seat on the flight but must buy a holiday package of some kind. But one can also buy inclusive tours using scheduled services. The only major feature which distinguishes ITCs and other forms of charter services from scheduled flights is that the passenger cannot buy a seat or a package holiday directly from the airline as scheduled passengers can but must do so through an intermediary such as a tour operator, travel agent, student union and so on. This distinction, too, may be cosmetic rather than real, since, in some cases the intermediary selling agent may be a subsidiary company of the charter airline or even its parent company.

While many scheduled airlines operate charters, the international passenger charter market is dominated by specialist charter carriers which are either privately owned non-scheduled airlines or charter subsidiaries of scheduled airlines (Table 1.5). In 1983 these specialist charter carriers generated 65 per cent of the total international non-scheduled passenger-kilometres with the balance of 35 per cent being carried by the charter flights of scheduled carriers (ICAO, 1984d). Several of the charter carriers are relatively large, with traffic levels exceeding those of many national scheduled airlines. Their size and importance can be gauged by the fact that the largest of them, Britannia Airways (UK), generates more passenger-kilometres on international services than any of the scheduled airlines of South America or Africa, more even than Eastern in the United States, or British Caledonian. The non-scheduled carriers are equipped with large and modern fleets of aircraft, usually bought new. In 1983 Britannia Airways operated a fleet of twenty-nine Boeing 737-200 aircraft and the following year it was among the first airlines in Europe to introduce the new Boeing 767. A second British charter airline, Monarch, was a lead customer for the Boeing 757.

A particular feature of the European inclusive tour industry is the strong tendency towards vertical integration between tour operators and charter airlines and in some cases with hotel groups as well. The largest non-scheduled carrier in the world, Britannia Airways, is part of the Thomson organization, which also owns Thomson Travel, Britain's largest tour operator, with interests in a number of hotels. Sterling, another of the larger charter airlines, is wholly owned by Tjaereborg International Holdings, a leading Scandinavian travel agency and tour organizer. Many more instances of vertical integration can be found in the UK and elsewhere in Europe.

Another feature of non-scheduled airlines is that as a group their financial performance has been better than that of scheduled carriers. They managed to continue making profits in the early 1980s at a time when many scheduled airlines were nosediving into deficit. In 1981, losses amongst the world's scheduled airlines reached their peak. IATA member airlines made a loss (after interest) of $1,900 million on their international services. In the United Kingdom all the larger scheduled airlines also made losses in 1981, even those operating charters in addition to their scheduled services. Yet in that year all the British charter airlines showed a profit except Dan Air and

Table 6.2 Profit or loss: United Kingdom scheduled and non-scheduled airlines – financial year 1981

	Profit or loss (after interest) (£'000)
Mainly scheduled airlines	
Air UK	− 11,040
British Airways	−113,719
British Caledonian	− 8,021
British Midland	− 3,636
Non-scheduled airlines	
Air Europe	+ 5,390
British Air Ferries	+ 798
Britannia Airways	+ 22,039
Dan Air (some scheduled)	− 243
Monarch	+ 754
Orion	+ 3,912
Tradewinds (cargo charters)	− 2,209

Source: CAA Annual Statistics 1982 (CAP 484).

Tradewinds which was a cargo airline (Table 6.2). The charter market is very competitive and some charter airlines do make losses or even go out of business. In 1981 two of the larger European charter airlines, Condor (Germany) and Balair (Switzerland), both made small losses. Nevertheless, the larger charter carriers have generally shown themselves more adept than many scheduled airlines at matching supply and demand in a way which both generates profits for the producers and meets consumer needs. A key element in this matching process is the ability of charter airlines to produce at low unit costs.

6.2   Non-scheduled cost advantages

6.2.1   DIRECT OPERATING COSTS

In order to appreciate how non-scheduled operators can produce such relatively low unit costs one must examine separately each element of costs for a charter service and compare it with the costs of a comparable scheduled service. To eliminate the effect of differing aircraft types and stage lengths any cost comparison must assume the use of similar aircraft on the same route. The London–Greece route would be a suitable example, since Boeing 737 and Boeing 757 aircraft have been used by both sectors of the industry on this route.

Flight operations are the largest single element of direct costs. Here, charter operators may enjoy some limited advantages. While in the early days of charter services flight crew salaries were lower than in scheduled airlines, this is no longer the case amongst most airlines in the UK and other European countries. The pilots' unions have ensured that salaries within each country are broadly comparable for pilots flying the same aircraft type. Fuel costs are likely to be similar for both charter and scheduled carriers if flying the same aircraft on the same route and paying the same price for fuel. The larger charter airlines should be able to negotiate equally favourable fuel prices at their home base because their uplift will be very high. If, however, they have only a limited number of charter flights to a particular destination, their fuel uplift at that destination may be rather limited and they may be unable to negotiate as good a price as the scheduled carriers. In the latter case they may have a cost disadvantage. Insurance costs will be broadly similar for both types of operators, as will en-route navigation charges. Charter operators may, on the other hand, pay lower landing fees by using cheaper airports, especially in their home country. Scheduled services between London and Greece fly from Heathrow but charter flights might use either Gatwick or Luton which are also in the London area. In the summer of 1984 a scheduled Boeing 757 flight at Heathrow with 150 passengers on board would have paid the airport £2,055, whereas the same aircraft with the same number of passengers on a charter flight from Luton would have paid £1,428 and at Gatwick £1,186. If the charter flight flew from Gatwick on Tuesday or Wednesday, which were off-peak days, the airport charge would have been only £338.

Maintenance costs for both charter and scheduled operations would be broadly similar if using the same aircraft on the same routes. Depreciation costs per hour would also be the same if both charter and scheduled airlines achieved the same utilization. In practice this is unlikely. First, because aircraft used by the scheduled airlines will be used on different routes, many of which are, as previously explained, relatively short. The need to use the London–Greece aircraft on other much shorter scheduled sectors inevitably reduces the annual utilization which that aircraft could have achieved flying only on longer sectors such as London–Greece or London–Palma which is what charter aircraft will be doing. Secondly, because during the peak summer months the charter airlines will be flying their aircraft night and day. Aircraft on scheduled short- to medium-haul routes have a limited 14–16 hour operating day since scheduled passengers do not like departing before 0800 or arriving after 2200; the night hours cannot be used. Scheduled short-haul aircraft frequently spend them on the ground; not so charter aircraft. Charter passengers seem prepared to put up with considerable inconvenience in order to fly cheaply. They will accept departures or arrivals at any time of the night, or at least some of them will. As a result, except where constrained by night bans or limits, charter airlines programme their aircraft to fly during night hours. They have an effective 24-hour operating day during the peak months. On the other hand, charter services have much more marked seasonal peaks and troughs so that in the off-peak winter months daily utilization of aircraft may drop below that of scheduled aircraft. This is more than compensated for by the very high peak utilization achieved by using the night hours. The significantly higher utilization obtained by charter airlines is illustrated in Table 6.3. In addition some charter airlines are able to lease out aircraft during their own off-peak periods to airlines in other parts of the world who face peak demand at that time. Thus Monarch in the UK leased some of its Boeing 737 aircraft in the winter of 1984 and 1985 to Pacific Western in Canada who used them for winter charters to the Caribbean. Air Europe had a similar arrangement with Air Florida. The net result is that European charter airlines achieve significantly higher aircraft utilization than their scheduled counterparts (Table 6.3). Air Europe, for example, in 1983 got more than twice as many flying hours out of its Boeing 757s than British Airways did. Higher aircraft utilization might also enable the charter airlines to achieve more flying

Table 6.3   Aircraft utilization rates: UK scheduled and charter services 1983

	Average daily Utilization (h)	
	Boeing 737-200	Boeing 757
Mainly scheduled		
British Airways	7·7	5·4
Charter only		
Air Europe	12·1	11·7
Britannia	9·7	
Orion	9·0	
Monarch	9·3	9·4

Source: CAA (1984a).

hours per flight crew member. On long-haul air services, scheduled airlines are not so restricted by the commercial need to avoid the night hours. Time zone changes make this difficult anyway. Consequently, on long-haul services, charter airlines have rarely managed to achieve higher aircraft utilization than scheduled airlines.

In terms of direct operating costs, a charter operator flying London–Greece may obtain some cost advantage by paying lower airport charges and, by achieving higher daily utilization for his aircraft, he may also be able to reduce his hourly depreciation costs. Since airport charges and depreciation together may account for about 10 per cent or so of total costs, savings in this area would only have a marginal effect on a charter airline's total operating costs. Flight crew might also be more productive. Conversely, the charter may have to pay higher prices for fuel at airports where their total uplift is not very high. Overall a charter operator is likely to achieve only marginally lower direct operating costs when competing with a scheduled carrier on a particular route and flying the same aircraft. The differences in direct costs are likely to be no greater than might exist between two scheduled airlines flying on that route.

6.2.2   INDIRECT OPERATING COSTS

It is in the area of indirect operating costs that the costs of charter and scheduled services begin to diverge markedly. Charter airlines flying to Greece or elsewhere save money by sub-contracting out most of the aircraft, passenger and baggage handling activities at their destination airports. This may be expensive on a per flight basis, but it means that they avoid a heavy year-round commitment. The seasonal nature of their operations means that they have no need for permanent staff or offices or other facilities at most of the outstations they serve. Even where they do need staff dedicated to their operations they may be in a better position to use seasonal staff. In contrast, British Airways or any other scheduled airline with daily or more frequent flights to Greece will almost certainly do most of its own handling. It will employ a station manager in Athens together with assorted other station and handling staff. It will have offices at the airport and perhaps off the airport as well, with associated rents and other costs. It will have vehicles and perhaps aircraft steps, baggage trolleys and other equipment. While it might employ some seasonal staff, a scheduled airline would have high year-round costs in Athens. Charter carriers are thus likely to have lower station and ground costs.

Charter airlines will also have lower expenditure on passenger services. They will do this by trying to have fewer cabin staff than a scheduled airline would have in the same aircraft type while providing the statutory minimum required for safety. Moreover, a higher proportion of the cabin staff will be seasonally employed and will not be a cost burden for the rest of the year. Some charter airlines employ as much as 50–60 per cent of their staff for their peak season only. By providing relatively poorer and simpler in-flight meals they will reduce the costs of in-flight catering. On long-haul charters, airlines will not normally have inter-lining passengers or passengers catching connecting flights the following day for whom they have responsibility. They thereby escape the hotel, food, transport and other costs associated with such passengers which scheduled airlines have to meet.

The largest savings obtained by charter airlines arise in ticketing, sales and promotion. Charter operations do not require large reservations computers or other expensive ticketing facilities, since the whole plane is chartered to one or perhaps a handful of agents or clubs who then become responsible for distributing the tickets and allocating the seats. The airline will probably print a simple book of tickets for each charter flight. Each book, resembling a book of large raffle tickets, will contain as many single sheets as there are seats on the aircraft. Each sheet or card will be one outward ticket marked with the date of the flight, the destination and the seat number. Part of the sheet may even be torn off and used as a numbered and labelled baggage tag. In some cases the outward and the return ticket may be incorporated on a single card. The airline merely prints books of tickets and hands over to the charterer a book for each flight chartered and has no further ticketing or reservation cost. The charterer then allocates the tickets as he feels best. A charter airline has minimal sales costs. Since it does not sell direct to the public, it has no retail sales offices or staff, nor does it pay commission to others for selling its tickets. Yet agents' commission is an important cost for scheduled airlines. In the financial year 1982 commission paid (net of commission received) represented 8 per cent of British Airways' operating costs and 6 per cent of British Caledonian's costs. A charter airline sells its services not to passengers but to travel agents, tour organizers, or other charterers. In the UK there are a small number of very large tour operators and a somewhat larger number of medium-sized ones. Perhaps less than fifty tour operators purchase up to about 90 per cent of the charter flights operated each year out of the UK. Thus a charter airline's annual selling and promotion costs may be no more than the cost of fifty or so lunches with the key buyers of charter capacity. The charter airline's managing director with a handful of back-up sales staff to do the detailed costings and negotiations is probably all that is required. There is no need to sell or promote its services to the travelling public so a charter airline is unlikely to have a promotion or advertising budget.

Enormous cost savings accrue to charter airlines from the virtual absence of ticketing, sales and promotion expenditure. In 1982 Britain's major international scheduled airlines spent more than £18 per passenger on ticketing sales and promotion (Table 6.4). For the smaller scheduled airlines concentrating on domestic services the per passenger figure was lower at £3–6. The contrast with the UK charter airlines is quite stark. The latter generally spent only a few pence each per passenger on ticketing and sales.

Charter airlines tend to have very much lower general and administrative costs because they require fewer administrative and account-

Table 6.4   Marketing costs per passenger: UK airlines financial year 1982

	Charter pax as percentage of Total pax (%)	*Ticketing, sales (including commissions) and promotion costs per pax (£)*
Mainly scheduled		
British Caledonian	7	22·37
British Airways	14	18·15
Air UK	1	5·61
Britsh Midland	21	3·08
Mainly charter		
Dan Air	80	1·25
Britannia	100	0·08
Monarch	100	0·07
Air Europe	100	0·04
Orion	100	Negligible

Source: CAA (1984a).

ing staff. Many functions which are crucial to scheduled airlines and absorb significant resources either do not exist within a charter airline at all or because of the different nature of charter operations require relatively few staff. A charter airline, for example, does not need a large planning department or forecasting staff or large numbers of accountants to sort out revenue and sales accounts and inter-airline ticketing debts.

A charter airline can make economies in virtually all areas of indirect costs. It can thereby reduce its total operating costs to levels well below those that can be achieved by a scheduled airline flying the same aircraft on the same routes. Because most of the savings in charter operations arise in indirect costs, while direct costs are broadly comparable for both charter and scheduled operations, one finds that indirect costs are a much lower proportion of the total costs of charter airlines than of scheduled airlines. In 1982 among UK scheduled airlines indirect costs accounted for between 35 and 40 per cent of total costs. But among charter airlines, with the exception of Dan Air, indirect costs were around 25 per cent and for Monarch they were well below 20 per cent (CAA, 1984).

Major savings in indirect costs, together with marginally lower direct costs, suggests that if flying similar aircraft a non-scheduled operator may have *total* round trip costs between 20 and 30 per cent lower than those of a scheduled operator on the same route. This is clearly insufficient to explain the wide differentials in charter and scheduled passenger fares which exist in the European market and which were illustrated earlier by reference to the London–Athens route in summer 1983 (Table 6.1). But the initial 20–30 per cent operating cost advantage is magnified by two key elements in the economics of non-scheduled air services: high seating densities and very high load factors.

6.2.3 HIGH SEATING DENSITY

Hapag-Lloyd, a large German airline, has operated Airbus A300s on charter flights from Germany to Greece, Spain or elsewhere in the Mediterranean in a 315-seat configuration. Scheduled airlines such as Lufthansa, Alitalia or Olympic flying on the same routes have generally had 265 seats or less on the same aircraft. (Table 5.6). By putting in 15–25 per cent more seats than its scheduled competitors, Hapag-Lloyd would have been able to reduce its seat-kilometre costs by nearly the same proportion. The scope for higher seating densities and therefore for even lower seat-kilometre costs is sometimes greater on wide-bodied aircraft. Non-scheduled airlines operating DC-10-30 aircraft would normally expect to have close to 380 seats in a charter configuration. Yet the same aircraft flown on scheduled services is more likely to have between 235 and 275 seats (Table 5.6). In this case the charter configuration increases the seating capacity by well over a third.

Several factors explain the ability of charter operators to push up the seating capacities on their aircraft. Non-scheduled aircraft are invariably in a single class layout and at a constant seat pitch. No space is lost accommodating first or business class passengers in separate cabins with greater leg room and low seat densities. The trend towards a three class cabin on medium- and long-haul scheduled flights has in many cases reduced the total seating capacity on aircraft that had previously had only two cabins for first and economy class passengers. Conversely, in Europe, airlines such as British Airways, which discontinued first class and adopted a business class concept but with economy class seating and seat pitch were able to push up their seating capacity. Whatever the cabin layout the charter configuration will also have lower seat pitch, that is, less distance between each row of seats, so that more seat rows can be installed within the length of the cabin. A 29-inch (73·7 cm) seat pitch would be acceptable in a short-haul charter layout, whereas 31–34 inches (78·7–86·4 cm) would be more normal for economy class seating on a scheduled flight. Charter airlines also tend to increase the floor area on the main deck of their aircraft available for seating by reducing the number of toilets and galley space and by eliminating other space uses such as coat cupboards and so on. Galley space can be reduced because in-flight catering tends to be simple and less lavish than on scheduled flights. The absence of first or business class passengers helps in this. In wide-body aircraft, such as DC-10s, the galleys may be placed on the lower deck with an internal lift providing access. This is possible since aircraft on non-scheduled flights do not have traffic rights for the carriage of freight so the aircraft hold is relatively empty.

6.2.4   HIGH LOAD FACTORS

Not only do non-scheduled airlines put more seats into their aircraft but they also fill substantially more of them. Whereas scheduled airlines would be pleased to achieve year-round passenger load factors on their international services of 65–70 per cent, charter airlines would be aiming for around 85 per cent. The stark contrast in the seat factors of the two sectors of the industry is illustrated in Table 6.5. While in 1983 one or two of the scheduled airlines achieved international seat factors of 68 or 69 per cent, which are considered very high by scheduled standards, the majority had seat factors of less than 65 per cent and some were less than 60 per cent. In contrast, over half the non-scheduled operators shown achieved very high seat factors of over 85 per cent while only one, World, had a seat factor below 80

Table 6.5 Passenger load factors on international services 1983

Scheduled	Seat factor (%)	Non-scheduled	Seat factor (%)
	United Kingdom airlines		
British Airways	65	Air Europe	88
British Caledonian	62	Dan Air	87
Dan Air	52	British Airways	87
British Midland	48	Monarch	86
		British Airtours	85
		Britannia	85
		Orion	83
	Other European airlines		
SAS	66	Scanair	90
Air France	64	Sterling	87
Swissair	64	Hapag-Lloyd (1982)	85
KLM	63	Condor (1982)	83
Alitalia	62		
Lufthansa	60		
	United States airlines		
TWA	69	Flying Tigers	91
Delta	68	Arrow	87
Northwest	65	Pan Am	86
American	65	Transamerica	82
Pan Am	60	World	77

Source: CAA (1984a); ICAO (1984f).

per cent. One can conclude that in general passenger seat factors are at least 20 per cent higher on non-scheduled than comparable scheduled services. Pan Am is one of the extreme cases with a seat factor of only 60 per cent on its scheduled flights but 86 per cent on its non-scheduled operations.

The achievement of such high load factors is not due to the non-scheduled operators themselves but to the efforts of the charterers, for it is they who have the responsibility for selling retail the seats they have bought wholesale. By careful programming and scheduling of flights and other components of the total package such as hotel beds, ground transport, tours and so on, the tour operators can achieve very high seat factors on the aircraft and high occupancy factors for the beds and other facilities they have booked. Vertical integration between tour organizers, who may be hotel owners too, and charter airlines facilitates the process of closely matching and programming the supply and demand for hotel beds and aircraft seats. Load factors must be kept high to ensure low and competitive prices.

Several features of the charter market help in achieving this.

Charter passengers are given limited flexibility in terms of choice of departure days and almost none on the choice of the return days. Particularly with inclusive tours, passengers can only stay for a fixed period at their destination; usually seven or 14 days on intra-European charters, or perhaps twelve nights on long-haul charters to East Africa. All the travellers on an outward flight will frequently come back together on the same return flight and on the same day of the week that they flew out on. Aircraft loads are not subject, as in scheduled operations, to the whims of different individual travellers who want to be away for different periods of time and travel on different days of the week. Moreover, once made and paid for, charter bookings are difficult to change and cancel except at a considerable cost to the passenger concerned. Ticket brokers are also used by aircraft charterers to fill up spare capacity on inclusive tour or advanced booking charters. The ticket brokers try to sell spare seats to travel agents or at a discount to the public. If things go really badly a tour operator with a large number of unsold seats on a flight he has chartered may cancel the flight (though he will pay a large penalty if he does that late in the date), and 'consolidate' his passengers on to someone else's flight where seats may be available. Both tour operators benefit from such an arrangement. Loads on individual flights are carefully monitored to ensure high load factors. A finely tuned and highly differentiated price structure for charter tours is used to induce a potential customer to travel on less popular days or times or seasons of the year. Such incentives include lower holiday prices, two weeks for the price of one, free car hire, no charge for a child, and so on.

Higher load factors substantially reduce the passenger-kilometre costs of charter as against scheduled services. The twin impact of higher seating densities and very much higher seat factors on the unit costs of charters can be illustrated by reference to two German airlines, Hapag-Lloyd and Lufthansa, both of whom have been flying Airbus A300 aircraft on European services. As previously pointed out, Hapag-Lloyd operated a charter configuration with 315 seats. Its average load factor in 1982 was 85 per cent. Assuming it achieved this on its Airbuses, this would have resulted in a load of 268 passengers. Lufthansa's scheduled A300s had 265 seats and its average load factor on its European scheduled services was around 55 per cent. On an A300 this would mean 146 passengers. Even if on a particular route the operating costs of the two airlines were the same, and we have seen that they are not, the costs per passenger round trip or per passenger-kilometre for Hapag-Lloyd would be about 45 per cent less than for Lufthansa, purely because it was carrying 268 passengers instead of 146. In other words, by spreading the total round trip operating costs over many more passengers the non-scheduled operator can significantly reduce the trip cost per passenger. The above example shows that the higher charter seating densities and load factor together have a greater impact on reducing the charter costs per passenger than do the savings in operating costs.

6.3 The Cascade and reverse cascade studies

The preceding analysis indicates that non-scheduled operations start with an initial round-trip cost advantage of between 20 and 30 per cent. This arises largely because of their lower indirect operating costs. By putting more seats into their aircraft they magnify this into an even greater cost advantage per seat-kilometre. Then, by filling 80–85 per cent of a larger number of seats, the costs per passenger-kilometre become even less *vis-à-vis* those of scheduled operators. The net effect may be to convert the round trip cost advantage of 20–30 per cent into a passenger cost advantage which may range from 50 to 65 per cent.

It is impossible to obtain operating cost data for comparable routes for both scheduled and non-scheduled services so inevitably there is some uncertainty about the precise level of the initial operating cost advantage enjoyed by charter operators. One of the very few published studies of non-scheduled costs was the so called 'Cascade' study in 1977. This was a joint study carried out by the British CAA and British Airways (CAA, 1977a; Appendix 6). It covered the same ground as the preceding analysis, but it looked at the comparative costs of the two sectors of the industry from a different viewpoint. Commencing with British Airways' scheduled cost per passenger on three sample intra-European routes, systematic adjustments were made for the known differences between charter and scheduled operations, so as to arrive at a derived charter cost per passenger. This was expressed as a percentage of the initial scheduled cost per passenger and on all three routes it was found to be around 36–39 per cent. The *derived* charter cost obtained was then compared with the *actual* charter in that year, which was 1975/6, and was found to be quite close. A Dutch 'cascade' study comparing the relative costs of KLM and a major Dutch charter operator on one route found that the derived charter cost was 54 per cent of the scheduled cost. But the analysis did not include commission and the scheduled operator was not operating a first class service so the scheduled seating density was higher than normal (CEC, 1981).

The British Cascade study found that on London–Athens both the derived and actual charter cost per passenger were around 35–37 per cent of the scheduled cost (Table 6.6). This corresponds very closely to the 1983 differential between the charter cost and the excursion fare (Table 6.1 above). If one examines the different adjustments that were

Table 6.6　Scheduled and charter cost per passenger on London–Athens route

	Charter adjustment to scheduled cost	Cost index
Total scheduled cost per pax (assuming 55% load factor)		100
1 Charter cost savings		
No sales commission	− 8	92
Higher aircraft and crew utilization (assumed 25% higher)	− 3	89
Lower charter 'standards' (i.e. lower landing fees, fewer cabin crew, lower handling and in-flight standards)	− 6	83
Cost not applicable (i.e. no sales, reservations or advertising; low overheads; higher bar sales	− 15	68
Higher charter peak : trough ratio increases fixed element of aircraft operating and station costs)	+ 4	72
2 Higher charter seating density		
Elimination of first class	− 6	66
Higher seating density	− 9	57
3 Higher load factor (assumed 85% on charters)	− 21	36
Derived charter cost as percentage of scheduled		36
Actual charter cost 1975/6 as percentage of scheduled		34–37

Source: Based on UK Civil Aviation Authority Cascade Study 1977.

made to scheduled costs to arrive at a charter cost which was 64 per cent lower, two elements stand out. Straightforward cost savings, after adjustment for the higher costs of meeting charter peaks, accounted for about 28 per cent of the 64 per cent cost reduction. The remaining 36 per cent was due to the increased seating capacity and higher load factors on charter flights. These figures correspond broadly to the cost savings suggested by the analysis earlier in the present chapter.

The UK Civil Aviation Authority carried out a similar study three years later using March 1978 costs and adopting a different approach. This second study considered the costs which a charter airline would incur if it were to offer a scheduled product. Unlike the earlier Cascade study, it defined charter rather than scheduled cost per passenger as its index base and instead of cascading down to a charter product it cascaded up to the scheduled cost. Hence it became known as the 'Reverse Cascade' (CEC, 1981, Annexe 6). Starting with a charter cost per passenger, at an assumed 85 per cent load factor, adjustments were made to allow for the intrinsic differences which a scheduled operation would impose. In the Reverse Cascade the charter cost represents 46 per cent of the derived scheduled cost, whereas, in the original Cascade study, the derived charter cost for the same route represented 39 per cent of the scheduled cost. The implication is that a charter airline using scheduled seating densities and load factors might well be able to operate a scheduled service at a lower unit cost than a scheduled airline would do. It seems that this lower estimated cost came about because the charter airline's estimates of what it would cost to retail the scheduled product were considerably lower than those actually incurred by scheduled airlines.

Both the Cascade and Reverse Cascade studies include some cost adjustments which are controversial. For instance, the assumption that charter costs are adversely affected by their higher peak : trough ratio might be questioned in view of the fact that despite this alleged handicap charters achieve much higher aircraft and crew utilization. The highly peaked nature of charter services also allows much greater use of seasonal labour which may reduce overall labour costs. Thus cost adjustments given in the various studies should be considered as indicative rather than precise. But all the studies do indicate that the charter cost per passenger will normally be less than half the scheduled cost and may be as low as a third. The precise relationship between the two will vary on each route and will clearly be affected by the cost efficiency of the scheduled and non-scheduled airlines competing on that route.

On many European routes the charter-scheduled passenger cost differential has tended to decline since the Cascade and Reverse Cascade studies were costed out. As a result of the fuel price escalation in 1978 and 1979, indirect costs have decreased as a proportion of total costs. Since charter cost savings arise primarily in the area of indirect costs, it is likely that such savings are slightly lower today in relation to total costs than they were before 1978. There have also been two significant changes in scheduled operations. Many scheduled airlines have replaced first class by a business class on their intra-European scheduled services. In the process the number of seats in their aircraft has been increased. At the same time there has been a determined effort to push up load factors, especially since 1980. As a result, scheduled load factors by 1983 were more likely to be around 60 per cent or higher, especially on Mediterranean holiday routes. This contrasts with the 55 per cent load factors assumed in the studies discussed earlier. These changes will have reduced the scheduled-charter cost differential on some routes.

The discussion so far has been concerned with short- to medium-haul charter operations within the Europe–Mediterranean area. Much of the analysis is equally relevant to long-haul charters across the North Atlantic or on other routes. Certainly such charters enjoy similar large savings in indirect costs which are magnified by higher seating densities and high load factors. But it is unlikely that long-haul charters obtain any savings in direct costs. What evidence there is does not indicate that charter airlines on long-haul routes achieve higher aircraft or aircrew utilization, while the relatively low frequency of long-haul charters may result in higher prices being paid for fuel at outstations. The only direct cost saving may be in airport landing fees through the use of airports with lower charges.

6.4 Planning and financial advantages

Apart from a straightforward operating cost advantage charter airlines enjoy other planning and financial advantages which are inherent in the workings of the charter market, particularly for ITCs. The peak period for ITC holidays is during the European summer from mid-June to mid-September. The retailing of those holidays begins the previous November or December with peak sales generally during January to March; though as a result of the economic recession in recent years the proportion of late sales in early summer has increased. Because of early sales the tour operators have to publish their summer brochures with full details of their various package holidays at the very latest by October of the previous year. For competitive reasons the very large tour operators try to produce their brochures even earlier. To do this they must plan and schedule their flights and 'buy' the hotel beds they need some months earlier. Hotel beds and flights for the summer season of 1986 would have been contracted for at the very latest by May or June 1985. The same pattern of charter contracts finalized up to a year in advance exists for winter ITCs. The markets for advanced booking and other forms of series charters basically function in the same way as the ITC market, though the charter contracts may not be closed so long in advance.

The commercial pressure on tour operators and travel agents to plan and sell their holiday packages so far in advance works to the benefit of the non-scheduled operators. By May or early June of one year a charter operator would expect to negotiate several contracts for a summer season of 24–26 weeks starting around the following April or Easter. Each contract may require several return flights per week and may involve hundreds or thousands of hours of flying. The routes to be flown, aircraft types, frequencies, days of the week and departure times will all have been specified. Staggered but high cancellation fees would also have been agreed. Thus if a charterer cancels a summer flight after February the cancellation fee might well be the full cost of the flight minus the out of pocket expenses that would be saved, that is for fuel, meals, *en route* navigation charges and airport fees. Charter operators are in an enviable position. Having negotiated contracts with their various customers they are in a position to know almost a year in advance the routes and frequencies they will be operating and the aircraft and crews they will need. They can plan their productive resources so as to ensure that supply precisely matches demand and that it does so as efficiently as possible. Even if demand falls below expectations and a charterer cancels some flights, the charter airline is safeguarded against loss by the high cancellation fees. Knowing their total revenue in advance, charter airlines can adjust and reorganize their costs to ensure that costs do not exceed revenues. Scheduled airlines normally do not know their revenues until the costs have been incurred and it is too late to make any significant adjustments.

The charter airline has further safeguards. The negotiated price for the charter is normally per round trip or per block hour for a minimum number of trips or block hours per season. If this minimum number is exceeded the trip or hourly cost may decline. But the price is based on the airline's input costs at a datum point and will include actual or forecast fuel prices, airport fees and navigation charges and assumed exchange rates for relevant currencies especially the dollar rate. The airline is obliged to advise the charterer of any net change of costs in relation to the datum costs a certain number of days before a flight. If costs have gone up there will be a surcharge to pay. If they have gone down the charterer may be entitled to a rebate. A minimum notice period of 90 days is often used so the charterer has time to pass on any surcharge to the passenger. This system of surcharges on the negotiated charter price insulates charter airlines against any sudden and adverse variations in their input costs. They cannot lose.

Once the contracts with the various tour operators and other charterers have been negotiated, the airline receives a series of advance payments. The size and timing of these advances will vary with each contract. It would not be unusual for an airline to receive 5 per cent of the total contract sum either on signing the contract or shortly afterwards. Another 5 per cent may be paid in December and in each subsequent month so that 25 per cent of the total has been paid by

April or the start of the summer season. Once flying commences the balance due on each flight has to be paid before the flight takes off. The purpose of these advance payments is to help the airlines' cash flow through the relatively slack winter months and to provide some security against cancellations by the charterers. The net result is that a charter operator gets paid in full before a flight even takes off yet a scheduled carrier may wait for months after a particular flight to collect all the revenues due from ticket agents, credit card companies and other airlines.

The charter operator's cash flow is also helped by the high volume of on-board sales of spirits, cigarettes, perfumes, watches and so on. For some reason on-board sales per passenger in Europe are much higher for charter than scheduled passengers. This may be due partly to the fact that many charter flights are from secondary airports with poor duty-free facilities of their own and partly to the high proportion of regular travellers on scheduled flights who may be less inclined to spend money on board. Monarch, one of the larger UK charter airlines, estimated that in 1983 its more than 1 million passengers spent around £2.50 per head on in-flight sales. This produced a handsome profit. Whereas some scheduled airlines are tending to reduce their in-flight range of goods on intra-European services or have done away with them altogether, non-scheduled operators are carrying more high-value goods such as expensive watches and perfumes. While in-flight sales are a positive element for non-scheduled operations the absence of freight revenue clearly reduces the potential revenue from any one flight. Authorizations for passenger charter flights from destination countries normally exclude the right to carry any freight. Thus the charter operator cannot top up his passenger revenue with freight revenue as his scheduled competitor can. The price at which he charters out his aircraft must therefore reflect this.

The charter airlines' planning and financial advantages described above are also the cause of their major headache, which is the constant fear of over-capacity in the market. Signed contracts to provide many hours of flying a year or so later can be used to facilitate the raising of loans to purchase aircraft to meet the charter contract. The ease with which finance can be raised once a contract has been signed may well induce new entrants into the market or existing airlines to expand their capacity too quickly. If too much capacity is available there is a strong downward pressure on charter rates. This happened in the UK charter market in 1981 when Laker Airways started offering its new Airbuses on charters for the 1982 summer season at charter rates per seat about 8 per cent below the 1981 rates. It forced the 1982 market rates down by 8 per cent yet Laker Airways itself collapsed early in 1982 before the summer season had started. An additional problem in recent years in the UK has been the move by a few large tour operators into charter airline operations. This is part of the trend towards vertical integration previously mentioned. The Intasun leisure group set up Air Europe in 1979 and a year later Orion Airways was launched by Horizon Travel. This was done partly because the tour operators were able to offset investment allowances on their newly purchased aircraft against their large profits and thereby reduce their tax liabilities. There were tax advantages to be gained by diversifying from tour operating into flying. The result was to increase the overall charter capacity in the market. The fear that more charter airlines will be set up reinforces the pressures towards vertical integration. As more tour operators become financially linked with particular charter airlines the scope for new airline entrants diminishes.

The early negotiation of charter contracts, the ability to adjust charter rates in response to changes in input costs and the high cancellation fees paid by charterers who cancel flights provide non-scheduled operators with a level of certainty and financial security that is unique in air transport. They can sell their product in advance, at a price which will be adjusted if their costs go up. They can then go out and procure the resources necessary to provide the capacity they have sold. Scheduled airlines are handicapped because they have to do the exact opposite. They first decide to provide a level of scheduled capacity, allocate resources to it and subsequently try and sell it. Scheduled operators must plan their output in advance, without knowing for certain how much of it they will sell. As a result, they face much greater problems in trying to match supply and demand than do the charter airlines.

6.5 Charter versus scheduled competition

There can be little doubt that non-scheduled operations enjoy several cost and other advantages when competing with scheduled air services. These advantages are particularly marked in the short-haul inclusive tour markets within the Europe–Mediterranean area. When faced with head-on competition with charters, European scheduled airlines have had difficulty in maintaining their market share. Some, such as Olympic Airways or the Portuguese carrier TAP, have tried to fight back by entering the charter market themselves. This is rarely a financial success since scheduled airlines can only match the prevailing charter rates at a loss. This is because they have to carry and recoup the high indirect and overhead costs of a scheduled airline. At the same time they lack the flexibility of a specialist charter operator. If aircraft are being used on both scheduled and charter flights they may be unable to use charter seating densities. They may also be unable to tender for all sectors of the charter market if aircraft have to be used for scheduled services for much of the day. The difficulties involved in competing directly in the charter markets has pushed European scheduled carriers in two directions. Many have set up separate but subsidiary charter companies with their own dedicated aircraft and crews. Subsidiaries such as Condor (Lufthansa), British Airtours (British Airways), Scanair (SAS) are now large and successful charter airlines in their own right. The second tendency has been the growth of so-called 'part-charters' on scheduled services within Europe. Under part-charter rules scheduled carriers can sell off blocks of seats to travel agents or tour operators who package the seats into inclusive tour holidays. First introduced between Britain and Spain in 1971, they quickly spread to several other routes where both governments approved. In some cases controls were introduced on the number of seats in scheduled aircraft that could be part-chartered. In many cases there may not be a separate part-charter fare but the airlines may give tour agents a discount on the group inclusive tour (GIT) fare. For example, on London–Athens in summer 1983 some agents were able to buy GIT seats at up to 20 per cent discount on the £164 round trip fare (Table 6.1). This produced an effective part charter rate of around £131 which compared favourably with charter passenger costs of £110–125.

The concept of part-charter on scheduled services is not merely a competitive response to low-cost charters but it also offers scheduled carriers other advantages. By mixing normal traffic and charter traffic scheduled carriers can fill up otherwise empty seats and improve load factors. In the process they may also be able to switch to larger aircraft sooner and thereby get the benefit of lower seat-kilometre costs. By mixing traffic in this way it may also be possible to sustain scheduled services on routes where the scheduled traffic would otherwise be insufficient to maintain adequate scheduled frequencies. But there is an inherent danger in scheduled airlines trying to match charter fares. Scheduled costs are much higher than charter costs. If the proportion of part-charter or other very low fare passengers is controlled and mixed with an adequate proportion of high-yield passengers, the total revenue on the scheduled service may be pushed up. On the other hand, too many very low-fare passengers are a recipe for financial disaster since scheduled costs are not low enough. Yet in their desperation to head off charter competition some European scheduled airlines ended up with too high a proportion of part-charter and low-fare passengers on some of their intra-European holiday routes. As a result, they frequently lost money on such routes without effectively stemming charter penetration. On the North Atlantic, following deregulation in 1978, various charter-competitive fares cut back the charter share of the market from 29 per cent to just over 11 per cent but they also ensured that many of the scheduled carriers made large losses on this route (Table 3.4).

In Europe, the charter airlines' response to part-charters on scheduled services has been to try and introduce seat-only sales on charter flights. The first step in this direction were the 'throw-away' inclusive tours or 'cheapies' introduced in 1975 when the British CAA authorized a small number of tour operators to offer ITC holidays which included only very simple ground arrangements. In time, such holiday packages, where the accommodation content was derisory and where the passengers were discouraged from using it, spread – despite attempts by governments at both ends of the route to control it. Effectively such 'throw-aways' enable passengers to buy a seat only on a charter flight while remaining technically within the regulations. In recent years the CAA has turned a blind eye to this. The logical next step is formal authorization for seat-only sales on charter flights. This was approved briefly on some charter services between UK and Jugoslavia in 1982 and 1983 but the Jugoslavs subsequently withdrew their approval. Tourist destination countries are loath to formalize the currently illegal practice of seat-only sales because they fear the repercussions on their own scheduled carriers. Yet there seems to be so much public pressure to do so that in the end they may have to give way. If not, travel agents and tour operators will continue to bend the rules to meet public demand for seat-only travel on charter flights. In some cases charter airlines themselves have set up subsidiary travel agencies to sell off to the public unsold seats or seats the agencies have actually bought from the parent charter airline. On the North Atlantic the advance booking charters are seat-only sales.

Part-charters and very low group inclusive or other charter-competitive fares on scheduled services and what are effectively seat-only sales on charter flights are further eroding the remaining distinctions between scheduled and charter services in the markets where both are allowed to operate. The two sides of the industry are moving closer together. On the North Atlantic route this process has been accelerated by United States deregulation which allowed US airlines previously certificated as 'supplemental', that is, charter, carriers to provide scheduled services. World Airways, Transamerica and others began operating on a limited number of North Atlantic scheduled routes. In the process they introduced many elements of charter economics, such as low indirect costs and higher seating densities and load factors, into scheduled operations. By doing this they were able to operate at costs which were about 25 per cent below those of the established scheduled carriers (Wheatcroft, 1982). Some new airlines, such as People Express and Virgin Atlantic, understood the implications of this and have tried to adopt charter features into their own scheduled services. Most of the long-haul scheduled carriers have yet to do so.

7

The Nature of Passenger Demand

7.1 The interaction of supply and demand

The discussion so far has concentrated to a great extent on supply aspects of international air transport. There is a tendency among airline managers to concentrate on supply considerations at the expense of demand factors. Within many airlines great emphasis is placed on operational safety and efficiency and on reducing costs of production. A large range of performance indicators are produced to enable the airlines to monitor various aspects of supply. Engine shutdowns per 1,000, hours punctuality, annual utilization of aircraft and crews, maintenance man-hours per aircraft, and unit costs per tonne-kilometre are just a few of the indicators used to monitor supply conditions. By contrast performance indicators on the demand or revenue side are relatively few and often less importance is attached to them. Too many airlines, among them smaller national carriers, assume that if their supply of services is efficient and low cost that is enough; profitability should follow. The international regulation of fares through the IATA and, especially within Europe, the extensive use of airline pooling agreements may have blunted initiative with regard to understanding and stimulating demand. Yet airline management is about matching the supply of air services which management can largely control with the demand for such services over which management has much less influence. To be successful in this an airline can be a low-cost operator or a high-cost operator. What determines profitability is the airline's ability to produce unit revenues which are higher than its unit costs. Low unit costs are no guarantee of profit if an airline is unable to generate even the low unit revenues necessary to cover such costs. Pan Am, one of the lowest cost international carriers in the world, in 1982 was losing a million dollars a day before interest, while Northwest, the world leader in terms of cost, made a small loss (Table 7.1).

Conversely, as the 1982 results for British Airways, Lufthansa or Swissair indicate, high unit costs are not necessarily a bar to profit if an airline can develop its markets in such a way as to ensure even higher unit revenues. Some airlines do this by setting out to position themselves at the top end of their markets, developing and catering for traffic which will produce high enough revenue to compensate for

Table 7.1 Operating results: selected airlines, financial year 1982

	Cost per available tonne-kilometre (US cents)	Revenue per available tonne-kilometre (US cents)	Operating profit or loss* ($ million)
Northwest	28·0	27·9	(− 8)
Thai International	31·2	35·0	+ 62
Korean (1981)	31·8	34·5	+ 78
SIA	33·1	34·0	+ 33
Air Canada	34·4	34·0	(− 21)
Pan Am	34·9	34·1	(− 373)
Air India	35·4	38·8	+ 63
JAL	35·5	35·1	(− 33)
Qantas	38·9	37·9	(− 32)
KLM	39·7	40·0	+ 15
American	39·9	39·7	(− 18)
TWA	41·0	39·7	(− 104)
Air France	42·5	41·3	(− 83)
British Airways	43·3	47·3	+ 286
Lufthansa	45·0	45·9	+ 56
Eastern	47·1	46·9	(− 19)
Swissair	52·7	53·3	+ 18
Alitalia	55·2	53·3	(− 55)

*Before interest and other non-operating items.
Source: ICAO (1983e).

those airlines' high costs. SAS and Swissair have been doing this very successfully in recent years on their international routes and New York Air has been doing it domestically in the United States.

To achieve this profitable matching of supply and demand it is crucial for airline managers to have a thorough understanding of the demand they are trying to satisfy. Such an understanding is fundamental to every aspect of airline planning. Aircraft selection, route development, scheduling, product planning and pricing and advertising are just some of the many decision areas which ultimately are dependent on an analysis of demand for the transport of both passengers and freight. As in all industries supply and demand for air services are not independent of each other. On the contrary, each affects the other. Aircraft types and speeds, departure and arrival times, frequency of service, air fares, in-flight service, the quality of ground handling and other features of supply will influence demand for an airline's services. Conversely, the demand will itself affect those supply features. The density of passenger demand, its seasonality, the purpose of travel, the distance to be travelled, the nature of the freight demand and other demand aspects should influence supply and will impact on costs. (The impact of demand patterns on costs have been discussed briefly in Ch. 5.) Thus airline planning is a dynamic and iterative process. An understanding and evaluation of the demand for air transport leads to the provision of services which themselves then affect the demand. New adjustments to the supply then take place to meet changes in the demand and this interactive process continues. The more competitive and unregulated the market, the more dynamic the interaction becomes and the greater are the headaches for airline managers.

The present chapter considers certain characteristics of the demand for air travel and examines the various factors which affect the level and growth of demand in any given market. This understanding of demand leads on naturally to an examination of the forecasting techniques most widely used by airlines.

7.2 The pattern of air travel

The bulk of air travel is either for business or for leisure. Business travel involves a journey necessitated by one's employment and paid for by the employer. The business traveller and the employer may in some cases be the same person, but even then the traveller will not be paying directly out of his own pocket but out of his firm's. The leisure market is further subdivided into two distinct categories, holiday travel and travel whose primary purpose is visiting friends or relatives (often referred to as VFR). Leisure travellers, unlike those travelling on business, invariably pay their own fares out of their own pockets. A number of important differences between the business and leisure markets stem from the fact that in the former case the passenger is not paying for his own travel whereas in the latter he is. These are discussed later.

There is, finally, a small proportion of air passengers who do not fit into the business, holiday or VFR categories. These include students travelling to or from their place of study, those travelling for medical reasons, and migrants moving to another country. They are normally grouped together as a miscellaneous category.

In the early days of international air transport the majority of passengers were travelling on business. The remainder were relatively wealthy leisure passengers. As the total air passenger market has expanded following the steady rise in personal incomes and the decline in the real cost of air fares, the proportion of business travel has fallen rapidly. In Europe business now generates about 30 per cent or less of international air travel while the proportion is slightly higher in the United States (ATA, 1983). In the UK the figure is below 20 per cent. In 1983, 12·3 million UK residents went abroad by air. Of these, only

18·5 per cent were travelling on business. Two-thirds, or 67·7 per cent were holiday travellers and 11·7 per cent were flying to visit friends and relatives. The remainder, approximately 2·1 per cent, were travelling for a miscellany of other reasons (*Business Monitor*, 1983).

Thus leisure travel, for holidays and to visit friends or relatives, accounts for around 80 per cent of the UK originating air travel market and its share is tending to increase. It is also significant that nearly half (46·6 per cent) of the 12·3 million UK residents flying abroad in 1983 went on inclusive tours, the majority of which would have been on charter flights. Charters thereby absorb a large proportion of the total holiday market. Conversely, business travel is almost entirely confined to scheduled flights. As a result, on many scheduled flights the business proportion of the traffic is much higher than the 18·5 per cent overall business share would suggest.

On short-haul scheduled routes out of London such as Frankfurt, Brussels or Paris business trips may generate as much as two-thirds of the total traffic. The business share goes down to about one-third on long-haul routes such as London to Los Angeles or Singapore and will be lowest at around 10 per cent on long-haul routes to Australia where the VFR traffic is particularly high (CAA, 1980).

While only about one in ten UK travellers going abroad does so to visit friends or relatives, in some markets such VFR traffic can be much more important. On routes to Canada, to the Caribbean or to South East Asia and Australia as much as a third of the UK originating traffic may be visiting friends or relatives.

In other regions of the world the split between business, holiday, VFR and other trips will vary. As a general rule the higher the personal disposable income of the population in a country, the greater is the proportion of holiday trips in the total international air travel generated by that country. Unless, of course, travel or foreign exchange restrictions are imposed on its citizens. Low incomes in most countries of Africa mean that business trips dominate on international air routes within the continent. Conversely, rapidly rising personal incomes in Japan and the newly industrialized countries of East Asia during the 1970s generated a rapid growth of leisure travel which partly explains the unusually high growth rates enjoyed by airlines in the region during the last decade (Table 1.2). VFR traffic tends to be significant on air routes joining countries between which there have been earlier population movements. Apart from the UK examples previously cited, there are many other air routes with an important VFR component. These include France to Algeria or Morocco, and the United States to the Philippines.

The air travel market is smaller than the number of passenger trips recorded since each individual traveller will normally make more than one flight. The relationship between the number of travellers and the passenger trips recorded varies on a route-by-route basis. It is greatly influenced by the proportion of business travellers on the route since they are most likely to be frequent users of air services. On many inclusive tour charter routes the number of travellers is probably close to half the number of passengers recorded on the route since each traveller will make both an outward and a return trip, while it is unlikely that he will make that round trip more than once a year. In scheduled markets the position is more complex, with a small proportion of frequent travellers generating a high proportion of the total passenger trips recorded. Such frequent travellers will usually be flying on business, but some may also be on leisure trips. In the United States in 1983, frequent flyers who took more than twelve trips in the previous year represented only 3 per cent of air travellers but took 31 per cent of all air trips (ATA, 1983). In 1978 the 25 million largely scheduled passenger movements recorded at London's Heathrow airport (excluding transit passengers) were due to about 6 million travellers making an average of four trips a year through the airport (CAA 1980). The average figure hides the fact that UK business passengers had each, on average, used Heathrow seven times during the year, while UK leisure passengers had used it 1·6 times each.

Travel motivation has an impact on frequency of travel but also on the duration of the trip. While business travellers fly more frequently they also take shorter trips. Among leisure passengers, those on inclusive tour holidays have the longest trips since such holidays normally are of fixed duration, often in multiples of a week. As the journey distance increases so does the duration of the trip, whatever its purpose. These two tendencies, longer trip duration for leisure travellers and longer duration for longer distance trips by all travellers, was clearly illustrated in the 1978 survey of Heathrow passengers. This showed that, remarkably, 22 per cent of business travellers on European routes out of Heathrow fly back the same day or the next. At the other extreme 68 per cent of leisure passengers to or from North America have trips lasting for more than two weeks.

7.3 Socio-economic characteristics

One would expect male passengers to make up the bulk of the business market, but the extent to which males dominate is perhaps surprising. In the UK only about one in ten business air travellers is a woman (CAA 1984a). The proportion is somewhat lower on UK domestic air services and lowest on international long haul. This pattern is indicative of the situation elsewhere in Europe too. In the United States the proportion of women among business travellers is close to three in ten (ATA, 1983). Traditionally, business travellers have been thought to be primarily middle and senior managers and executives and established lawyers, architects, consultants or other professionals. Their seniority inevitably meant that they would be in the middle to upper age group, that is, early 30s to mid-50s. However, the business market appears to be undergoing a fundamental change. The internationalization of the world's trade and industry and the fall in the real cost of air travel, together with the speed advantage offered, has resulted in recent years in a growth of business travel by more junior staff and skilled workers. The 1978 survey of air passengers at London's airports found that nearly one-quarter of business passengers were supervisory clerical and junior managerial or professional staff or skilled manual workers (CAA, 1980). Such passengers would tend to be younger and on lower incomes than the more traditional business passenger.

The leisure market manifests a more even split of passengers between the two sexes, though in many European and North American leisure markets women if anything predominate. The most recent survey in the United Kingdom, that of passengers at the Scottish airports, indicated that in 1982 55 per cent of leisure passengers on Scottish international air services were women. The proportion of women rose to 63 per cent among international VFR passengers (CAA, 1984b). In the United States women are dominant in the leisure market, generating well over half the total air trips. Among leisure passengers the age distribution is wider and more evenly spread than among business passengers. The propensity to travel by air for all forms of leisure is highest in the UK among those aged from 16 to 49 years. It tapers off among those aged 50 years or older, though still remaining high. Conversely, the very young, those below the age of 16 years of age, who represent a quarter of the population, account for less than 5 per cent of leisure air travel. The most significant socio-economic variable affecting the demand for leisure travel is personal or household income since leisure trips are paid for by the passenger, who may also be paying for a spouse and one or more children As a result those with higher incomes generate a disproportionately large share of the leisure market. The 1982 survey of passengers using Scottish airports indicated that the 60 per cent of the international air trips were generated by the 15 per cent of the population at the top of the income scale. In many Third World countries with low average disposable incomes, international air travel may be limited entirely to the 5–10 per cent of the population with the highest incomes. Elsewhere international leisure travel may be more widespread but still with a predominance of higher income earners.

Apart from sex, age and household income, passenger surveys may also ascertain other socio-economic features of the passengers on a route. These may include size of family, the number of people travelling together, the social class of passengers, the type of industry or profession that business travellers are engaged in, and so on. An appreciation of the socio-economic characteristics of passenger demand in each market is helpful to airlines in planning their advertising, promotion and sales activity. It can help them in deciding where to advertise and what features of their services to emphasize in their advertising campaigns. Such knowledge of the market may help to a certain extent in product planning and in determining tariff policies and possibly even in forecasting. But in the latter areas knowing the breakdown of one's passengers by purpose of travel and trip duration and an awareness of their booking patterns may be more useful than knowing their socio-economic characteristics.

7.4 Market segmentation

Traditionally airlines have segmented their markets on each route by trip purpose. Some airlines do this simply by dividing their passengers into business and non-business or leisure passengers. Others make a three- or fourfold division into business, leisure, VFR and other. Market segmentation in this way is invaluable since the different market segments have different growth rates and respond differently to internal variables such as fare changes or to external factors such as exchange rate fluctuations or economic recession in a particular country. Understanding the size and the characteristics of each market segment on each route is essential for forecasting demand, for many aspects of product planning such as scheduling or in-flight service and especially for pricing. Airlines without such detailed knowledge of their markets are likely to get into difficulties when trying to match supply and demand.

In recent years there has been a growing awareness among airline managers that this simple approach to market segmentation based on trip purpose has some shortcomings. First, it tends to place too much emphasis on the demographic and socio-economic features of the passengers. Age, sex or social class are perhaps less important than appreciating passenger needs and requirements when travelling by air. Surely it is more important for an airline to know whether a passenger will cancel his reservation at the last moment or whether he is prepared to pay a lower fare for an inconvenient departure than to know his sex or age? Secondly, traditional market segmentation oversimplifies the motivational factors involved in travel decisions. All business air travellers cannot be grouped together and assumed to have similar demand characteristics and needs any more than can all holiday passengers. A senior manager or engineer requiring to go to another country immediately because of an unexpected crisis has different transport requirements and demands than a salesman who plans his regular overseas sales trips months in advance. Equally the family holidaymaker buying his annual two-week inclusive tour package holiday at a sunshine resort places different demands on the air services than the holiday maker going independently and making his own accommodation arrangements or the couple going for a weekend break to Paris from London or to Hong Kong from Manila.

Many airline planners now believe that market segmentation should be based not on a straightforward fourfold division based on journey purpose but on a more complex division related partly to journey purpose but partly also to passenger needs. Thus the business segment may be further subdivided into routine business and emergency business. The holiday segment of the leisure market could be split into an inclusive tour segment, into a multi-destination touring segment and a weekender segment. Other ways of segmenting the market can also be used depending on each airline's appreciation of what are the key segments of its market. The point about more complex market segmentation is that each segment should have distinctive needs and

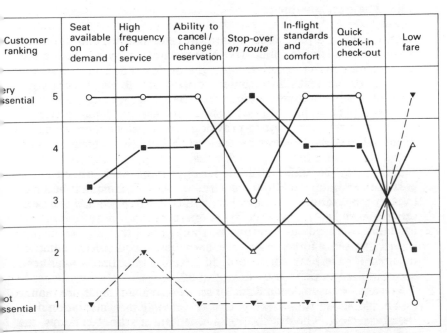

Figure 7.1 Market segmentation by trip purpose and passenger needs. Only a sample of possible market segments is shown here. ▼----▼ , holidaymaker two-week holiday; △———△ , weekend holiday; ■———■ , routine business; ○———○ , emergency business.

expectations such as the need or otherwise to change reservations or
routeings, the need to make stop-overs, the ability to pay particular
fare levels, expectations in terms of in-flight service and comfort and
so on. Variations in needs are shown in Figure 7.1 for four of the
many possible market segments on a medium-haul route such as
London–Athens or Singapore–Colombo. The significance of this
more sophisticated approach to market segmentation is that it can
help airlines in their forecasting and marketing, but it can be especially
helpful in product planning and pricing. It can help them in relating
fares more closely to the costs imposed by the different segments and
also in working out the various conditions attached to different fares
to prevent the slippage of passengers from high to low fare categories.
There is a problem, however. The more complex and sophisticated the
market segmentation, the more complex and costly is the market
research which is necessary to establish and monitor the market
segments and their needs. Smaller airlines will tend to stick to a more
traditional approach.

7.5   The peak problem

Like many transport industries, particularly those dealing with
passengers, the airline industry is characterized by marked daily,
weekly and seasonal peaks and troughs of demand. The pattern and
intensity of the peaks and troughs varies by route and geographical
area. Peak flows become a serious problem when they begin to impose
cost penalties on the airlines involved. In meeting demand at peak
periods an airline may have to provide extra capacity not only in terms
of aircraft and flight crews or cabin staff but also in terms of staff
and facilities in other areas such as sales or engineering. Such extra
capacity may be under-utilized during the off-peak periods. The
greater the ratio of peak to trough traffic the more difficult it becomes
to ensure utilization of peak capacity in off-peak periods. Such peak
capacity then becomes very costly to operate since it must cover all its
fixed and overhead costs during the short period that it is actually in
use. Expressed another way, one finds costly equipment and staff
required for the peak sitting around virtually unutilized or, at best,
under-utilized in periods of low demand.

Seasonal peaks in demand for air services to and from each country
or on particular routes arise as a result of either institutional or
climatic factors. The distribution and length of school holidays, the
patterns of annual holidays for factories and offices, religious festivals
such as Christmas, the Chinese New Year or the Haj pilgrimage and
the distribution of major cultural and sporting events are the main
institutional factors creating seasonal traffic peaks. Climatic factors

are important through their effect on holiday patterns or by disrupting surface modes of travel. Where institutional and climatic factors coalesce then seasonal peaks become very marked. In the European area traditional summer holidays for schoolchildren and employees coincide with climatic conditions in the Mediterranean basin which are ideal for seaside holidays and which are markedly better than in north-western Europe. During the summer months there is an outpouring of people moving southwards from north-western Europe. The effect on airline peaks is dramatic, particularly for the non-scheduled operators who cater for much of this demand. In North America, the Christmas holiday season coincides with very cold winter weather in Canada and parts of the United States while Florida and the Caribbean bask in warm sunshine. These conditions create a peak of demand for air services to the Caribbean area in late December and early January.

Daily or weekly peaks are related to the pattern of working times and days during the week. Business travel creates daily demand peaks usually in the early morning and early evening and weekly peaks on Mondays or possibly Tuesdays and on Fridays. In those Muslim countries which have Thursdays and/or Fridays as days of rest the business peaks will be different. Leisure traffic is responsible for a peaking of demand at the weekends, particularly during the peak season. The split of traffic on any route between business and leisure influences the nature of the daily, weekly and seasonal variations in demand.

The daily and weekly peaks in demand generally pose a less severe handicap since there is enough flexibility in most airlines' operations to enable them to make sensible use of spare capacity during particular periods of the day or the week. Maintenance and training flights can be programmed for such slack periods or aircraft can be leased out for charter work. Many international airlines find that on scheduled routes with a high business component demand falls off at the weekend and they can reduce their frequencies on Saturday and Sundays. A few, such as the Portuguese carrier TAP, use this spare weekend capacity on charter flights to meet the needs of the leisure market which prefers weekend travel.

It is the seasonal peaks of demand which create more problems and impose the greatest costs. Seasonal peaks are especially marked for non-scheduled airlines catering for the inclusive-tour holiday market. As previously pointed out (Ch. 6), they partly overcome their problems by flying their aircraft and crews intensively day and night during the peak period and thereby achieve very high annual utilization for both aircraft and crew. Some may also try to lease their aircraft during their low season to carriers, scheduled or non-scheduled, in other parts of the world who may have a different seasonal pattern of demand. For scheduled airlines seasonal peaks, though less marked than for non-scheduled airlines, may be more difficult to cope with.

The peak : trough variations in monthly passenger flows in 1983 for a selection of routes radiating from London are shown in Table 7.2. On all routes except two, peak traffic exceeds off-peak traffic by at least 50 per cent. As expected, the greatest variations are on European charter services where the peak traffic may be many times greater than the lowest month's traffic. Among scheduled routes, it is the North Atlantic services followed by those to the Middle East which have the greatest relative excess of traffic at peak periods. Airlines on the North

Table 7.2   Seasonal variations on London routes 1983

	Routes to or from London	Lowest month (000s)		Peak month (000s)		Peak as percentage of lowest month (%)
1	European scheduled					
	Athens	16	Feb.	42	Aug.	260
	Amsterdam	61	Feb.	105	Sept.	159
	Paris	146	Feb.	203	Sept.	139
2	European charter					
	Athens	1	Feb.	46	Aug.	5398
	Geneva	4	Oct.	32	March	721
	Malaga	23	Feb.	66	Sept.	285
3	North Atlantic scheduled					
	New York	74	Feb.	204	July	276
	Los Angeles	32	Feb.	89	Aug.	275
	Toronto	17	Feb.	46	Sept.	261
4	Africa scheduled					
	Nairobi	8	May	14	Aug.	182
	Lagos	27	Feb.	42	July	156
	Johannesburg	21	Sept.	29	Dec.	136
5	Asia/Australasia scheduled					
	Singapore	14	Feb.	24	Aug.	168
	Hong Kong	30	Feb.	46	Aug.	153
	Melbourne	20	Nov.	26	Aug.	131
6	Middle East scheduled					
	Kuwait	9	Nov.	23	Aug.	260
	Dubai	7	Feb.	13	July	195
	Jeddah	11	Nov.	20	Sept.	187

The heading above the table reads: *Number of passengers (total both ways)*

Source: CAA, UK Airports (monthly).

Atlantic route have to provide about two and a half times as much capacity to meet peak demand as off-peak. It is also noticeable that most peak months are in the European summer period, that is July to September, and the lowest month tends to be February. There are exceptions, the most notable being on charter services to Geneva which show a winter peak related to the skiing season. The pattern of seasonal peaks and off-peaks will be different on routes in other parts of the world.

A scheduled airline operating on routes with different peak periods can try and shift aircraft and other resources between routes according to the season so as to ensure high utilization. But Table 7.2 shows that an airline such as British Airways operating a range of services out of London, its home base, would have only a limited scope to do this since on many London routes peaks and troughs of demand fall at the same time of the year. Many other airlines face this same problem. As a result the capacity provided by scheduled airlines on international services in the peak season is substantially higher than in the low season (Table 7.3). Some airlines, such as TWA, are offering more than twice as many international seat-kilometres in their peak month as in their lowest month. Conversely, Asian carriers have a less peaky

Table 7.3 Peak : trough capacity imbalance on international services 1982: seat-kilometres available in peak month as a percentage of lowest month

Rank	North American	(%)	European	(%)	Asia/Australasia	(%)
1					SIA	116
2					Thai International	120
3					Qantas	123
4			Swissair	124		
5					Korean	125
6					JAL	126
7			Lufthansa	130		
8					Air India	132
9	Pan Am	137				
10			Air France	139		
11			British Airways	140		
12			KLM	141		
13			Alitalia	142		
14	American	144				
15	Air Canada	163				
16	Eastern	185				
17	Northwest	212				
18	TWA	212				

Source: ICAO (1984c).

output profile than American or European carriers and this may be an added cost advantage for them.

The high costs of meeting peaks of demand could be offset either wholly or partly by operating at very high load factors during peak periods or by charging higher fares at such periods. The question of peak period pricing is discussed in a later chapter on airline revenues. But as far as load factors are concerned, only one of the eighteen airlines in Table 7.3 achieved a passenger load factor in the peak month of 1983 of over 75 per cent and several had peak load factors of 65 per cent or less. At periods when demand is so high that one would expect scheduled airlines to capitalize by filling every seat, in fact about one out of every three seats on international services remains empty. Such relatively low load factors at peak periods aggravate the economic penalties arising from the need to provide sufficient capacity to meet peak demands.

Several factors explain the inability of the scheduled airlines to achieve much higher load factors at peak periods. During the peak month or peak period there are considerable variations in demand. There are peaks and slumps within the peak. To maintain public goodwill and to facilitate the planning of flight operations airlines cannot afford to change schedules and frequencies every week or even every month. Timetables are planned and published many months in advance and the daily or weekly capacity offered during a timetable period will aim at achieving load factors of over 80 or 90 per cent on certain peak days or times in the certainty that at other times load factors will slump to low levels. On routes where airlines are free to compete in terms of frequencies offered, commercial pressures may push airlines to over-provide capacity at peak periods or on peak days so that they may even fail to achieve the expected high load factors. An added problem is that on many routes there is a directional imbalance in the traffic flows. The period of peak demand in one direction may correspond with an off-peak level of demand in the opposite direction. Directional imbalances in traffic levels exist on many routes and usually arise from institutional differences in the markets at each end of the route such as the timing of annual holidays. Such directional imbalances are particularly marked on some long-haul routes such as the North Atlantic or Europe to Australia. Finally, airlines may be unable to match the capacity they offer closely enough to the demand to ensure very high load factors at peak periods. This is because in trying to reduce the number of aircraft types in the fleet, the aircraft on some routes may be too large in relation to the demand. Aircraft size and frequencies can not always be tailored precisely to the demand levels in each market.

Coping with the seasonal variations in demand is a major headache for some airline managements since they affect so many aspects of airline operations. Pricing policies, operating schedules, maintenance and overhaul checks and advertising campaigns all need to be carefully manipulated in order to minimize the adverse effect of traffic peaks and slumps on aircraft and crew utilization and on load factors and through these on unit costs. To mitigate the adverse impact of highly peaked demand, airlines may also lease in aircraft or try to use seasonally employed labour during peak periods. Whatever techniques are used to diminish its impact the peak remains a problem to a greater or lesser extent for all airlines and is an underlying constraint in many aspects of airline planning.

7.6 Factors affecting passenger demand

The demand for passenger services arises from the complex interaction of a large number of factors which affect the different market segments differentially. Those factors fall broadly into two groups: the general economic and supply-related factors that influence demand in all markets, and the more particular factors that may influence demand on some routes but which may be totally absent on others.

Of the general factors affecting demand, the price of air transport and the level and distribution of personal income in the markets served are perhaps the most important. Much of the growth of air travel during the last 30 years can be explained by the falling real price of air transport (as discussed in Ch. 1) and by growth in personal incomes. Accelerated rates of traffic growth in particular markets at particular times have usually been due either to rapid growth in personal incomes or to falling air fares. The more general economic conditions also impact on traffic growth. The world economic climate and the rate of economic growth in particular countries or regions of the world influence demand in a variety of complex ways. They determine the level of industrial and economic activity in each country and more generally the level and nature of international trade. The level of economic activity and trade directly influences the growth of demand for business travel. Indirectly, it also influences leisure demand since it affects the level and growth of personal incomes. Economic factors such as personal incomes or industrial activity have to be understood within a demographic context. The size and the distribution of the populations served by a route impose a major constraint on the level of potential demand. Thus, despite rapidly rising personal incomes in Singapore, the potential demand for Singapore originating air travel is strictly limited by the small size of the island's population of only 2·5 million. This explains SIA's critical need to develop fifth and sixth freedom traffic. Conversely, Japan originating leisure traffic has barely scratched the surface of the potential demand given Japan's population of around 120 million and its rapid economic growth. While rapid population growth may in theory increase the size of the air market in practice it may have an adverse effect if it results in lower per capita incomes or in a larger population but with with a disproportionate share of young children who are unlikely to be air travellers. Both these phenomena have been evident in Morocco and Algeria, countries with birth rates well above average.

Demand and supply do not only interact through the price mechanism. Various supply conditions other than price affect demand. In the short term, frequency, seat availability, departure and arrival times, number of *en-route* stops and other supply features influence the level of demand and the distribution of that demand between competing carriers. In the long term it is the improvements in the overall speed and convenience of air transport that have had the most significant effect on demand. This is particularly true over medium- and long-haul distances where the speed advantage of air increased so dramatically in the 1960s and 1970s that effective surface competition by rail, road or sea has largely disappeared.

In addition to the above general considerations several other factors which may be particular to individual routes also influence demand levels. Demand for holiday trips is related to the tourist attractiveness of particular destinations. In order to be attractive and have a tourist potential, resort areas or towns need two things: they must enjoy certain preferably unique scenic, climatic, historical or cultural advantages; they must also have the right infrastructure to cater for tourist needs such as sufficient hotel beds and of the right standard, adequate ground transport, restaurants, entertainments, shopping facilities and so on. Tourist facilities in themselves may not be enough. They must be priced correctly for the market they hope to attract and in relation to competing destinations. Changes in the relative price levels of hotels and other facilities in a tourist resort area may accelerate or retard traffic growth on particular air routes. Changes in the relative costs of holidays in a country may come about as a result of internal economic conditions or even government decisions. But they may also be generated by fluctuations in the exchange rates. When the pound sterling was worth $2·20–2·40 there was a large influx of UK tourists to the United States. Conversely, when in 1983 and 1984 the value of sterling was down to between $1·50 and 1·20 the UK became very attractive for American tourists. Ultimately, of course, leisure travel is also related to taste. Tourist destinations can inexplicably fall into or out of favour. Between 1978 and 1981 leisure travel between the UK and Greece grew at an average rate of over 20 per cent per year.

Suddenly in 1982 the demand failed to grow and in 1983 it declined. This reversal was attributed largely to a switch of demand to other destinations, notably Spain. Comparative inclusive holiday prices may have favoured Spain but it was also a question of changing tastes.

The visiting friends and relatives demand is clearly affected by earlier population movements and migrations that are very specific to particular routes. The heavy volume of demand on routes between France and Morocco, Algeria or Tunisia is related to the large number of immigrants from these countries living and working in France. There is little VFR traffic on routes between North Africa and the UK. On the other hand traffic demand between the UK and Canada, the West Indies, Pakistan, Australia or from Singapore to southern India or Sri Lanka can only be explained by earlier population movements. The same is true of the demand between the United States and Israel or the United States and Ireland. Many earlier migrations of population were related to the colonial period of history. Colonial ties have also resulted in linguistic and cultural links between particular pairs of countries which generate certain types of leisure travel but also considerable student travel. Large numbers of Singaporean, Malaysian or Hong Kong students go to the English-speaking countries, such as Australia, the UK or the United States to study. Students are an important component of demand on the air routes between their home countries and their places of study. The cultural and linguistic ties also generate travel for cultural events, for conferences and so on. Such ties affect trading patterns and thereby influence business travel. Population migrations for work or settlement are still going on. The United States, Canada and Australia are still attracting and allowing immigrants from certain other countries and these swell the number of air passengers on the respective routes. In other parts of the world there are relatively dense traffic flows generated by movements of migrant labour such as those from the Philippines, South Korea or Pakistan to Saudi Arabia and other Middle East states.

The demand for business travel is related to several factors not just the level of trade and commercial interaction between two city pairs. It would seem that the nature of industrial, commercial and other activities in an airport's hinterland is an important determinant of the level of business travel demand. Certain activities appear to generate more business trips than others. In Britain manufacturing industry generates a disproportionally high level of business travel (CAA, 1980). Administrative capitals obviously generate a great deal of government-related travel. Equally there is some evidence that major international ports generate a disproportionate amount of business air travel. Then there are very specific industrial situations which may stimulate often for a short term a rapid growth in demand for air services. The exploration and development of a new oilfield or the construction and commissioning of a new industrial complex would be two such examples.

The pattern and growth of demand on any route can only be understood by reference to the economic and demographic characteristics of the markets at either end of the route and to the supply features of the air services provided, of which price is the most important. But one must also consider any particular circumstances affecting demand on that route such as the tourist attractiveness of one or both ends of the route, the historical and cultural ties between the two markets served, the impact of exchange rate fluctuations, earlier or current population movements, and so on. These various factors provide an explanation of the growth and current level of demand on a route. Changes in any of them will affect the growth of demand in the future. But ultimately, the demand for air travel, like that for most goods or services, seems to be most closely related to its price and to the income levels of its consumer.

7.7   Income and price elasticities of demand

Historically, leisure travel has shown a marked responsiveness to personal income levels. Early surveys of air passengers, such as those done at the University of Michigan (Lansing and Blood, 1964), established that two things happen as people's personal incomes rise. First, they spend more on all non-essentials. This includes greater expenditure on travel by all modes. Second, air transport which is the high cost but more comfortable and convenient mode for longer journeys becomes more competitive with surface travel and there is a shift of demand from surface modes to air. In other words, higher incomes result in greater expenditure on longer distance holiday and VFR travel and at the same time a higher proportion of that expenditure goes on travel by air rather than surface. The relationship between income changes and demand for air travel can be measured by an income elasticity. This is arrived at quite simply by dividing the percentage change in demand generated by an income change by the percentage change in personal income which generated that shift in demand:

$$\text{income elasticity} = \frac{\text{percentage change in demand}}{\text{percentage change in income}}.$$

Thus, if a 3 per cent increase in personal income results in a 6 per cent growth in demand for air travel then the income elasticity is 6 per cent divided by 3 per cent equals $+2 \cdot 0$. This means that every 1 per cent variation in income will induce a 2 per cent change in demand.

In examining traffic development on a route or group of routes over time in order to establish what the impact of income changes has been, a number of problems arise. The first is how to isolate or exclude the impact of other variables, such as fare changes, on demand. This is done by using multiple regression techniques which in turn pose certain methodological problems discussed in the following chapter. Secondly, there is the question of how to measure personal income. Ideally one would like to use a measure of the personal disposal income, after adjustment for inflation, of the population in a market or of the populations served at either end of a route. But disposable income data is not always available and countries tend to calculate it differently. Proxy measures have to be used for disposable income. Per capita gross domestic product is used most frequently. This is itself problematical in that it assumes a fairly even distribution of income among a country's population which frequently is not the case. The British Airports Authority in its forecasts uses an index of consumer expenditure as a readily accessible measure of the income available to consumers in different countries (BAA, 1978). Thirdly, since air travel for leisure is a relatively new form of expenditure one can assume a high rate of growth in the early stages of increasing incomes and then a gradual saturation as people on high incomes get to the stage where they cannot easily consume more leisure travel. If income elasticities are changing over time it may be misleading to base forecasts on elasticities derived from past data. Finally, there may be difficulties in establishing different income elasticities for the different segments of the leisure market, such as inclusive tours, independent holidays or for VFR travel.

One would not expect the demand for business travel to be closely related to per capita income since business travellers' expenditure patterns are not related to their own personal incomes but to the needs of their employers. On the other hand, several studies have found that gross domestic product or some other measure of a country's national income or wealth does correlate with the volume of business traffic generated. It is not difficult to accept that business activity and travel will increase as a nation's total wealth grows. Thus it has proved possible to establish income elasticities for business travel but based on changes in national rather than per capita income.

Most demand studies in recent years have produced results indicating income elasticities for various categories of passengers which are usually between $1 \cdot 5$ and $2 \cdot 5$. In 1976 the British Airports Authority carried out a forecasting study of traffic for 12 major West European airport authorities (BAA, 1978). Using data for the period

1965–1975 it produced aggregated income elasticities which were as follows:

	income elasticity
short-haul leisure	2·3
long-haul leisure	2·0
short-haul business	1·6
long-haul business	1·2

These figures indicate the lower income elasticities for business travel which are a feature of most studies (e.g. DoT, 1978, 1981). Subsequently, using more recent data and on a more disaggregate basis, the British Airports Authority calculated income elasticities which it could use for forecasting traffic demand through London's airport (BAA, 1981). The predicted income elasticities for the international leisure segments are shown in Table 7.4. The BAA no longer calculates income elasticities for business demand since it finds that trade is a more significant variable for business travel than income.

The responsiveness of demand to price or fare changes can also be measured in terms of an elasticity coefficient:

$$\text{price elasticity} = \frac{\text{percentage change in demand}}{\text{percentage change in price or fare}}.$$

Table 7.4 Predicted income elasticities for international leisure trips to and from London's airports

Leisure segment	1981–5	1985–90
Short haul		
UK resident	0·8	1·1
Non-UK resident	1·8	1·6
North Atlantic		
UK resident	2·0	1·7
Non-UK resident	1·6	1·3
Middle East		
UK resident	2·0	1·7
Non-UK resident	1·3	1·0
Long haul (excluding North America and Middle East)		
UK resident	2·3	2·0
Non-UK resident	1·3	1·3

Source: BAA (1981).

Unlike income elasticity, price elasticity is always negative since price and demand must move in opposite directions. If the fare goes up demand is expected to fall and vice versa. So there is invariably a negative sign in the equation. If fares go up 3 per cent and demand drops 6 per cent then the price elasticity is $(-6\%) \div (+3\%) = -2 \cdot 0$.

Most of the problems previously mentioned which have to be faced when estimating income elasticities also arise in price elasticity studies, but there are some additional ones too. In examining traffic and fare data for a route or several routes over a period of time which fare should one choose to indicate price changes? Not only will there be several fares on each route but the number of fares and their relative levels may have changed over time. Problems multiply when fares vary by season of the year. Some analysts might use the basic economy fare or the most widely used fare or, if it is available, the average yield obtained by the airline. Alternatively, some have overcome this problem by establishing different price elasticities for different fare groups (Staszheim, 1978). It is the real level of the fare in constant value terms that is significant, not the current level. Therefore fares have to be adjusted for price inflation so as to establish the real cost of air travel in relation to the cost of other goods and services. On international routes this means making different adjustments at each end of the route. An additional problem in establishing fare elasticities is posed by the inclusive tour (IT) passengers who have no knowledge of the cost of the fare within their total holiday package price. Moreover, IT fare changes will have a disproportionately small impact on the total holiday price paid by the prospective IT consumer.

In so far as business travellers do not pay for their own travel one would expect them to be relatively insensitive to fare changes. This should be reflected in lower price elasticities for business travellers or for high fare traffic categories which are composed primarily of business travellers. An examination of price elasticities in some of the more recent studies illustrated in Table 7.5 shows this to be true. Whereas non-business travel tends to have price elasticities greater than $-1 \cdot 0$, the price elasticity of business travel is less than $-1 \cdot 0$ and in the case of first class travel on the North Atlantic it was as low as $-0 \cdot 65$. Conversely, the most price-sensitive market segments are those at the lower end of the market, that is the high discount fare groups and, in Europe, the inclusive tour segment of the market.

Economic textbooks deal at length with the concept and the mathematics of elasticity. It is not opportune to discuss the complexities of the concept here. Suffice it to say that in order to make pricing and marketing decisions an airline manager needs to have a feel for the price elasticity of the various market segments on the route or routes he is dealing with. Without such a feel he may make major planning and pricing errors. He basically needs to know whether his

Table 7.5   Price elasticities in recent studies of international travel

Type of travel	Price elasticity	Study or source
Total North Atlantic		
First class	−0·65	Straszheim (1978)
Economy	−1·5	
High discount	−2·7	
High discount and promotion	−1·8	
Australian international		
To Australia	−1·9	Smith and Toms
From Australia	−1·8	(1978)
UK originating		
Inclusive tour leisure	−2·4/−4·6	Department of Trade
Other leisure − Western Europe	−2·4/−2·2	(1978)
Other leisure − rest of world	−2·6	
Business − rest of world	−0·9	
UK resident leisure travel		
Short haul	−1·0	BAA (1981)
North America	−0·7	
Middle East	−1·0	
Long haul (excluding North America and Middle East)	−1·5	

markets are price elastic or inelastic. If the price elasticity of demand in a particular market is greater than −1·0, that is, if it is −1·1, −1·2 or more, the market is considered to be elastic. This means that a change in the price or fare has a more than proportional impact on demand. If the fare is reduced demand will grow more than in proportion. Although each passenger will be paying less than before, there will be many more passengers travelling with the result that the total revenue generated will go up. Conversely a fare increase in an elastic market has such an adverse effect on demand that total revenue will decline despite the fare increase. When the price elasticity is less than −1·0, as in the case of the first class market on the North Atlantic route where one study puts it at −0·65 (Table 7.5), demand is inelastic. Fare changes have a proportionally smaller impact on demand levels. In such market conditions, fare increases will generate greater total revenue because demand will not fall off very much. On the other hand, fare reductions will stimulate some traffic growth, but it will be proportionally less than the drop in fare, so total revenue will decline.

The easiest way of appreciating the pricing and revenue implications of different price elasticities is to consider a simple example. Let us assume that on a short-haul international route, an airline is flying a daily return service with a 200-seater aircraft. It is the only operator and the fare is $100 one way. The daily traffic and revenue on the route can be summarized thus:

total seats offered per day (200 each way)	400
business passengers (approx. 50 each way)	100
leisure passengers (approx. 50 each way)	100
daily seat factor	50%
revenue from business market (100 × $100)	$10,000
revenue from leisure market (100 × $100)	$10,000
total revenue per day	$20,000

Because of an increase in fuel costs, the airline needs to increase revenue on the route by about 4 per cent. In the short term costs cannot be reduced in other areas so the marketing manager is required to generate the additional revenue through tariff changes. The instinctive reaction would be to increase fares by 6 per cent or so. However, earlier market research had established that, while business demand is relatively inelastic to fare changes with an elasticity of $-0 \cdot 8$, the leisure market is price elastic with an elasticity of $-2 \cdot 0$. Using these price elasticities the marketing manager estimates the traffic and revenue impact of a 10 per cent increase in the fare from $100 to $110.

The business price elasticity of $-0 \cdot 8$ tells him that for every 1 per cent increase in the fare the airline will lose $0 \cdot 8$ per cent of its market. Thus a 10 per cent fare rise results in an 8 per cent loss of business travellers. So their daily number will decline from 100 to ninety-two. Leisure traffic, being more elastic to price changes, will drop more, by 20 per cent (or $-2 \cdot 0$ per cent for each 1 per cent increase in fare) to eighty passengers on average each day. The revenue implications of a 10 per cent fare increase are surprising:

92	business passengers at $110	$10,120
80	leisure passengers at $110	$ 8,800
172	passengers:	total revenue	$18,920

seat factor = 43%

Revenue from business travellers would go up because though fewer would travel the drop in traffic is more than compensated for by the higher fare they are all paying. But leisure passengers react in larger numbers to the higher fare and total revenue from this segment of the market would go down markedly. The net result is that if the airline followed an instinctive reaction and increased the fare by, say, 10 per cent, it would end up with a significant fall in traffic, and a collapse of the seat factor from 50 to 43 per cent. This in turn would lead to a drop in total revenue. Too often airlines fail to appreciate that increasing fares may reduce rather than increase their total revenues.

What would be the effect of reducing the fare by 10 per cent to $90? Both business and leisure demand would increase. Using the price elasticities as before the traffic and revenue implications can be calculated.

108	business passengers at $90	$ 9,720
120	leisure passengers at $90	$10,800
228	passengers: total revenue	$20,520

seat factor = 57%

The lower fare would generate twenty-eight more passengers each day and the seat factor would jump to 57 per cent, a creditable improvement from the current 50 per cent. Most of the additional passengers would be leisure passengers, who are more price elastic, and revenue from this sector of the market would increase. While there would also be more business travellers, business revenue would decline because the 8 per cent increase in passenger numbers would not be sufficient to compensate for the 10 per cent drop in the fare paid. Total revenue would increase by $520 which might do little more than cover any additional costs such as in-flight catering imposed by the extra twenty-eight passengers. Cutting fares would produce a better revenue result than increasing the fares but it still fails to generate the additional revenue required.

Examination of the above figures suggests that revenue could be maximized by a two-fare price structure. The airline should charge the business travellers more because their demand is relatively inelastic to price. But it should charge less to the price-elastic leisure market, knowing that lower fares will generate proportionally more demand and thereby increase total revenue from this market segment.

92	business passengers at $110	$10,120
120	leisure passengers at $90	$10,800
212	passengers: total revenue	$20,920

seat factor = 53%

By introducing separate fares for each market segment, the airline can increase its total revenue by 4·6 per cent and its seat factor by three points to 53 per cent. The net revenue gain might be less because there may be some extra costs involved in carrying twelve more passengers. This solution also presupposes that the airline can create effective tariff 'fences' to prevent slippage of business passengers into the low fare market. Simply put, the above example illustrates the principle that in price elastic markets low fares may increase total revenue and that conversely, where demand is inelastic, higher fares will generate higher total revenue.

It must be emphasized that even on a simple route the best pricing solution is dependent on two variables, the price elasticities of the different market segments and the market mix, that is the proportion of the total market represented by each segment. In the above simplified example the pricing policy adopted might be different if business travellers represented 90 per cent of the market or if the price elasticity of leisure demand was $-2\cdot4$ instead of $-2\cdot0$.

The concept of demand elasticity can be taken further to establish the reaction of passenger demand to changes in other variables. For instance, it is possible to calculate a journey time elasticity of demand. This would show that business travel is the most responsive to reductions in journey time and VFR demand probably least responsive. There is also the concept of cross-elasticity. This measures the impact on the demand for air travel of changes in the price of competing goods or services. One study has established the cross-elasticity of demand for international leisure air travel from Australia with respect to changes in domestic air fares or domestic hotel rates (Taplin, 1980). Changes in fare structure and levels on the North Atlantic route have resulted not only in changes in the total demand but also in significant shifts of demand between fare types, between scheduled and charter and also to some extent between seasons, since fares vary by season. One or two studies have attempted to establish cross-elasticities within the air market (Kanafani *et al.*, 1974).

Different studies even of the same markets inevitably seem to produce different income and price elasticities. Airlines may have difficulties in choosing between them. Larger airlines may carry out their own studies to establish elasticities on the routes they are most interested in. If they can overcome the data and methodological problems they must still face up to the fact that the elasticities are based on historical traffic data which may be influenced by particular variables other than fare or income which have not been included in their analysis. There is the additional problem that price, income or other elasticities are changing over time. This is inherent and inevitable. Since elasticities are based on proportional changes in demand such proportions change as the total demand changes. The pragmatic and methodological problems involved in establishing elasticities should not induce airlines to abandon the concept. Some understanding of elasticities is so crucial for pricing, marketing and forecasting that they cannot be ignored. Even an approximate appreciation of price and income elasticities for the major market segments will help airlines make more soundly based decisions.

8

Forecasting Demand

8.1 The need for forecasts

Forecasting is the most critical area of airline management. An airline forecasts demand in order to plan the supply of services required to meet that demand. Broadly speaking tactical or operational decisions stem from short-term traffic forecasts covering the next 6–18 months or so, and are included in the airline's operating plan and budget for the current and the coming financial year. Aircraft scheduling decisions, maintenance planning, advertising and sales campaigns, the opening of new sales offices are among the many decisions which ultimately are dependent on these shorter-term forecasts. There are in addition a range of strategic decisions, many related to an airline's corporate plan and objectives which stem from long-term forecasts. Decisions on aircraft procurement, the opening-up of new routes or markets, the training of new flight crews, investment in new maintenance facilities and similar strategic decisions all stem from longer-term forecasts of up to five years or longer. Almost every tactical or strategic decision taken within an airline stems ultimately from a forecast. At the same time, forecasting is the area in which mistakes are most frequently made and the one about which there is least certainty. There is no absolute truth in forecasting, no optimum method that can guarantee accuracy. Instead, airline forecasters use any one of a range of forecasting techniques, of varying mathematical complexity, each of which has advantages and disadvantages, none of which can ensure consistent accuracy. Yet forecasts have to be made since so many decisions flow from them.

The annual budgets and the longer-term plans on which so many supply decisions hinge start with forecasts of passenger and freight traffic. Forecasting involves different types of forecasts, each of which pose different methodological problems. In the first instance, airlines need to forecast traffic growth assuming a continuation of current operating conditions with no dramatic changes in fares or in other supply factors. They will forecast the global growth of passenger and/or freight traffic on a route, group of routes or geographical region. Such forecasts represent the total demand from which the airline then has to predict its own share and its own traffic. Such forecasts essentially involve an assumption that traffic growth will continue in the future very much as it has done in the past.

Airlines must also be able to forecast the response of demand to a change in the conditions of supply. Such changes may include an increase or reduction in the real level of fares, a change from narrow- to wide-body aircraft, a marked increase in frequencies or a change in departure times. A significant change in supply conditions may be under consideration by the airline itself or change may be imposed by one or more of its competitors. In either case, an airline must be in a position to forecast traffic reaction to such change.

A somewhat different forecasting problem exists when an airline is trying to forecast demand on a new route which is under evaluation. This may frequently be a route on which there have been no direct air services at all previously, or it may be a route on which the airline concerned is a new entrant. In either case the airline has no experience and little or no historical traffic data on which to base its forecasts. This is particularly so if the route has had no previous air services at all. Forecasting in such circumstances is clearly very difficult with a high risk of error and may require different forecasting techniques to those normally used.

Finally, there is the question of segmental forecasting. Passenger traffic on a route is composed of identifiable market segments related partly to purpose of travel and partly to service requirements. Such segments may be further categorized by point of origin. The earlier analysis of demand factors indicated that each market segment is likely to have differing demand elasticities and to be growing at different rates. It should therefore be possible to produce more accurate forecasts by forecasting the growth in each market segment separately and then aggregating them rather than by forecasting the total traffic from the start. Some airlines already do forecasts using two market segments, business and non-business, or possibly three based on fare type. It is only a handful of airlines that have the resources to carry out more extensive segmental forecasting. In the future, however, planning requirements and the need to improve the accuracy of forecasts may push more airlines to consider this disaggregate forecasting.

The aim of the present chapter is not to suggest the best way of forecasting but to review some of the problems of forecasting and the alternative techniques which are most commonly used in the international airline industry, without going too deeply into their mathematics. As a result, this is not an exhaustive review since some forecasting tools, little used by airlines, are not examined. The forecasting methods more widely used by airlines, often in combination, fall broadly into three groups of growing complexity: qualitative methods, time series projections and causal methods.

8.2 Qualitative methods

8.2.1 EXECUTIVE JUDGEMENT

Of the numerous forecasting techniques available to airlines executive judgement is one of the most widely used, usually to modify and adapt other more mathematical forecasts. Such judgement is based on the insight and assessment of a person, who often may not be a forecaster, but who has special knowledge of the route or market in question. For instance, the country or area managers of an airline are frequently asked to predict traffic growth on their routes. Their knowledge will include an understanding of recent and current traffic growth and of economic and other developments likely to affect future demand. They weigh up the factors involved and therefore their judgement and their predictions may be quite soundly based but the approach is basically crude and unscientific. The more detailed and the more long-term the forecast the more likely it is that executive judgement will prove inadequate. On the other hand executive judgement as a forecasting tool has two distinct advantages. It is quick. Forecasts can be made almost instantaneously and do not require any detailed assessment or working out of data. In addition, the person making the forecast may be aware of extraneous and particular factors which may affect future demand on a route, which the more data-based techniques would not pick up. It is for this reason that many airlines subject their data-based forecasts to assessment and possible modification by certain key managers and executives.

8.2.2 MARKET RESEARCH

A wide range of market research techniques can be used by airlines in order to analyse the characteristics of demand for both passengers and freight. These techniques will include attitudinal and behavioural surveys of passengers and hopefully those not travelling by air. They will also involve studies of hotel and tourism facilities, surveys of travel agents and business houses, analyses of trade flows and other business interaction and so on. Such studies might be commissioned from specialist market research companies or they might be carried out by the airlines themselves. Many larger airlines, in any case, carry out regular and systematic surveys of their own passengers so as to build up a profile of their needs and characteristics. Others carry out such surveys on an *ad hoc* basis when a specific question needs to be resolved. The aim of all this is to derive empirically an understanding of how demand for air transport varies between different sectors of the population or, in the case of air freight, between different industrial sectors. This knowledge can then be used in combination with forecasts by others of sociological, demographic or economic change to predict future levels of demand.

In many circumstances such an empirical approach to forecasting may be more appropriate than the more econometric methods. On an air route where the demand for air travel is suppressed by the inadequate number of hotel beds at the destination, a study of hotel and tourism infrastructure projects at that destination may produce a better indication of future travel flows than would an analysis of past traffic trends. Equally the forecasting of air freight demand often lends itself to the use of market research studies, especially on routes where freight flows are relatively thin. On many routes the erratic and irregular growth of air freight makes time series analyses or other econometric techniques difficult to use. Air freight forecasting models have generally been less successful than models for forecasting passenger demand. On most air routes the goods freighted by air fall into a limited number of clearly defined commodities. Exports by air from many developing countries are usually confined to one or two commodities while imports are quite different and cover a wider, though still limited range of goods. As a result, air freight forecasts may often fruitfully be based on market research analyses of trade developments in a few key commodities.

Market studies are particularly useful as a forecasting tool when past traffic data is inadequate or non-existent, thereby prohibiting the use of time series and possibly of econometric forecasts too. This happens on many routes from developing countries and is obviously the case on entirely new routes. In these circumstances market research may be the only way of evaluating future demand. Market research also helps airlines to forecast demand reaction to changes in supply conditions and to gain an appreciation of their different market segments if they wish to get involved in segmental forecasting.

8.2.3 DELPHI TECHNIQUES

The Delphi approach requires the building up of a consensus forecast based on the views of individuals who are considered to have sufficient expertise to be able to anticipate future trends. The process is an iterative one, possibly involving several rounds of consultation. In simple terms, a group of experts may be asked to give their forecasts of growth in a region or market. These forecasts are used to build up a composite forecast. This is then communicated to each expert who may wish to revise his own original forecast in the light of what other experts are predicting. The individual forecasts from this second round of consultations can be used to arrive at an agreed or consensus forecast. This is the principle of the Delphi method. In practice, the consultative process can be more or less complex depending on the amount of information which is exchanged between the experts. The Delphi technique is more suitable for aggregate forecasts of growth in major markets or regions rather than than for individual route forecasts. As a result it is little used internally by airlines but it is the basis for the industry-wide forecasts produced annually by IATA. These are regional forecasts for nearly twenty route areas, such as Europe–Middle East or Middle East–Far East. Forecasts of passengers in each direction are produced as well as forecasts of freight traffic. The forecasts cover the current year and a five-year period ahead and are revised each June, sometimes with interim revisions during the winter. The forecasts are based on a concensus of expert opinion and are arrived at in a series of steps.

The first step involves the development of explicit forecasting assumptions at a meeting of airline forecasters and key experts from outside the airline industry. The purpose of this meeting is to develop the best possible background scenarios and explicit regional assumptions for the changes in the real level of tariffs and in the major economic indicators affecting demand. The assumptions and data bases are communicated to the airlines participating in the forecasting exercise. The airlines are then requested to submit their own forecasts for the industry as a whole and for each route area or market on which they operate. Airlines are free to use whatever forecasting method they prefer in arriving at their own forecasts and can even make alternative key assumptions if they wish to. The results of this first round are distributed to all participating airlines for review before the finalization meeting. This takes place in early June. The experts review the consolidated regional forecasts, make adjustments in the light of more recent developments and may also consider econometric forecasts made by some member airlines. The IATA forecasts are then finalized and widely distributed throughout the world. These forecasts represent a concensus of expertise within the airline industry. As such they are used by smaller airlines as inputs into their own forecasting processes and by larger airlines as a counter check to their own internal forecasts. Airport authorities, aircraft manufacturers and governments also refer to the IATA forecasts.

8.3 Time-series projections

Time-series or trend projections represent the forecasting technique most widely used by international airlines. Many smaller airlines do little else. Essentially the technique involves a projection into the future of what has happened in the past. It assumes that whatever factors affected air traffic in the past will continue to operate in the

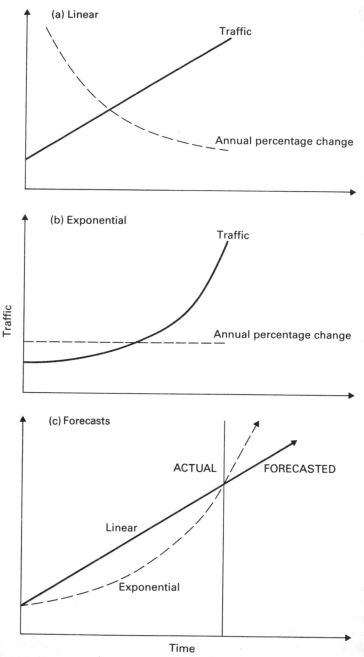

Figure 8.1 Types of traffic growth: (a) linear, $y = a + bt$; (b) exponential, $y = a(1 + b)^t$; (c) actual and forecasted.

same manner in the future. The only independent variable affecting traffic is time and as time progresses so will traffic.

To establish the relationship between traffic, the dependent variable, and time, the independent variable, it is essential to have accurate and detailed traffic statistics for the route in question. Without such data, trend projections cannot be used. The first step in the forecasting process is to plot the time series data on a graph so as to show monthly or annual traffic totals against the appropriate month or year. Drawing a freehand curve through the points should indicate whether the traffic trend on the route is exponential or linear (Fig. 8.1). An exponential trend is one where traffic seems to grow by a constant percentage with each unit change in time. This means that the absolute increase in each time period in passenger numbers or freight tonnes is greater than in the previous period. This is because each successive growth is a constant percentage but of a larger preceding total. The equation of the exponential curve is given by

$$\text{traffic } (y) = a (1 + b)^t,$$

where a is a constant and b is the rate of growth and t is time. A linear or straight-line trend is one where the traffic increases by a constant absolute amount with each unit of time. It is expressed in the form

$$\text{traffic } (y) = a + bt,$$

where a and b are constants and t is again time. Because changes for each unit of time are by a constant amount and the total traffic is growing, the percentage growth is gradually declining. There is therefore a fundamental difference between the impact of exponential as opposed to a linear growth trend on forecasts of traffic growth. Exponential growth means ever greater annual or monthly traffic increments though the percentage change may be more or less constant. Linear growth would indicate constant increments and declining percentage changes. Deciding which trend best represents developments of a route will therefore have a major impact on forecasts, especially longer-term ones. There is also the possibility that growth on a route may be linear in its early stages and then become exponential or vice versa. An added problem is that at times it might be difficult to decide whether an exponential or linear trend fits the data best, yet choosing between them will produce quite different forecasts.

It has been observed that some air routes or markets after achieving very rapid growth for a number of years reach a plateau where traffic growth flattens off. It is frequently assumed that this plateau level is reached when the market is in some sense saturated. If this has happened or is happening on a route the trend of past traffic data may best be described by growth curves which asymptotically approach an upper limit such as a logistic curve or a Gompertz curve. Both of these are S-shaped and indicate declining absolute and relative growth as markets reach maturity. In practice, international airlines tend not to use logistic or Gompertz trend curves for forecasting. Most time-series forecasting is either exponential or linear. Of these the former is probably more widely used both because of its simplicity and also because past air traffic trends do often appear to be exponential.

The workings and implications of different time-series techniques can best be appreciated by using them to make forecasts for an actual route. The route chosen is London to Nice, a short-haul scheduled route with virtually no charter traffic and relatively little indirect traffic transiting via Paris or elsewhere. To make time-series forecasts a minimum of 7–10 years of past traffic data is required and some forecasters suggest that one should not forecast for a longer period ahead than about half the number of past years for which statistics are available. For the London to Nice route traffic data 12 years to 1983 was examined (Table 8.1). This indicated that although passenger movements almost doubled between 1972 and 1983, growth was at times erratic with two years, 1974 and 1977, in which traffic actually declined. In practice many larger airlines would hesitate to forecast so far ahead on the basis of time-series projections alone. Nevertheless, a five-year forecast to 1988 does enable one to see clearly the impact

Table 8.1   Total   passenger   traffic,   London–Nice   (both   ways) 1972–1983

	Terminal passengers ('000) 1	Annual change (%) 2	Three-year moving average pax ('000) 3	Annual change (%) 4
1972	140·6			
1973	148·5	+ 5·6	143·8	
1974	142·4	− 4·1	151·6	+ 5·4
1975	163·8	+15·0	158·6	+ 4·6
1976	169·6	+ 3·5	166·9	+ 5·2
1977	167·4	− 1·3	174·0	+ 4·3
1978	185·0	+10·5	187·4	+ 7·7
1979	209·9	+13·5	206·7	+10·3
1980	225·1	+ 7·2	225·4	+ 9·0
1981	241·2	+ 7·2	245·0	+ 8·7
1982	268·8	+11·4	259·3	+ 5·8
1983	268·0	− 0·3		

Source: CAA (1982).

of different techniques. While the analysis which follows relates to annual traffic volumes and forecasts the annual traffic for 1988, the same forecasting methods could be used with monthly or weekly traffic data. Problems of seasonal traffic fluctuations might arise but these could be adjusted for.

The London to Nice data underlines some of the difficulties faced in forecasting. To start with, examination and plotting of the traffic data does not make it easy to decide whether past growth is linear or exponential. As a result both exponential and linear forecasts will be made in the analysis which follows. Another major problem facing the forecaster using time-series analysis is how far back should he go in examining past traffic data. In the case of London to Nice ten-year data to 1983 meant 1974 would be the first year. This was known to be a year in which traffic slumped because of the first oil crisis. There was subsequently a very large jump in traffic in the following year, 1975. Using a maverick low year as the starting point might produce less accurate forecasts. So the forecaster may decide, as has been done here, to go back and extend the time series by two years to 1972. This then raises a different question. Is data and traffic so far in the past a good reflection of what will happen five years in the future? Would it not be logical to take a shorter time series? Is the recent past a better indicator of the future than the more distant past? There is no absolute answer to this enigma. The forecaster must choose the time series which he feels in each case will best allow him to make a realistic forecast. To do this he must ensure that his stream of data embodies the underlying trends and encompasses complete cyclical variations if any exist.

8.3.1 EXPONENTIAL FORECASTS

(a) Average rate of growth Many airlines, especially the smaller ones and those that have relatively new routes with only a short stream of data, base their forecasts on the average of the past rates of growth. This approach has the advantage of simplicity. In the London to Nice case, adding up the annual percentage change each year from 1972 to 1983 and dividing by eleven, which is the number of observations, produces an average annual growth of $+6\cdot2$ per cent. Using the formula

$$y = a(1 + b)^t,$$

where a is the actual traffic in 1983; b is the growth rate and t is the number of years forecast, then

$$1988 \text{ traffic} = 268 \times (1\cdot062)^5 = 362\cdot0.$$

In this and subsequent equations, traffic volumes are given in thousands.

In the London to Nice case the number of observations is relatively small, only twelve; and this is so with many airline forecasts. But it does raise some doubt as to whether + 6·2 per cent is the true average growth rate. It is possible to estimate mathematically what the possible range of values for the true growth rate might be. The true growth rate at a 95 per cent level of confidence would be 6·2 ±4·2. If one were to adjust the 1988 forecast accordingly, the range would be very wide. It is for this reason that most airline forecasters would ignore the implications of having a relatively small number of observations.

(b) Moving average growth The use of annual average growth rates should be based, in theory, on data series which are long enough to show what are the random variations and what are shifts in underlying trends. Where the time series is not very long and where there are very marked fluctuations in traffic growth from year to year, some forecasters will use moving averages as a way of flattening out wild traffic variations so as to understand the underlying trends. In order to do this normally three (or more) observations are added together and the average calculated. This is then given as the actual observation for the middle of the three years (or months if one is using monthly data). For London to Nice the actual traffics for 1972, 1973 and 1974 were added together and divided by three. This produced a three-year moving average of 143,800, which was the traffic attributed to 1973, the middle year (Column 3 of Table 8.1). Then 1972 was dropped and the average for 1973, 1974 and 1975 calculated and attributed to 1974 and so on, the final moving average being for 1982. The choice of the number of observations for the moving average is up to the forecaster whose aim is to eliminate sudden short-term traffic variations without losing sight of longer-term changes. But moving averages cannot be used with small data sets since one effectively loses data at each end. Examination of the moving average data for London to Nice in Table 8.1 (columns 3 and 4) shows a flattening out effect. Traffic does not decline in any single year and the growth in the good years is not as high as the unadjusted annual figures would suggest. The highest growth was 10·3 per cent in 1979, following which there seems to have been a downward trend in the underlying growth rate.

The annual average rate of growth can be calculated from the annual changes in the moving average figures (column 4 in Table 8.1). In this case it was 6·8 per cent. Using this to forecast 1988 traffic, then

$$1988 \text{ traffic} = 259.3 \times (1 \cdot 068)^6 = 384 \cdot 8.$$

The use of a moving average here seems to have identified a faster underlying growth than was evident previously.

(c) Exponential smoothing Some forecasters believe that the recent past is a better pointer to the future than the more distant past. It follows that in projecting past traffic growth into the future greater weight should be given to the more recent observations. Mathematically, the technique for doing this is similar to the moving average but adjusted to give a particular weighting to recent as opposed to more distant observations. In a simple form,

$$y + 1 = \alpha y + \alpha(1 - \alpha)y - 1 + \alpha(1 - \alpha)^2 y - 2 + \alpha(1 - \alpha)^3 y - 3 \ldots,$$

where α is a smoothing factor $(0 < \alpha < 1)$, y is the number of passengers in year y, and $y + 1$ is the first year forecast. The greater the value given to α the greater will be the weight given to the more recent observations. The forecaster can himself decide the value of α. The above formulation is relatively simple but some smoothing techniques can be quite complex. The best known is the Box–Jenkins model. This is a sophisticated and complex model requiring a large number of observations. Though airline forecasters make reference to Box–Jenkins (Nguyen Dai, 1982), few if any actually use it. Simpler formulations are available. One of these is the Holt–Winters model, which uses a smoothing technique to deal with time-series data containing a trend variation. Since the London to Nice traffic data showed a clear trend pattern the Holt–Winters model was used. The 1988 forecast produced on this basis was 326,200 passengers. This is much lower than the other exponential forecasts because the effect of the smoothing technique is to give much greater weight to the fact that in 1983 traffic declined marginally. While exponential smoothing techniques have been widely used in some other industries, their use is still fairly limited within the airline industry. There is, however, a growing awareness that by giving greater weight to the more recent observations, forecasters may be in a position to improve the accuracy of time series projections.

8.3.2 LINEAR TREND PROJECTIONS

(a) Simple trend The underlying assumption is that a straight line best represents the trend of the traffic over time and that traffic increases by a constant amount with each unit of time. The technique involves drawing a straight line through the time series so as to produce a best fit. This is normally done by the least squares method though other mathematical techniques are also available. The least squares criterion requires that the line fitted to the data should be the

one which minimizes the sum of the squares of the vertical deviations of the data points from the line. Some of the points are likely to be above the line, and therefore positive, and some below the line, and so negative. These would cancel each other out if one were merely trying to minimize the sum of the deviations. By using the squares of the deviations this problem is avoided.

In fitting a line of the form $y = a + bt$ to the time-series data so as to satisfy the least squares criterion, there remains the problem of how closely the straight line corresponds to that data. The goodness of fit is measured by an index known as the coefficient of correlation (R) or the square of this quantity (R^2), which is strictly speaking the co-efficient of determination. In practice the R^2 coefficient is used most frequently. If the fit of the straight line to the data is very poor the value of R^2 approaches zero. If the fit is very good the value of R^2 will be close to 1.0. Within the airline industry experience suggests that accurate predictions using linear trend lines require very high coefficients of determination. They should be above 0·90 and preferably higher.

Fitting a trend line to the London to Nice data produced the following result:

$$y = 111 \cdot 9 + 12 \cdot 7t, \qquad R^2 = 0 \cdot 939.$$

This indicates that a trend line starting at 111,900 passengers and growing by 12,700 passengers per year (t) produces a good fit with the actual traffic in each year since the coefficient of determination at 0·939 is high. To forecast traffic in 1988 one needs to add 12,700 passengers for each year of the 17 years from 1972 to 1988 to the starting figure of 111,900:

$$\text{1988 traffic} = 111 \cdot 9 + (12 \cdot 7 \times 17) = 327 \cdot 8.$$

Trend projections are simple and easy to use. But they can only be used if the data exhibits some regularity without wide fluctuations. Many air routes, however, do exhibit very pronounced traffic variations with large jumps in traffic followed inexplicably by sudden slumps. In such conditions, fitting trend lines with an adequately high coefficient of determination may prove difficult. One possible solution is to use moving averages.

(c) Moving average trend Unusually large variations in the past traffic volumes can be reduced by calculating moving averages and establishing a new time series. This should now contain only the trend component in the traffic and it should be easier to fit a trend line. Using the moving average data for London to Nice (as previously

given in column 3 of Table 8.1) the following trend line and forecast was calculated:

$$y = 119 \cdot 9 + 13 \cdot 1t, \qquad R^2 = 0 \cdot 961,$$
$$1988 \text{ traffic} = 119 \cdot 9 + (13 \cdot 1 \times 16) = 329 \cdot 5.$$

On London to Nice the use of a moving average trend produces a forecast which is very close to the one based on the unadjusted trend. This is because the London to Nice traffic does not exhibit wide fluctuations and therefore using a moving average trend has relatively little impact. It has only been done here for illustrative purposes.

As a result of using alternative time-series techniques five different forecasts of the London to Nice passenger traffic in 1988 have been produced. They are summarized in Table 8.2. The difference between the highest and the lowest forecast is around 58,000 passengers a year, equivalent to four round-trip flights a week with an Airbus A310 at about a 60 per cent seat factor. The range is very wide and could play havoc with any airline's strategic fleet planning decisions. Which forecast should the forecasters and planners go for? As a group the exponential techniques in this particular case produce higher forecasts than the linear trends. This seems to be frequently so in airline forecasts and may be an additional reason why airlines prefer working with exponential rather than linear projections. They prefer to be optimistic in their forecasts.

Over time every airline's forecasting group has developed, in the light of its experience, a preference for a particular approach to forecasting involving only one or two of the methods proposed above. Few airlines would bother to calculate more than a couple of time-series forecasts.

Table 8.2   Alternative time-series forecasts of London–Nice traffic in 1988

Forecasting method	1988 forecast Number of pax
Exponential forecasts	
1 Average annual rate of growth	362,000
2 Moving average	384,800
3 Exponential smoothing (Holt–Winters)	326,200
Linear trend projections	
4 Simple trend	327,800
5 Moving average trend	329,500
Difference between highest and lowest forecast	58,600

Throughout the world the majority of airlines use time-series projections as the starting point for their forecasting exercises. They are simple to use provided that adequate statistical information on past traffic flows is available. They require little else. They are also likely to be reasonably accurate for shorter-term forecasts. It is relatively easy to forecast tomorrow's traffic if you know today's or to forecast next week's traffic if you know the average traffic handled in recent weeks. Beyond 18 months or so the risk of error with time-series forecasts increases as various external factors begin to impact on demand. Time-series projections allow airlines to make individual forecasts for each route. Annual forecasts can be disaggregated into monthly forecasts reflecting seasonal variations without too much difficulty. Alternatively, time-series forecasts can be built up using monthly rather than annual data.

Although they are widely used, time-series forecasting methods do have a fundamental underlying weakness. They are based on the assumption that traffic growth and development are merely functions of time. As time changes so does demand. Yet our earlier analysis of demand showed that many factors affect the level of demand, such as the level of trade or of personal income, and that these factors are themselves changing over time. Even if these did not do so, there are numerous supply factors, of which the most critical is the tariff level, which are invariably changing and affecting demand in the process. It is clearly an over-simplification to relate demand purely to changes in time. Time can only be a very poor proxy for a host of other critical variables. The longer ahead the time-series projection the less likely it is to be accurate as there is more time and scope for demand to have been influenced by changes in one or more of the many independent variables.

There are two ways in which airline forecasters can try to overcome this underlying weakness. Most airlines start by making time-series projections. They then modify these projections on the basis of market research findings and executive judgement and turn them into forecasts. In this way they can allow for the impact of the expected changes in demand factors and of planned changes in supply which they themselves control. As an alternative a few airlines, usually larger ones, may try to use causal forecasting techniques which relate traffic growth not to time but to a series of assumed causal factors.

8.4   Causal models

The underlying principle of all such models is that the demand for passenger transport or for air freight services is related to and affected by one or more economic, social or supply factors. Therefore, the starting point must be to identify and select the factors, known as the independent variables, which must be assessed in order to forecast the dependent variable that is the level of passenger or possibly freight traffic. The second step is to determine the functional relationship between the dependent variables and the independent variables selected. This means specifying the form of the model to be used. Normally for airline forecasting it will be a regression model. Other model forms such as gravity-type models are used in other areas of transport but rarely in air transport. The third step in the forecasting process involves the calibration of the model and the testing of the mathematical expression for the relationship between the dependent and the independent variables. Should the tests show that the relationship established through the model is significant and statistically robust then one can move on to the final step. This involves forecasting the independent variables or using other people's forecasts in order to derive from them the forecasts of air traffic.

8.4.1 REGRESSION MODELS

Most econometric forecasts of air traffic tend to be based on simple or multiple regression models, where traffic is a function of one or more independent variables. The two variables most frequently used are the air fare and some measure of per capita income. Thus, for a route such as London to Nice, one might consider a model of the form:

$$T = f(F, Y, t), \tag{8.1}$$

where T is the annual number of passengers travelling between London and Nice; F is the average fare in real terms; Y is an income measure such as gross domestic product or consumer expenditure per head; and t is some underlying time trend. Fare level, income levels or other economic variables have to be adjusted for inflation and expressed in constant value or real terms. The choice of fare is critical. Ideally only change in the lowest fare should be considered as only this should affect the total market; changes in other fares would only affect the market mix. On many routes it is not as clear-cut as that since the number of seats for sale at the lowest fare may be strictly limited in number. Many analysts will choose the average yield rather than the lowest fare as the fare variable. Income levels pose the additional problem of identifying those whose income one considers is the variable affecting demand. In the above case should one use a global figure of UK per capita income and another for French income or should one try to establish the income levels in London and those in Nice? If one adjusts the fare level for inflation, one would have to make adjustments to the fare in French francs for Nice-originating traffic and a different adjustment to express the sterling fare in constant terms. This kind of problem would induce many forecasters to develop two separate directional models for the route based on origin of travel. For London-originating passenger traffic going to Nice the formulation would be

$$T_L = f(F_L, Y_{UK}, t_L), \qquad (8.2)$$

where T_L is the London-originating passenger traffic on London–Nice; F_L is the real sterling air fare from London; Y_{UK} is the per capita income in the UK; and t_L is the time trend for London-originating traffic.

In order to convert fares, income or other independent variables into numbers of passengers a constant (K) has to be incorporated into the equation

$$T_L = Kf(F_L, Y_{UK}, t_L). \qquad (8.3)$$

Most airline forecasting models assume that the relationship between the independent variables is multiplicative, that is to say the effects of each of the variables on traffic tend to multiply rather than to add up. The independent variables must represent quite different influences on demand, otherwise the multiplicative relationship may not apply. Expressing the multiplicative relationship between the dependent and the independent variables in logarithmic form turns the relationship between the logarithms into a linear one:

$$\log T_L = K + a \log F_L + b \log Y_{UK} + c \log t_L + u, \qquad (8.4)$$

where u is an error term and a, b and c are model parameters, and the higher their value the more impact changes in the corresponding variables will have on the traffic level.

It is not essential for the model to be log–linear but many empirical studies of demand have found this to be a useful and relevant form.

Many forecasters may decide to go further and relate the percentage change of traffic from one year to the next to the corresponding percentage change in the independent variables, in this case fare and income. The model is then expressed as follows:

$$\Delta \log T_L = K + a \Delta \log F_L + b \Delta \log Y_{UK} + c \log t_L + u, \qquad (8.5)$$

where $\Delta \log$ is the logarithm of the percentage change variable in question over the previous year. Effectively a and b are now the demand or traffic elasticities. The value of a is the fare elasticity of UK-originating traffic on the London to Nice route and b is the income elasticity of that traffic. It is through regression models of this kind that the price and income elasticities discussed in the preceding chapter are derived.

Having specified the regression model and the independent variables to be initially included, the model is calibrated to past traffic levels and changes in the independent variables. It is usual for time-series data to be used, that is, past data over a period of time. Less frequently a model may be calibrated using cross-sectional data, that is, data at one point in time but covering many routes. Using an iterative process based on the estimation of ordinary least squares the regression model establishes the value of the constant term (K) and of the coefficients a, b and c.

It is normal for several model formulations to be tested before the independent variables to be used for forecasting are finally selected. While fare and income levels are the most frequently used many others have also been found to give good results on particular routes or markets. Models for forecasting business travel may well use trade as an index of industrial production instead of income as a variable (BAA, 1981). Models on routes where holiday traffic is dominant may include hotel prices, currency exchange rates or some other variable that is especially relevant to tourism flows. Quality of service variables may also be introduced into the model. The simplest of these is a speed or journey time variable though a few more complex models have included frequency, load factor or some other service variable (Ippolito, 1981).

Having fitted the data and established the value of the constant (K) and of the coefficients, the forecaster needs to find out how statistically sound his model is. He can only use it as a forecasting tool if he is convinced of the reliability of relationships the model purports to have established. A number of statistical tests can be used for this purpose. The most straightforward is the coefficient of multiple determination $(\bar{R}^2)$ which measures the closeness of fit of the time-series data to the regression model. A very close fit will produce a coefficient approaching $1\cdot0$, whereas a low coefficient of, say, $0\cdot5$ or less would indicate a poor fit. Using time-series data one would ideally expect to obtain a coefficient of $0\cdot9$ or more if one wanted to use the model for forecasting with some degree of confidence. The $\bar{R}^2$ coefficient may also be used to choose between models with different combinations of independent variables.

While the $\bar{R}^2$ value tells the forecaster how well traffic variations fit variations in the independent variable it does not tell him how traffic is related statistically to each of the independent variables separately. This is done by partial correlation coefficients. These measure how closely traffic is related to any one of the independent variables when all other variables are held constant.

Other tests to establish the validity of the model and the significance of the relationships it purports to measure include Student's t test and the F statistic. The latter is an alternative to the coefficient of multiple determination and is found by comparing the explained variance of the data to the unexplained variance. It is not the aim of the present book to deal in detail with the conduct and significance of the various statistical tests which can be carried out. These are covered adequately in many statistics textbooks and in one or two specialist air transport texts (Taneja, 1978).

While academic economists have developed quite sophisticated and apparently robust econometric models for forecasting air traffic, airlines tend to use fairly simple models, often models which may not be as statistically sound as, in theory, one might wish. One such model was developed in 1977 for forecasting Air Algerie's traffic between Algeria and France. The model took the form

$$\log T = K + a \log GNP + b \log F + C \log S, \qquad (8.6)$$

where T is the number of passengers carried by Air Algerie between Algiers and Paris; GNP is a measure of the combined real GNP of France and Algeria weighted in proportion to the share of Algerians in the total traffic; F is the average yield per passenger-kilometre on all Algeria–France routes; S is the average speed of all Algeria–France air services.

Effectively the independent variables were income, price and a quality of service variable which was speed. The time series on which the model was based was for the eight years 1968–1975. This was rather short, though a similar model for total air traffic between the two countries had a 10 year data base. Using the ordinary least squares method the coefficient worked out as follows:

$$\log T = 1 \cdot 0963 + 1 \cdot 4476 \log GNP - 1 \cdot 4135 \log F + 0 \cdot 2471 \log S,$$
$$(0 \cdot 7890) \; (8 \cdot 3352) \qquad (-2 \cdot 3490) \qquad (0 \cdot 6656) \quad (8.7)$$

where the respective Student t values are given in parentheses below the main equation, $\bar{R}^2 = 0 \cdot 9732$, the standard error is $0 \cdot 0381$, $F(3 \cdot 5) = 60.60$ and the value of the Durbin–Watson statistic is $3 \cdot 24$.

The model established a price elasticity of $-1 \cdot 4$ on the Algiers–Paris route and an income elasticity of $+1 \cdot 4$. Since the high t-test values validated the significance of the coefficients, the model was used to carry out ten-year forecasts to be used for fleet planning purposes.

Whereas the Air Algerie model was used for specific route forecasts, econometric models are also used to forecast traffic development in particular markets. Thus the British Airports Authority (BAA) has divided the traffic at its London airports into thirty-four discrete market segments based on purpose of travel, place of residence of passengers and type of route. Each market segment has its own causal model and its traffic is forecast separately. For instance, leisure traffic by UK residents on the North Atlantic is a function of UK consumer expenditure, North Atlantic fares, the sterling–dollar exchange rate and an autonomous trend related to the opening up of new routes and new gateway points (BAA, 1981). The UK Department of Transport (previously Trade) has used a similar approach in forecasting total UK air traffic (Green, 1978; Department of Trade, 1981).

Very high coefficients of multiple determination are not in themselves a guarantee of causality or even of a close relationship between the independent and the dependent variables. A high coefficient of determination may be produced if the error terms produced by the regression equation fall into a pattern. This is is called autocorrelation and may occur either when a significant independent variable has been left out or when there is a marked cyclical variation in the dependent variable. One can test for autocorrelation using the Durbin–Watson d statistic. The values of d which will enable one to assess whether autocorrelation is present are related to the number of observations and the number of independent variables. As a general rule, if the Durbin–Watson statistics are below 1·5 or above 2·5 the forecaster will be concerned with the possibility of autocorrelation. The high Durbin–Watson statistic of 3·24 on the Algiers–Paris model (equation (8.7) above) would suggest the existence of negative serial correlation. Another problem which might exist despite high coefficients of determination is that of multicollinearity. This occurs if the independent variables are not statistically independent of each other. For example air fares and fuel prices may move more or less in unison. Therefore including both as independent variables would result in multicollinearity and would pose difficulties in interpreting the regression coefficients. In particular, they could no longer be strictly considered as elasticities. One can test for multicollinearity by using a matrix showing the correlation between the independent variables. Variables showing a high correlation, say 0·85 or higher, should not really be included in the same model. The possibility of autocorrelation and multicollinearity are two key problems for the airline forecaster using econometric models. There are other more obscure ones, such as heteroscedasticity, which are dealt with in detail in the specialist texts (Taneja, 1978).

Having developed and tested models such as those described above, an airline needs to obtain forecasts of the independent variables used in order to be able to derive from them forecasts of future air traffic. In doing this, particularly for longer-term forecasts, one should not necessarily assume that the elasticities remain constant over time. It is inherent in the way that elasticity is measured that it must change over time as total traffic grows. Because of this many forecasters build changing elasticities into their predictive processes. Changes in elasticity values can be derived mathematically or they can be assumed. The BAA, for example, in its own forecasts assumes a decline in the income elasticities of most market groups (see Table 7.3).

It is while forecasting the independent variables that some form of sensitivity test may be introduced into the forecasting process. Airlines might consider what would happen to the economy of a particular country and its per capita income if industrial growth did not turn out to be as fast as predicted by the government concerned. Alternatively, they might evaluate the impact of a disruption of oil production in the Middle East on the price of fuel and ultimately on economic growth or on the future level of air fares. These sensitivity tests may produce band forecasts suggesting a range of possible traffic outcomes rather than point forecasts.

For decisions dependent on forecasts over a two-year time span or less airline managers tend to prefer point rather than band forecasts. Decisions have to be taken and giving a range of forecasts is no help to the decision makers. They want precise traffic estimates. They expect the forecasters to have assessed the risks and the sensitivity of the forecasts to external variables and to have made the point forecasts in the light of such assessment. When it comes to strategic decisions stemming from the airline's corporate plan, band forecasts become useful. They should force the airline to maintain flexibility in its long-term planning decisions. An airline must avoid taking decisions which lock it into a size and level of production which it cannot easily vary. This is particularly true of aircraft purchase or other major investments. Band forecasts emphasize the uncertainty inherent in forecasting.

8.4.2 AIR FREIGHT MODELS

The factors affecting the growth of air freight are complex and often fickle. The tonnage of freight moving on any route is subject to sudden and unexplained variations. There is the added complication that unlike passengers who tend to return to their point of origin, freight movements are unidirectional. There is a multitude of commodity freight rates on any route and such rates have also tended to be less stable than passenger fares. Much freight capacity is produced as a by-product of passenger capacity and as a consequence there is frequently an overprovision of freight capacity with a strong downward pressure on freight rates. Tariffs charged often bear little relationship to the published tariff so that even establishing tariff levels is difficult.

As a result of all these complexities it has often been difficult to relate past freight growth to one or more independent variables, particularly in relation to individual routes, though one of the early studies did develop a model relating freight tonne-kilometres to freight rates, an index of US industrial production and a time trend (Sletmo, 1972).

The few causal freight models which have been developed have tended to be used for forecasting global air freight demand or demand in large markets rather than on individual routes. For example, the aircraft manufacturer McDonnell Douglas produces inter-regional air freight forecasts using a simple model where freight tonne-kilometres are a function of regional gross domestic product and a regional real yield variable (McDonnell Douglas, 1980).

ICAO uses econometric models for its long-term forecasts of the world's scheduled air traffic (ICAO, 1983c). Using data for the period 1960–1981 ICAO has developed two separate models, one for passenger traffic and one for air freight. The freight model takes the form:

$$\log FTK = 0 \cdot 375 + 1 \cdot 62 \log EXP - 0 \cdot 48 \log FYIELD \qquad (8)$$
$$(8 \cdot 4) \qquad\qquad (1 \cdot 6)$$

where FTK is the number of freight tonne-kilometres; EXP is the world exports in real terms; $FYIELD$ is the freight revenue per freight tonne-kilometre in real terms.

Most route by route forecasts for freight are based on a combination of executive judgement, market research and, where appropriate, time-series projections. Frequently such forecasts are on a commodity by commodity basis since the number of separate commodities being freighted by air on any route is usually fairly limited. A few airlines such as the US cargo carrier, Flying Tigers, have tentatively tried to use both time-series projections and regression models but with uncertain results (Garcia-Fuertes, 1980). In the late 1970s British Airways also experimented with econometric models for freight flows but with little success and subsequently has placed greater emphasis on time-series analysis and on assessing the factors affecting particular commodity flows. The development of causal models of individual commodity flows may ultimately prove more rewarding than attempts to model total freight flows on particular routes.

8.4.3 ASSESSMENT OF REGRESSION MODELS

The advantage and strength of causal forecasting models is that they are logical. They relate demand to changes in factors which one would expect to have an impact on demand. The models chosen must therefore be logical too, despite the findings of any statistical tests. A model with a high coefficient of determination should not be used if the independent variables are intuitively wrong. The forecaster's direct experience of market conditions and knowledge gained through market research can provide an insight into demand behaviour which may ultimately be more useful than that obtained through statistical analysis and mathematical correlation. The models used must be logically consistent. If that is the case, it follows that if one can forecast the independent variables for three or more years, then one should be able to derive longer-term traffic forecasts with a lower risk of error than if one were using time-series projections where demand is related purely to changes in time. Herein lies the strength of causal forecasting but also its weakness. For by using a causal model in the interests of logical consistency and greater accuracy the airline forecaster transposes his problem. Instead of having to forecast air traffic he must now use someone else's forecasts of the independent variables and if these are not available he must make his own. Many governments, central banks and other institutions do make forecasts of gross domestic product, consumer expenditure, trade and of other economic indicators which might be used as independent variables. Such economic forecasts are not always reliable, nor are they necessarily long term. Where more than one institution is forecasting a particular variable the forecasts do not always agree. If the air fare is one of the independent variables used, then this should in theory be easy for an airline to forecast since it is under airline control. In practice it is difficult for the airlines to predict fare levels more than two or three years hence, without getting embroiled in forecasting oil prices or changes in other factors that may affect future fare levels.

Causal techniques pose some further problems too. Like time-series analyses they also depend on the availability of historical data. Clearly to calibrate the models one needs not only good air traffic data but also adequate and accurate statistics going back many years of independent variables being used in the model. In most developed countries these should be available. In many Third World countries adequate data is either unavailable or possibly unreliable. Where data *is* available the complexity of the modelling work is daunting and time-consuming, especially if an airline wishes to develop separate forecasts for key markets or major routes, each requiring separate models.

It should be borne in mind that econometric forecasting, despite its inherent logic and mathematical complexity, is not a mechanistic exercise. Judgement is involved at all stages from the model specification to the choice of independent variables and more especially in the choice between alternative forecasts of those independent variables.

8.5 Choice of forecasting technique

It is clear from the preceding analysis that there is no certainty in forecasting; no forecasting tool that can guarantee the accuracy of its predictions. Even very similar forecasting methods may produce widely diverging forecasts. Whatever the uncertainties, however, airlines can not avoid making forecasts because so many other decisions stem from them. Their forecasters must make a choice between the numerous forecasting techniques open to them. Several factors will determine that choice.

The starting point is to determine the prime objective of the forecast. Is it to forecast traffic growth; is to to predict the reaction of demand to some new development such as a fare increase or frequency change; or is it to forecast the traffic on a new route? While all techniques enable one to make a forecast of traffic growth under normal conditions only a few are suitable for forecasting traffic reaction or demand on a new route (Table 8.3). If an airline is planning to open up an entirely new route it has little choice but to use a qualitative technique or a causal model.

Having determined the forecasting techniques suitable for the type of forecast being undertaken then speed and data availability become important criteria. A quick forecast means either executive judgement or a straightforward time-series projection. Data availability is crucial for certain of the techniques. Time-series projections need accurate and detailed traffic data over a reasonable period of time. Regression models need all that but also adequate data on the independent variables included in the model. If either traffic data or data on the various socio-economic variables is unavailable and unobtainable then the forecaster is obliged to turn to qualitative methods. Cost may be an important consideration too. Smaller international airlines may not be prepared to meet the high costs of market research while sophisticated causal forecasting for them would mean using consultants and consultants do not come cheaply. In fact, many smaller airlines are dependent on aircraft manufacturers for their long-term forecasts.

If speed, data availability and cost are not a constraint then airlines might choose between the forecasting techniques open to them on the basis of their predictive accuracy. This is a difficult judgement to make. The various techniques are listed in Table 8.3 and their accuracy for short-, medium- and long-term forecasts is indicated on a three-point grading of poor, fair and good. But the gradings are to a certain extent subjective and influenced by one's personal experience and judgement. Different forecasters would use different gradings. Inevitably most techniques are fairly accurate for short-term forecasts and some are also reasonable for two-year forecasts. Beyond that time

Table 8.3 Attributes of airline passenger forecasting techniques

	Qualitative methods			Time-series projections				Causal model
	Executive judgement	Market research	Delphi	Annual average growth	Exponential smoothing	Linear trend	Linear trend on moving average	Regression analysis
Accuracy								
0–6 months	Good	Good	Fair/good	Fair/good	Good	Fair/good	Good	Good
6–24 months	Fair	Good	Fair/good	Poor/fair	Fair/good	Poor/fair	Fair	Fair/good
5 years	Poor	Poor/fair	Fair	Poor	Poor/fair	Poor	Poor/fair	Poor/fair
Suitability for forecasting								
Traffic growth	Good	Good	Good	Good	Good	Good	Good	Good
Traffic reaction	Fair	Good	Fair	n.a.	n.a.	n.a.	n.a.	Good
Traffic new routes	Poor	Fair	Poor	n.a.	n.a.	n.a.	n.a.	Fair
Ability to identify turning points	Poor/fair	Fair/good	Fair/good	Poor	Fair	Poor	Poor/fair	Good
Ready availability of input data	Good	Poor/fair	Poor	Good	Good	Good	Good	Poor/fair
Days required to produce forecast	1–2	90+	30–180	1–2	1–2	1–2	1–2	30–90
Cost	Very low	High	Low	Low	Low	Low	Low	High

Abbreviation: n.a., not applicable.

span there is some doubt, but it is likely that qualitative or causal techniques will produce the more accurate forecasts. These techniques are also the most likely to be able to identify and predict turning points in the underlying growth trends. In theory causal models should produce the better results but some aviation experts suggest that there is no compelling evidence that econometric techniques produce more accurate air traffic forecasts than do the simpler and more straightforward approaches (de Neufville, 1976).

Within most international airlines a range of forecasting techniques is used. Faced with differing planning requirements airlines carry out both short- to medium- and longer-term forecasts. The former tend to be based on time-series projections frequently modified by executive judgement and by market research findings. The precise time-series technique or techniques used by each airline will depend on its experience and the judgement of its forecasters. Where new routes are being evaluated, the airline's preference may well be to use market research methods to forecast potential demand. For longer-term forecasts beyond a year or two, many smaller airlines continue to use time-series projections despite doubts about the accuracy of such methods for longer time spans, while some of the larger airlines switch to causal models. Ultimately, so many exogenous and unpredictable factors may affect air transport demand that forecasts beyond 3–5 years ahead must be thought of as being very tentative.

Pricing Policies and Fare Structures

9.1 Objectives of airline pricing policy

Pricing is a crucial element in airline management. It is the mechanism whereby the demand for air services is matched with the supply. The airline's primary aim must be to sell the capacity it is prepared and able to offer at prices which will generate sufficient demand to ensure an adequate level of profit. A great deal hinges on what each airline considers an adequate profit. For some state-owned airlines it may mean little more than breaking even. For others it may be measured in terms of an adequate rate of return to shareholders or a target rate of return on the value of the assets employed. Some airlines may go further and set out not only to produce a target rate of return on their current assets, but also to generate an adequate reserve fund to self-finance, as far as possible, the acquisition of new assets. Singapore Airlines appears in recent years to have followed this latter objective. Thus even the profit objective in airline pricing may have different implications for different airlines. There is also a temporal dimension to the profit objective. While some airlines may be concerned more with current profits, others may place the emphasis on longer-term profitability. They may be prepared to forego profits in the short term to ensure their longer-term objective.

International airlines will normally have a clear profit objective but it will only be one of a number of corporate objectives. These other objectives may also impinge on pricing policy. Expansion into new routes and new markets figures large in many airlines' corporate objectives. Expansion may be an objective in its own right or the ultimate aim may be rapid growth or the attainment of a particular size of operation. Many airlines want to be big! There may be cost advantages from growth but ultimately the purpose of growth seems to be more akin to a revenue-maximizing objective. If the development of new markets or rapid growth are objectives of an airline's pricing policy, then the pricing strategies it adopts must be coloured by this fact. We have already seen in discussing the impact of deregulation (Sec. 3.9 and Table 3.1) how new entrants, such as

Braniff or Northwest moving into markets with established carriers have tried to capture market share by offering lower tariffs.

The adverse cost impact of large seasonal or even daily variations in demand may induce airlines to use the pricing mechanism as a way of evening out these fluctuations. This might be done by using high tariffs to restrain peak demand and lower tariffs to stimulate off-peak traffic. Such a policy may adversely affect the total revenue generated compared to a policy of expanding the supply of services at the peak periods. But revenue maximization may be less important in the short term than reducing unit costs through a reduction in the peakiness of demand and hence of supply.

Pricing has a further role. It should in theory be a guide to new investment. Where the number of consumers who are prepared to pay the full cost, including a reasonable profit, of the goods or services they consume exceeds the supply, then the producers have a clear indication that if they can supply more at the same or a lower price demand will be sufficient to generate further profits. Conversely, if consumers in total do not generate sufficient revenue to cover the full costs of particular services then it would be foolhardy to invest in the expansion of such services. If pricing is to be used as a guide to further investment then the prices of different services should reflect their costs of production. If not, demand may be artificially high or it may be suppressed. On two or three occasions very low tariffs on the North Atlantic route as in 1978–9 generated a surge in demand which pushed up load factors to high levels. Many airlines misread the signs and increased the capacity on offer. This was a recipe for financial suicide. The low tariffs were only feasible if mixed with a certain proportion of high fare business and first class traffic. Putting on extra services to cater exclusively for the low yield traffic was ruinous since the revenue generated was insufficient to cover the costs. The pricing mechanism if used as a guide to further investment must be used with care.

In short, few international airlines have a single overriding objective in their pricing policy, although the attainment of profitability looms large especially for privately owned airlines. Most want their pricing policy to achieve a number of internal objectives. But they may also have externally imposed objectives. Some national airlines are required by their governments to stimulate incoming tourism. This may well require a low fare policy irrespective of its repercussions on the financial fortunes of the airline itself. The attempt to attain different pricing objectives simultaneously may produce conflicts and contradictions in pricing policy. Such conflicts and complexities in pricing are further increased because the same airline may be pursuing different objectives on different parts of its network. It may be trying to maximize profits on some routes, especially those in which there is little or no tariff competition, while on other routes its prime objective may be increasing its market share or its rate of growth. Inevitably within any airline different pricing objectives will prevail at different times and in different parts of its operations.

9.2 Inherent instability of airline tariffs

Profitability, which appears to be an important objective for most airlines, depends on the interplay of three variables, the unit costs, the unit revenues or yields and the load factors achieved. Airline managers must juggle with all three to produce a profitable combination. This is a dynamic and interactive process made more difficult by the pricing instability inherent in the airline industry. The industry is characterized by short-run marginal costs which are close to zero. The marginal cost of carrying an extra passenger on a flight which is due to leave with empty seats is no more than the cost of an additional meal, an airport passenger charge and a few pounds of fuel burnt as a result of the extra weight. The problem is that even when operating with high load factors of 70 per cent or more there will be many empty seats. These cannot be stored or sold later. If they are not sold at the moment of production, the seats and the seat-kilometres generated are lost forever. The same considerations apply to unsold freight capacity. An airline committed to operate a published schedule of services for a particular season or a tour operator committed to a series of charter flights find that their short-run total costs are fixed and cannot be varied. Therefore it makes business sense to try and maximize revenues. Having sold as much capacity as possible at normal tariffs, the airline or tour operator is tempted to sell any remaining empty seats at virtually any price above the very low marginal cost of carrying the additional passengers.

The problem is to prevent slippage or diversion of traffic prepared to pay the normal tariffs into the low tariffs. If that happens then the total revenue generated may decline. In markets where tariffs are regulated and enforced, diversion is prevented or minimized by the conditions, the so-called 'fences', which circumscribe the availability of the very low tariffs. (See Sec. 9.6 below.) In markets where tariffs are not regulated or, if regulated, are not enforced, the low marginal cost of carrying an additional passenger (or freight consignment) has a strong downward pressure on all tariffs, including the normal economy, business or first-class fares. The inherent instability in such markets is made much worse if there are no controls on capacity or if the entry of new carriers is easy. It is in conditions of over-capacity that airlines are most likely to resort to marginal cost pricing. Following the total deregulation of the United States domestic system the relationship between costs and tariffs has largely disappeared. Tariffs are determined by competitive factors and on many routes tariffs approach long-run marginal costs while on others only short-run marginal costs have any relevance to pricing. Since short-run marginal costs are close to zero and long-run marginal costs are below average costs, losses are likely to ensue.

In less regulated international markets the price instability is aggravated by a number of additional factors. One of these has already been mentioned and that is the tendency of new entrants in established markets to try and capture market share by undercutting existing tariffs. The most significant factor and the most widespread, even affecting regulated markets, is the availability of sixth freedom capacity. While the point-to-point, third and fourth freedom carriers on a route may be trying to maintain an adequate mix and level of different tariffs, sixth freedom carriers operating via their own home base may be prepared to charge almost anything to fill empty seats with traffic that they would otherwise not have had. The sixth freedom operators' tariffs will be particularly low if they want to compensate passengers for having to stop over for a night *en route* to their destination. In 1984 the lowest fares between the UK and South East Asia were with Aeroflot via Moscow and between London and India with Syrian Arab. If such sixth freedom carriers begin to capture significant market shares the direct carriers must react by reducing their own fares. In most long-haul international markets there is a great amount of spare sixth freedom and sometimes fifth freedom capacity slushing around and depressing tariffs. On some routes there may be the additional problem of the marginal carrier, that is the airline for whom the route is marginal to his total operation. He may therefore be unconcerned by low fares on the route, particularly if he sees them as a way of attracting traffic on to the rest of his network. This has certainly happened with new entrants on the North Atlantic or the trans-Pacific routes.

On other routes price instability may be increased by the actions of financially weak or subsidized carriers. Weak airlines may drop their prices in competitive markets in order to generate sufficient cash flow to meet their day-to-day payments. Brannif was effectively doing this in some international markets before its collapse in 1982. Some national airlines may continue operating on certain routes at yields and load factors which are uneconomic because of their ability to rely on subsidies to cover their losses. In the process, however, they depress the market for other carriers. Finally, the tendency for airlines to sell seats *en bloc* or on a part-charter basis to tour operators or travel agents reduces the airlines' ability to control the tariffs at which those seats will ultimately be sold to the public.

The low marginal cost of carrying additional traffic together with the other factors discussed, which undermine price stability, means that international airlines often have a strong incentive to reduce tariffs or introduce illegal discounts. The characteristics of international airline operations are such that tariffs are not enforceable unless the airlines themselves decide to enforce them. Even government controls are ineffective without airline acquiescence, since airlines can find countless ways in which to circumvent regulatory tariff restrictions. Without airline self-control and enforcement of tariffs and tariff conditions the inherent instability of air transport markets may well push tariffs to levels at which no operator can make a profit except for short periods. It is this fear above all else that pushes airlines to try and reach agreement between themselves on tariffs and on enforcement. A striking example has been the yield improvement programmes instituted in 1977 by the Orient Airlines Association, several of whose member airlines have been standard bearers of deregulation and critics of IATA. Yet they continue to come together periodically to establish minimum selling prices or maximum discounts on air services between their countries.

9.3   Alternative pricing strategies

In developing their pricing strategies international airlines must bear in mind both their pricing objectives and the inherent instability of airline tariffs. Broadly speaking, two alternative strategies are open to them. The first is to relate each tariff to the costs incurred in providing the services used by those paying that tariff. This is 'cost of service' pricing, more frequently referred to as cost-related pricing. The alternative is to base tariffs for different categories of service not on costs but on what consumers are able and willing to pay. This is market pricing or demand-related pricing, although in more traditional textbooks the concept has been called 'charging what the traffic will bear'.

In recent years it is regulatory authorities such as the CAB in the United States, several European governments (CEC, 1981) or the Commission of the European Communities (CEC, 1984) which have argued most strongly in favour of cost-related pricing. The CAA as long ago as 1977 outlined the fundamental principles to be pursued in developing airline pricing policies (CAA, 1977a). It suggested that 'charges ... should be at the lowest level which will cover the costs of efficient operators, including an adequate return on capital; each charge should be related to costs, and that tariff provisions should be rational, simple and enforceable ...'.

The arguments in favour of cost-related pricing hinge on the twin issues of equity and economic efficiency. It is considered inequitable that some consumers of air services should be charged more than the cost of providing those services either to generate excess profits or in order to cross-subsidize consumers who are paying less than the full cost of the services they consume. From this point of view the 50 per cent discount for children under the age of 12 years is clearly inequitable. It does not cost less to carry a child than an adult and by charging children only 50 per cent of the fare other adults have to pay more to compensate for the revenue loss. If tariffs are not cost related then they may well be discriminatory. That means that certain consumers will be discriminated against not on the basis of costs they impose but on the basis of their age, or their marital status or for instance because they want to spend less than six nights at their destination.

There are efficiency implications as well. If prices are above cost for some services, then demand for those services will be suppressed even though it would be profitable to supply that demand at prices that were cost related. Conversely, prices below cost may generate excess demand for particular services and induce airlines to expand such services even though consumers are not meeting their full costs. This would clearly be a misallocation of resources. Unless tariffs are cost related, inefficient, high cost airlines will continue to operate, protected by high tariffs. Consumers are thereby denied access to lower cost facilities. In reasonably competitive markets where there are several existing airlines or potential new entrants tariffs for different services will tend to the level of the most efficient operator, as happens in the European charter market. In markets where there is no price competition or ease of entry for new carriers there are no competitive forces to push tariffs to the level of the lowest cost operator. Tariffs will be agreed bilaterally or through IATA and will represent a compromise between the pricing strategies of the carriers on the route, each with different cost levels. There may also be a tendency to charge what are effectively monopoly prices for certain inelastic market segments. Market forces cannot ensure that tariffs reflect the costs of the most efficient suppliers. Regulatory authorities and other bodies, such as consumer associations, have argued that it is primarily in regulated markets that cost-related pricing is needed to ensure equity and that tariffs reflect the costs of efficient suppliers. Cost-related pricing is supported both on social grounds in order to reduce discrimination between consumers and on economic grounds in the belief that it creates pressures towards improved airline efficiency and a sounder allocation of productive resources.

On the other hand, several arguments can be put forward against the principle of cost pricing. The first of these is that there is no satisfactory way for transport industries to allocate costs to particular users, because of the incidence of joint costs and of the high proportion of fixed costs that have to be allocated arbitrarily. Joint costs arise when in producing one service another is inadvertently provided. A daily scheduled flight aimed at a business market produces freight capacity whether or not there is a demand for freight services. Its operations will also inevitably result in vacant seats which might be sold off to meet tourism demand. How is one to allocate the costs of that flight between business passengers, who were the prime objective in setting up the flight, and freight or holiday travellers? Any allocation of joint costs must have an element of arbitrariness in it. The same applies to certain fixed direct operating costs and to indirect costs. In practice many but not all of the problems of airline cost allocation can be overcome, as the following section indicates. But some arbitrariness remains and it is argued that many airlines end up calculating what is more akin to an average cost for all users rather than a separate cost specific to different categories of users. Another argument against cost-related pricing is that on some routes such a pricing strategy would not generate sufficient revenue to cover costs and would therefore fail to ensure the continued operation of services. On a simple route with one fare and one class of service a cost-related fare may not generate sufficient demand to ensure profitability. On the other hand, if two market segments with different price elasticities can be identified, then the airline concerned may generate higher revenue by charging two separate fares to the two market groups even though there may be no difference in the cost of transporting them. Without discriminatory but market-related tariffs the services might be abandoned and all consumers would be worse off. Such a case was illustrated in Section 7.7 when discussing the concept of price elasticity. Finally, attempting to improve efficiency by setting tariffs at the levels of the lowest cost operator may be meaningless in international air transport. Most air routes are dominated by the third and fourth freedom carriers of the two countries at either end of the route. These airlines may have quite different costs for reasons quite unconnected with questions of efficiency. The prevailing wage levels in each country may be different, as may the price of fuel or other factor inputs. Exchange rate movements may also have an adverse impact on one airline's costs. Cost-related pricing would produce a different set of tariffs for each airline yet the lower tariffs may not necessarily be those of the most efficient carrier in terms of the resources used.

From an airline viewpoint demand-related pricing strategies make sense. A scheduled airline that is committed to a published timetable of flights and has brought together the productive resources to operate that timetable finds that its short-run total costs are more or less fixed. In those circumstances it needs the freedom to price its services in such a way as to be able to generate sufficient revenues to cover its costs. This may mean charging more than cost to price-inelastic segments of the market and less than cost to elastic market segments. In competitive conditions competition between carriers will ensure that market-related pricing is not abused to produce excessive profits for the airline. Where effective competition does not exist then there may well be a danger of excessive profits being made through discriminatory pricing with or without some capacity control. Government intervention to monitor costs, tariffs and airline profits may be necessary to prevent this happening, though there must be some doubt as to how effective government intervention can be. Some deregulation of tariffs and capacity controls would be the most effective way of minimizing the likelihood of excessive profits. Meanwhile, airlines can argue that they should have the freedom to offer a range of services at a range of prices which meets some or all segments of demand in a way which ensures the continued supply of such services whether or not individual prices are cost related.

While in the short term a strategy of market-oriented tariffs makes sense as a way of maximizing revenues, it does not in itself guarantee profitability, especially in price-competitive markets. Because of the inherent instability in airline tariffs which are due to very low short-run marginal costs, market-related tariffs may reach such low levels that the total revenue generated is insufficient to cover total costs. This is particularly so if extra capacity is provided to cater for the demand generated by the low tariffs. While revenue maximizing might be a short-term pricing objective, in the longer term airlines are likely to adopt a profit-generating or loss-minimizing objective. In that case they must ensure that each separate category of traffic they carry, whether passengers or freight, covers the costs which it imposes on the airline. This, together with the need to evaluate the feasibility of aircraft investments, of new routes and of different products, pushes airlines to consider carefully the costs of the different services they provide. Whatever pricing strategy they are forced to adopt by the market conditions on each route or part of their network the starting point for their pricing procedures should be and normally is an evaluation of the costs of the different services they provide. An understanding of the relationship between pricing and costs is fundamental to effective airline management.

9.4 Setting passenger tariffs

In allocating costs to routes airlines have to make some arbitrary decisions, particularly with regard to the allocation of certain overhead and fixed costs. Studies of European and other international airlines have indicated that there tends to be considerable uniformity in the allocation methods used (ECAC, 1981, ICAO, 1983b). Where there are marked divergences in the allocative process they tend to be in smaller cost items which have relatively minor impact on the total route costs. There are three major cost categories that need to be identified. The first are the costs which are directly attributable to each route, that is those costs which were previously described in Table 4.3 as the variable direct operating costs. They are the costs which would be escaped if a particular service or route was not operated at all. They include fuel costs, variable flight and cabin crew costs, landing and *en-route* charges and so on. Most of these are easy to identify and cost specifically for each route. The one difficult area is that of direct maintenance. This is allocated either on the basis of block hours flown on each route or a combination of block hours and number of landings. If a station at an airport on a route is used only for the service being costed then all the staff and other ground expenses associated with that station should be attributed to the service. Probably around half or more of the total costs are route specific and can be directly attributed to each route. The second cost category is that of the fixed or standing direct costs. These comprise aircraft standing charges, that is depreciation and insurance, the fixed annual flight and cabin crew costs, and engineering overhead costs. Most airlines tend to convert these costs into a cost per flying hour or more usually per block hour for each aircraft type. They then allocate them to each route on the basis of the block hours generated on that route. The third category of costs that needs to be allocated is that of the indirect operating costs. These include the station and ground costs that are not route specific; passenger service costs on the ground, including passenger insurance; ticketing, sales and promotion costs and the general and administrative overheads. These tend to be allocated on the basis of some output measure. Ticketing, sales and promotion costs are frequently attributed on the basis of the revenue contributed by each route. The other elements of indirect costs tend to be allocated either on the basis of capacity tonne-kilometres or revenue tonne-kilometres. Both these measures penalize long-haul routes where tonne-kilometres generated are high but earning potential may be relatively lower because of the tapering effect of distance on costs and fares. Using revenue earnings as the basis of allocating all indirect costs may appear more equitable, but would bias costs against shorter routes.

In allocating costs to specific routes certain costs which are passenger or freight specific should be excluded from the exercise so that they can be allocated to particular categories of traffic later on. On the passenger side these include the cost of in-flight services such as meals, free drinks, papers and give-aways as well as the costs of cabin staff. The costs of particular ground facilities such as first or business class lounges should also be identified. Having established the costs of a particular route, but excluding the freight- or passenger-related elements, it is relatively easy to convert the route costs into a cost per one-way flight. At this stage the joint route costs have to be split between passengers and freight. This might be done on the basis of the capacity payload or usable volume available for the two types of traffic (IATA, 1984b). It might be done on the basis of the tonne-kilometres expected to be generated by each, or even on the forecast revenue split. On routes primarily intended for the carriage of passengers some airlines might allocate virtually all the costs to the passenger side. This is a grey area in which it is difficult to argue that any solution is optimal. Once a proportion of the route costs have been allocated to the passenger side then the next step is to calculate the cost per category or class of passenger.

To understand the process whereby one arrives at a cost per passenger it is easiest to examine an example. To do this one might consider the case of a DC-10 on a long-haul flight with three cabins each with a different seating configuration and seat pitch producing twenty-four first, thirty-one business and 178 economy seats. If the route costs per economy seat is assumed to be 100, then it is possible to establish what the cost of the first and business class seats should be after allowing for the extra space they require because there are fewer seats abreast and a longer seat pitch. Such an analysis (line 5 of Table 9.1) indicates that purely on the basis of their space needs the ratio of fares in the three classes should be 243 : 144 : 100. An adjustment might also be made for the greater proportion of space allocated

Table 9.1 Unit costs of different classes on a long-haul DC-10

	First (F)	Business (J)	Economy (Y)
1. Cost per economy seat			100
2. Seat pitch (inches)	55	38	34
3. Seat cost index allowing for seat pitch	162	112	100
4. Number of seats abreast	6	7	9
5. Seat cost index allowing for pitch plus seats abreast	243	144	100
6. Planning load factor (%)	50	60	80
7. Cost per pax adjusted for load factor	486	240	125
8. Cost per pax including passenger specific costs	506	250	130
9. Cost per pax if Y = 100	389	192	100

to toilets and galleys although this has not been done here. What if the planned load factors of the three classes were different too? Differences in planned load factor can be used to convert the cost index per seat into an index of cost per passenger (lines 6 and 7 of Table 9.1).

Finally, the passenger-specific costs need to be added into the costing exercise. These include the cost per passenger of the different in-flight services such as meals, drinks, films, headsets and newspapers and of any exclusive ground facilities. The higher ratio of cabin staff to passengers in first and business should also be adjusted for. In broad terms passenger-specific costs in business class on a long-haul flight are likely to be about twice as high and for first class passengers about four times as high as those in economy class. Typical passenger-specific costs have been added to the passenger cost indices in Table 9.1, producing a final index of relative costs per passenger. The significance of these indices is that having earlier calculated the total cost per flight of operating a DC-10 on the route in question the relative tariffs which need to be charged for each fare class can be derived. If purely cost based the business fare should be twice as high as the normal economy fare and the first class fare four times as high. A study of IATA airlines' actual costs has shown similar relationships (IATA, 1984b).

The analysis so far has indicated that it is possible to identify the costs of transporting passengers in three separate cabins each offering different products in terms of seat density, comfort and in-flight service. If basing fares purely on cost this would result in a simple structure of three separate fares or two separate fares if aircraft are configured in a two-cabin layout. A simple tariff structure such as this may be adequate on routes where capacity and fares are closely controlled and regulated and where competition from charters or indirect sixth freedom carriers is minimal. In more competitive market conditions or in situations where total demand at the cost-related fares is insufficient to cover costs airlines may need to introduce some market-related fares. The latter will inevitably be various categories of low promotional fares aimed at generating new segments of demand or at diverting demand from other airlines or other routeings. In economic terms the aim would be to take advantage of the high price elasticity of demand of the low fare market segments.

In this context airlines may introduce off-peak fares at less than cost to generate off-peak demand and hopefully an increase in total revenue. But they may well need to do more than that. Airlines will try to identify the needs and demand characteristics of particular market segments on a route (an example was given in Fig. 7.1). They must assess whether existing tariffs and tariff conditions are attractive to each particular market segment and are generating sufficient demand from that segment. If particular market segments are not adequately catered for the airlines may need to examine their costs and fares to see whether either can be adjusted to meet the needs of those market segments. In doing this airlines are conscious of the low marginal cost of carrying additional passengers and of the short-term need to maximize revenue. This awareness has led to the development of a number of different pricing strategies.

Some of the current tariff strategies can be understood by reference to Figure 9.1. This shows the demand on a long-haul route for a daily DC-10 flight with a three-cabin configuration similar to the one previously analysed from the cost point of view. The figure shows the demand expected in a particular week, say six months from now, and is based on the airline's forecast of traffic and its knowledge of the distribution of traffic during the week. At the front of the aircraft twenty-four first class seats are blocked off and sold at first class fares and thirty-one seats are sold at business class fares. There will be daily variations in demand for these two classes but the airline has based the two tariffs on achieving relatively low average load factors of 50 per cent in first and 60 per cent in business. These give enough scope for meeting weekly peaks. In the economy class cabin, where there are 178 seats, projected demand at economy or similar fares peaks on

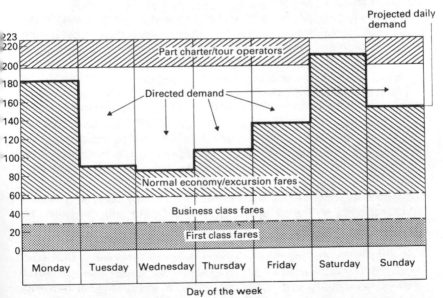

Figure 9.1 Projected demand for daily DC-10 with three-cabin configuration. Forecast demand for 1 week in 6 months time. Directed demand fares: in advance (for example, APEX and Super APEX) and last minute (for example, stand-by, 'Instant' and 'Late purchase').

Saturdays and Mondays but is relatively low on other days, especially during mid-week. At existing fares which are cost based, it cannot generate more demand. So the fares must be reduced in order to stimulate new market segments. This might be done in a number of ways. One partial solution would be to sell a block of seats to one or more tour operators or travel agents on a part-charter basis or some other basis which enables them to package the seats into inclusive holidays or to sell them in some other way. Ideally these seats should be sold at low prices and well in advance and the tour operators should be committed to pay for the seats contracted whether or not they are eventually resold by them. No part-charter or tour-basing seats would be contracted for on Saturdays since normal demand is sufficiently high.

Having sold some seats *en bloc* the airline can also introduce the concept of directed demand to sell the remaining seats which it expects to remain unsold at the normal economy tariffs. Directed demand means pushing passengers into flights or days of the week which are of the airline's choosing. In the case illustrated in Figure 9.1 directed demand fares would not be available on Mondays or Saturdays. Such fares normally take two forms: firstly fares requiring advance purchase, perhaps a minimum of 15 or 30 days before departure, such as APEX or budget fares. This enables airlines to ensure that such demand is directed to particular flights or days of the week. Passengers have a reduced choice but pay a price below the normal economy fare. The second type of directed demand fares are those that can only be purchased at the last moment or within 24 hours or so of departure. Passengers paying stand-by, 'late purchase' or 'instant' fares can only travel if seats are empty at the time of departure. These tend to be the cheapest fares.

There are other types of fare used to sell off spare seats but block sales to tour agents and various categories of directed demand fares are the most common. It could be argued that such fares are cost-related in the sense that they reflect the very low short-run marginal cost of selling an additional seat. Alternatively, it could be said that by insisting that certain of these fares can only be brought directly from the airline, the commission paid to travel agents is saved. Other cost savings may include the absence of stop-over or interlining rights. So these fares should be priced lower than normal economy. In practice the pricing of these various promotional fares tends to be market related. It is influenced by competition from charters or other scheduled carriers and by the price elasticity of demand at the lower end of the market. A major problem with these low market-oriented fares is how to prevent passengers prepared to pay higher fares from switching to the lower tariffs. Fences of various kinds have to be introduced to prevent slippage. These are discussed later. Another aspect of this same problem is how to prevent large numbers of bookings at low fares from reducing the capacity available for selling at the normal economy or excursion fares and thereby reducing the total revenue per flight. This requires very tight reservations control to ensure that no low fare seats at all are sold for some days except at the last moment and that the number available on other days of the week is strictly related to the predicted spare capacity. Reservation computers can be programmed to deal with this so as to prevent overselling of the low fares.

The practical application of these different pricing strategies can be seen by examining British Caledonian's passenger tariffs on the London–Hong Kong route in the summer of 1984 (Table 9.2). It is evident from Table 9.2 that the ratio of first and business to economy fares was 246 : 145 : 100. British Caledonian operated DC-10s on this route. Our earlier analysis of DC-10 seat costs suggested that on space grounds alone the cost ratio of the three classes should be 243 : 144 : 100 (line 5 of Table 9.1). This indicates that British Caledonian's pricing strategy was cost related but did not allow fully for different load factors or levels of in-flight service in the three classes. The group inclusive tour fares corresponded to the concept of part-charter or tour fares and there was a range of directed fares involving both advanced and late purchase. Some of these were half or less of

Table 9.2 London to Hong Kong fares, June–September 1984

	British Caledonian one-way fare (£)*	Index (Y = 100)
First class	1,230	246
Executive/club/business	725	145
Executive point to point	630	126
Economy	500	100
Excursion (90 day)	840 (return)	84
Advance purchase		
Basic	235	47
Shoulder	255	51
Peak	310	62
Late/instant purchase		
Basic	225	45
Shoulder	240	48
Peak	290	58
Group inclusive tour		
Basic	512 (return)	51
Peak	590 (return)	59

*British Airways and Cathay Pacific fares were similar with minor exceptions. Student, ship crew and government fares also available.

the normal economy fare. The Hong Kong example shows that airlines may well use cost-related and market-related pricing in combination, adapting their pricing strategies to market and competitive conditions as British Caledonian obviously does.

9.5   Choice of price and product strategies

The fare charged is only one aspect of the product or service provided by an airline to different classes of passenger. Other product features include frequency, ability to stop-over, the quality and nature of ground and in-flight services and so on. These have not been analysed in the present discussion but they too are elements of an airline's product, although price is usually the most important. In planning the supply of services on each route it serves an airline must also decide on the various price and product mixes which it feels will generate the level of demand it requires. In markets which are less regulated and where there is a high degree of price competition the pricing options available are much wider but the choice between them more difficult to make.

Given the objectives of its pricing policy, an airline must examine the costs of the different products it can put into the market in relation to its assessment of what potential consumers are prepared to pay. It must also consider its own positioning within each market. Is it setting out to meet the needs of all market segments or is it trying to attract only certain segments? It could concentrate on only the high fare and high product quality end of the market, as Swissair and SAS have done in recent years. By going for the top end of the market such airlines aim for high yield traffic and accept that this may mean lower load factors (Table 7.1 above). Some airlines choose a single product, single fare strategy. This usually involves a very low fare requiring very high load factors to break even. This was the Laker strategy and more recently the strategy adopted by People Express and Virgin Atlantic on the North Atlantic route. A pricing strategy must also be acceptable to the airline's own government and to the government at the other end of the route unless the route is one where tariffs are effectively deregulated. The other government's response will be dependent on the interests of its own airline and in particular on the relationship of the tariffs proposed to its own airline's costs and objectives.

In more price-competitive markets the pricing strategy may need to be dynamic and changing in response to price or product changes introduced by competing airlines. Airlines have many difficult decisions to make. Should they match a competitor's lower fares when they know the competitor has lower unit costs or is heavily subsidized by his government? What proportion of its capacity should an airline offer at price-competitive fares? Is there any point in undercutting a competitor's tariff if he is going to match those lower tariffs? These and other considerations will affect the pricing strategy and tariffs levels that airlines adopt in each of their markets. The ultimate aim must not be forgotten, however: that is to bring supply and demand together in such a way that the airline achieves its corporate objectives.

9.6 Passenger fare structures

9.6.1 FIRST, BUSINESS AND ECONOMY CLASS FARES

Partial or total deregulation of airline tariffs on many routes, together with differences in the pricing strategies of major international airlines, have made it increasingly difficult to identify what one might call normal fares. Up to the late 1970s most international air routes had two basic fares, a first class and an economy fare. The first class was generally 30–40 per cent higher than the economy. On a handful of routes there was also a supersonic fare for Concorde services which involved a 15–20 per cent surcharge on the first class tariff. Under the IATA tariff agreements which prevailed on the majority of international air routes, the conditions of service that went with each of those fares were also specified. These included the maximum permitted seat-pitch, the contents of meals, minimum bar prices and so on. In recent years on many major international markets such controls of conditions of service have been abandoned even on routes where the IATA tariffs still prevail.

That simple pattern of two basic fares has also changed. Deregulation of tariffs on air routes to and from the United States, the introduction of three-class cabin layouts on many long-haul services and a generally more flexible attitude to pricing among many governments and airlines has resulted in a more variegated and complex pattern of basic fares. In addition to the first and economy fares there is now also a business or executive class fare, which is sold under various names, but which in price terms is positioned between first and economy. Even that three-tier structure of normal fares is complicated on some routes by the availablility of a premium level of first or business fares which give passengers access to a particular part of the cabin or to a quality of service not available at the normal fares. On many European routes there may be a published first class fare but no first class capacity available since many European carriers from 1980 onwards abandoned first class altogether on short- and medium-haul routes and now offer only business and economy cabins. In 1983 Thai International began introducing the same concept on some of its own regional services. It should also be borne in mind that as a result of the introduction of country of origin rules or the double disapproval concept into many United States bilateral agreements and in one or two elsewhere, there are routes where each airline's three basic fares may differ from those of its competitors. Conversely there are still major route groups where the simple two-tier structure of first and economy fares still prevails. This is so on most routes to Africa and within Africa.

Point-to-point tariffs have an agreed IATA mileage attached to them. This is normally the great circle distance between the two points. In travelling from one point to the other passengers can deviate from the IATA distance by up to 15 per cent in mileage terms (20 per cent on some routes) without any increase in the normal fares. This freedom may not apply to some of the promotional fares. The free 15 per cent add-on to the permitted distance allows passengers to take quite circuitous routes to reach their ultimate destination, often with stop-overs *en route* at no extra cost. This is particularly so on tickets to distant destinations where a 15 per cent deviation on a distance of several thousand kilometres can give passengers considerable scope for round-about routeings. On a few very long-haul routes there may be several sets of normal fares depending on the routeing taken. This is done partly to avoid misuse of the 15 per cent add-on. Thus, between London and Sydney there is one set of fares for services via the Eastern Hemisphere or the trans-Siberian route, and higher fares for travel via the Atlantic or the polar routes.

9.6.2   DISCOUNT FARES

Discount fares are those promotional fares which are expressed as a percentage discount on the normal fares and which are generally applicable over large geographical areas. The most widely accepted and used are the 50 per cent discount on the full fares for children under 12 years of age and the 90 per cent discount for infants under 2 years of age but without the right to a seat. Child discounts on promotional fares, if available, are frequently lower. In Europe the discount is only 25 per cent while on Pacific routes it is 33·3 per cent. In particular traffic conference areas there may be discounts for students travelling to or from their places of study, there may be spouse discounts for husbands and wives accompanying their partners on business trips or publicly available group discounts. There may also be discounts for military personnel or ships' crews. Traditionally, the aim of discount fares has been partly developmental to encourage demand from particular groups within the community and partly social through the choice of groups to be encouraged, that is families with young children or students. Interestingly, child discounts are not normally available on charter flights.

9.6.3 PROMOTIONAL FARES

Promotional fares are various low fares, usually with one or more restrictions on their availability, which offer passengers significant savings on the normal economy fares. They are not of general application, as discount fares tend to be, but are separately negotiated and agreed for each point-to-point link. Promotional fares have tended to be most widely used on routes where there is charter competition, such as within the Europe–Mediterranean region or on the North Atlantic, and on routes where there is considerable over-capacity arising from the operating of fifth freedom or indirect sixth freedom carriers. They have been least developed on routes where the airlines concerned have wanted to maintain high fares or have believed that demand was likely to be inelastic to fare reductions. The latter is the case on many international routes to and within Africa.

The early development of promotional fares was aimed at stimulating particular market segments, such as off-peak demand or the demand for inclusive tours, while taking advantage of the low marginal cost of scheduled air services once airlines were committed to a published timetable. Off-peak fares, night fares and group (GTX) or individual inclusive tour (ITX) fares were of this kind. Subsequently a wide range of promotional fares has been developed. The economic rationale for some, such as advanced or late purchase fares, has been examined earlier. Fundamentally there can be only one justification for them. They must increase an airline's net revenue and hopefully its profits too. They can only do this by increasing traffic by a greater amount than is needed to overcome both the revenue loss, arising from the lower fares and the possible diversion of higher fare traffic, and the cost increase caused by the higher volume of traffic. Promotional fares involve considerable risk. There is the risk that newly generated traffic will not come up to expectations or alternatively that it might be so heavy that it will displace higher fare traffic. Tight reservations space control is necessary to ensure that this does not happen. The other risk is that too many passengers will be diverted from full fares or other high fares and will travel at the promotional fares thereby deflating total revenue. To minimize this risk 'fences' or conditions are attached to each promotional fare. Such fences will not last very long unless they are seen by the public to be reasonable or 'fair'. Each promotional fare tends to have one or more of the following fences:

(a) Duration limits Most promotional fares have a minimum and maximum stay limitation. Within Europe, several categories of promotional fares include a requirement that the passenger must stay at least one Saturday night at his destination and no more than one month or, in some cases, three months. On the North Atlantic route a 7 or 14 day minimum stay with a two-month maximum is common. Inevitably duration limits mean that passengers must buy return tickets. The primary aim of most duration limits is to prevent usage of these fares by normal business travellers who, as previously pointed out (Sec. 7.2) prefer short trips and avoid weekends away from home.

(b) Departure time limitations It is also common to limit the availability of many promotional fares to particular times of the day, or days of the week or seasons. The aim here is to generate off-peak demand or to try and fill up seats that would otherwise be expected to remain empty because of the timing or day of particular flights.

(c) Purchase time restrictions In order to be able to direct demand more effectively than can be done with departure time limitations, restrictions on the timing of purchase have been introduced for many promotional fares. These require either advance reservation and simultaneous full payment a minimum number of days before departure or late purchase, normally within 24 hours before the flight or actually at the time of departure or late purchase, normally within 24 hours before the flight or actually at the time of departure. Advance payment also reduces airline costs by improving its cash flow.

(d) Routeing conditions Many promotional fares can only be bought as round-trip fares. In some cases, the return trip must be booked at the time of reservation and neither the outward nor return booking can subsequently be changed except by forfeiting a substantial part of the fare. The aim is to reduce passenger flexibility, thereby making the fares unattractive to business passengers or independent holidaymakers, while at the same time ensuring high load factors by cutting out last minute changes and no-shows. Higher load factors by reducing unit costs justify the lower fares. A number of additional routeing restrictions might also be used as a way of reducing the costs of handling low fare traffic. These include reduced or no stop-overs between the origin and ultimate destination; a point-to-point restriction which prevents both stop-overs and use of the 15 per cent distance add-on rule; and a no 'open-jaw' rule to force passengers to start their return trip from the original destination point. Finally, some very low fares may preclude interlining; that is, they cannot be used by the passenger except on the airline which issued the ticket. This prevents any revenue loss by the airline from pro-rating (Sec. 9.8 below) of the ticket with other carriers. In a few cases restrictions aimed at reducing costs may be combined with normal fares. For instance, on the London to Hong Kong route there is a low point-to-point business fare (Table 9.2).

(e) Inclusive tour requirements There is finally a range of promotional fares which are not publicly available but which can be purchased by travel agents or tour operators and used to package into inclusive tours. Such packaged holidays normally include accommodation but might involve some other element such as car hire or tickets for a cultural or sports event instead of or in addition to the accommodation. On some routes there is a single inclusive tour fare while on others there may be a separate IT fare for individuals and a lower fare for groups. IT fares have been aimed at meeting the needs of the independent holidaymaker. At the same time on some routes they may allow scheduled airlines to compete with charters in the package holiday market. As such they are a defensive response.

Most promotional fares whose names tend to differ by region will have conditions attached to them involving several of the above limitations. On certain routes the complexities of the numerous fares available and the conditions attached to them have posed administrative problems for both airline staff and travel agents and have become counter-productive in marketing terms. Airlines are under both internal and external pressure to simplify tariffs. In this process of simplification the concept of 'unbundled' fares has gained ground. More and more low, unbundled fares now give the passenger none of the the traditional flexibility or rights which were costly for the airline. They provide nothing more than direct, uninterrupted carriage from origin to destination and back at the times and on the flights originally booked for.

On some routes with well developed promotional fares a high proportion of the total traffic may be travelling on such fares. IATA estimates that in 1983 three out of every four passengers on the North Atlantic route were travelling on promotional fares of various kinds (IATA, 1984a). The proportion was probably too high and this may partly explain the chronic losses suffered by many scheduled carriers on their North Atlantic routes. Attempts at effective reservations capacity control appear to have broken down as a result of over-capacity and competitive pressures. In other very competitive markets too, airlines have found themselves selling virtually their entire economy cabin at promotional fares. On London to South East Asia routes APEX fares have become effectively the standard economy fare, with hardly anyone paying the full economy tariff.

An ICAO study of the September 1982 tariffs on a large sample of city pairs around the world found that round-trip excursion fares, the oldest established and most common promotional fare, were available on two-thirds of all routes and generally offered a 30 per cent reduction on the economy fare. Advance purchase excursion (APEX) and other similar low promotional fares (e.g. European PEX and Eurobudget) were becoming increasingly prevalent and were available on about one-quarter of all city pairs. They predominated on routes between Canada, Mexico and the United States, across the Atlantic and across the Pacific. These often referred to as deep discount fares, were found to be on average 40 per cent lower than the normal economy fares. Individual inclusive tour fares were found to exist on one out of every five routes and were generally about 35 per cent below the economy fares (ICAO, 1983b).

9.6.4   CONCEPT OF FARE ZONES

An innovation in pricing strategy was introduced in May 1982 with the signing by the United States and ten member states of the European Civil Aviation Conference of a memorandum of understanding setting up agreed fare zones on the North Atlantic. Reference 'fares' were established in each direction on the North Atlantic route based on an agreed cost formula. In practice the reference fare was based on the standard foreign fare levels (SFFL) which had been established in 1980 by the CAB on the basis of US airline costs. Five pricing zones, or bands, each covering one fare type, were then established in relation to the reference fare. For example, the economy class fare zone was from 20 per cent below to 20 per cent above the reference fare. Any airline offering an economy fare at any level within the agreed zone would have it automatically approved by both governments on that route. It could also set a particular fare outside its zone but in that case specific approval would be needed from the governments concerned. If airline costs, such as the price of fuel, rise or fall the reference fare or the SFFL can be adjusted through the agreed cost formula or through arbitration. Since the fare zones are expressed as percentages of the reference fare they move up or down automatically with that fare.

The 1982 memorandum of understanding has been renewed regularly since then. The advantage for North Atlantic carriers is that if IATA or bilateral fares fall within the bands or zones they were automatically approved by the CAB and since its demise by the US Department of Transportation. Some IATA tariff agreements have also introduced fare bands but with a somewhat different objective. The IATA agreed business class fare on London to New York may be expressed as a zone to allow airlines to offer different elements of service. For instance, while the normal business class may be eight abreast on a Boeing 747 an airline with a premium six abreast business class might charge 25 per cent more and still be within the business fare band. Fare zones are an attractive innovation in that they can be used to introduce a more competitive pricing environment while maintaining some regulatory controls over the level of the reference fare and the width and relative level of the different zones. This is a compromise position which governments or airlines hostile to total deregulation of pricing might accept. For this reason the concept of fare zones is likely to be more widely adopted. Early in 1984 the European Commission espoused the concept of what it called 'zones of flexibility'. Its draft directive on European air fares contained provisions for the introduction of such tariff zones within Europe (CEC, 1984). Though the directive was unlikely to be agreed by the Council of Ministers for some years it was indicative of the direction in which pricing strategy was moving.

9.7 Geographical differences in fare levels

Annual analyses by ICAO of the normal economy fares on international routes around the world show considerable variation in fare levels between geographical areas (Table 9.3). Economy fares per kilometre on international routes in Europe are the highest in the world and they are 50–70 per cent higher than international fares within North America. On long-haul intra-regional routes the divergence between unit fare levels is lower but still quite marked with the lowest fares being found on the North Atlantic and across the

Table 9.3 Differences in average normal economy fares by distance and international route group, 1983 (September)

| Route group | *US cents per passenger-kilometre by distance (km)* | | | | | | |
	250	*500*	*1000*	*2000*	*4000*	*8000*	*12000*
Regional routes							
Europe	34·8	27·6	22·0	17·5	13·9		
Middle East	28·5	23·6	19·5	16·2			
Africa	22·3	19·1	16·3	13·9	11·9		
South America	23·1	19·1	15·8	13·0	10·8		
Asia/Pacific	20·3	17·9	15·7	13·8	12·1	10·6	9·9
North America	22·1	17·1	13·2	10·3	7·9		
Intra-regional routes							
Europe–Asia/Pacific			20·4	17·0	14·2	11·8	10·7
South Atlantic				11·9	11·5	11·2	
North Atlantic				12·1	10·6	9·8	
North–Mid Pacific				10·8	9·1	8·2	
World average	28·1	23·3	19·3	16·0	13·2	10·9	9·8

Source: ICAO (1984a).

North Pacific. Wide differences between route groups in the unit level of economy fares can be caused by any one of several factors. The most important is likely to be the differences which exist in the unit costs of operating in different geographical areas as a result of variations in the costs of inputs such as fuel or labour or in the pattern of demand. Several studies have examined such regional cost differences (ECAC, 1981; AEA, 1982; ICAO, 1983b). The degree of price competition also appears to have pushed down the economy fares particularly in markets where there is also considerable frequency and capacity competition. There may in addition be an element of cross-subsidization with above average fare levels on some routes compensating for fares that are perhaps too low on others. However, the level of economy fares might not in itself be a sufficient indicator of the prevailing fare levels on any route if there are a large number of promotional fares on that route. European fares are a case in point. While economy fares within Europe are particularly high, European scheduled routes which face charter competition tend to have a wide range of low promotional fares as on the London to Athens route discussed earlier (Table 6.1).

Our earlier analysis of airline operating costs showed that unit costs declined as sector distance increased. It is not surprising, therefore, to find that unit fares also decline with distance (Table 9.3). In fact the ICAO analyses show a close correlation between increasing route distance and falling unit fares in all major markets except on routes across the Atlantic and to a lesser extent on some trans-Pacific routes (ICAO, 1983a). It is important to recognize that even if there is a consistent relationship between fare level and distance that relationship may not be entirely cost based. There are strong indications, at least within Europe, that the taper in fares with distance is less than the taper in costs (ECAC, 1981). This is true of both economy and promotional fares. As a result, the break-even passenger load factor tends to be much lower on longer routes than on shorter ones.

Other cost variables appear to have even less impact on fare levels. Fares show no close relationship to the traffic density on a route even though thick routes lead to cost economies. The differentials between the first, business and economy fares do not always reflect the cost differences which arise as a result of the different space and service features of the three classes. Traditionally, first class fares have been under-priced in relation to the costs imposed by first class passengers. This was one reason why first class was progressively abandoned within Europe from 1980 onwards. While fare differentials between different classes have increased in recent years as a result of improved costing, on the lines of the exercise carried out on a long-haul DC-10 earlier in this chapter, there are numerous routes where the differentials do not adequately reflect cost differences.

9.8 Determinants of airline passenger yields

For an airline the level of passenger fare is less important than the yield it actually obtains. Yield is the average revenue per passenger, per passenger-kilometre or passenger tonne-kilometre performed. These all measure the average revenue per unit of output sold. The projected yield per passenger on a route will indicate to airline planners the break-even seat factor; that is, the percentage of available seats that they need to fill in order to cover the passenger-related costs. The higher the yield the lower will be the break-even seat factor.

The range of passenger yields achieved by different airlines, some of them based in the same geographical area, is surprisingly wide (Table 9.4). European carriers have exceptionally high passenger yields, though this did not save Air France from making a large loss in 1982 (Table 7.1) because their costs were relatively high (Table 5.1) and their load factors too low. The lowest passenger yields are generally achieved by Asian carriers. Yet by combining low passenger yields with low costs and relatively high load factors they achieve profitability, though of course overall performance depends on the combined passenger and freight yields. The outstanding example is

Table 9.4 Passenger yields on scheduled services 1982 (US cents per tonne-kilometre performed)

Rank	North American		European		Asia/Australasia	
1			Swissair	109·8		
2			Lufthansa	103·6		
3			Alitalia	96·6		
4			Air France	90·6		
5	Eastern	89·3				
6			British Airways	88·2		
7	Air Canada	78·4				
8	American	75·8				
9	TWA	75·5				
10					Air India	74·1
11					JAL	73·0
12			KLM	72·7		
13	Pan Am	70·5				
14					Qantas	69·8
15	Northwest	68·8				
16					Thai International	66·4
17					Korean*	64·9*
18					SIA	55·1

*1981 data.
Source: ICAO (1984c).

Singapore's SIA, whose passenger yield is exceptionally low, only about half that of some European airlines. But SIA's passenger load factor in 1982 was 74 per cent, ten percentage points or more higher than that of all the European and North American carriers in Table 9.4 except British Airways. This, together with SIA's low costs, ensured high profits. SIA's low yield and high load factor are clearly interrelated. Its low pricing strategy was used to increase its market share on many routes and to push up its load factors. The low comparative costs of SIA and other Asian carriers have enabled them to pursue low fare strategies.

The passenger yields indicated in Table 9.4 are global figures for each airline's total operations including its domestic services. Direct comparisons may therefore be somewhat misleading. Yet even when operating on the same or neighbouring routes airlines end up achieving markedly different yields as evidenced by US carriers on North Atlantic or Latin-American routes (Table 3.1). Why do yields vary so widely between carriers? The discussion so far has tacitly assumed that an airline can determine its revenue levels and its yields through the pricing strategies it adopts and in particular by the structure and level of passenger tariffs. In practice this is only partly so since the relationship between fares and yields achieved is much more complex and is influenced in varying degrees by a number of factors of which the fare structure itself is only one.

It has already been pointed out that marked differences exist in the level of fares between regions and even between neighbouring routes. In addition, the number, availability and level of discount and promotional fares will also vary. But the yield per passenger on a route depends less on the level of the individual fares and more on the traffic mix; that is, the number of passengers travelling at each of the different fares. While an airline in many cases may not be a free agent with regard to the structure and level of fares on its routes, it has somewhat greater freedom in determining the traffic mix on its flights. It does this through its positioning in the market, through its selling and marketing strategy and, if necessary, through strict reservations control. The latter is to ensure that its targeted traffic mix is not undermined by overselling of particular fare categories. The more varied and complex the fare structure, the more difficult it becomes to try to control the number of seats sold at each of the different fares. At the same time the degree to which an airline can achieve its desired traffic mix may depend on the degree of real price competition on each route. If competitive pressures become too strong it may have to abandon or change its targets.

Given the inherent instability in airline pricing discussed earlier one finds that in some markets there may be illegally discounted fares in addition to the approved promotional fares. They are illegal in the sense that they have not been approved by the governments concerned. It is on routes where there are many fifth freedom carriers and numerous opportunities for sixth freedom operations that discounting is most prevalent. Such routes include South East Asia to the Middle East or Europe to East Asia. Less frequently airlines may introduce illegally low fares if they have been unable to persuade other carriers or governments that the approved fares are just not low enough. They may want lower fares as a means of stimulating the total market. Thwarted by the regulatory system, they may go it alone. Airlines set on discounting tend to conform to tariff regulations in their own countries and to ignore the rules abroad. There are numerous tricks of the trade that airlines use. One is to sell a ticket at an illegal discount but show a legal fare on the ticket while marking the ticket as non-endorsable. This means the passenger cannot use it for carriage with any other airline. As a result the ticket will not go through inter-airline clearing and the discrepancy between the fare paid and the fare shown on the ticket will not become apparent. A secret coding on the ticket will tell the airline's own accountants what the actual ticket price paid was. Illegal discounting of normal or promotional fares either out of choice or as a result of competitive pressures further dilutes the average yield.

Another major source of revenue dilution arises from the pro-rating of revenue from interlining passengers. An interline passenger travelling with a single ticket on two or more sectors is charged the end-to-end fare, not the sum of the separate fares on each sector. Because of the taper of fares with distance the end-to-end fare to be charged is normally less than the sum of the separate fares. Pro-rating is the method used to share the revenue earned between the different sectors flown. The basic principle is to share the revenue in proportion to the fare of each sector expressed in fare construction units (FCU) which are effectively the US dollar fares. The FCUs for each sector are agreed through IATA or by the airlines concerned. The method of pro-ration using FCUs is illustrated in Table 9.5. For a club class ticket used to fly London to Athens via Vienna the revenue dilution is considerable. The airline carrying the passenger on the London to Vienna leg receives 19 per cent less than the full club fare for that sector. On the Vienna to Athens leg the revenue shortfall is 31 per cent or almost one-third. The same basic method is used to pro-rate cheaper fares as well if such fares allow interlining. Pro-rate calculations based on FCUs have become increasingly complex in some markets, especially where airlines on the same routes offer different fares.

Pro-rate dilution is greatest when passengers take advantage of the 15 or 20 per cent additional mileage rule to travel on a circuitous routeing between their origin and their destination, particularly if

Table 9.5 Pro-ration of London–Athens club ticket used London–Vienna–Athens (spring 1984)

	Separate club/economy fares	FCUs*	Pro-rate calculation	Revenue dilution
London–Athens	£280			
London–Vienna	£181	342	$£280 \times \dfrac{342}{651} = £147$	−19%
Vienna–Athens	£224	309	$£280 \times \dfrac{309}{651} = £133$	−31%
Total FCUs*		651	£280	

*FCU, fare construction unit.

travelling long-haul. The end-to-end fare has then to be split over several sectors. Pro-rate dilution will also increase if a domestic sector is included in the ticket and the domestic airline insists on receiving the full fare or a high proportion of it, leaving even less revenue to be shared between the international sectors. Pro-rated interline traffic may represent as much as a third or more of an airline's total traffic and it is particularly prevalent on routes serving geographical gateway airports such as Heathrow, Amsterdam or Singapore which are major interlining centres. A study of forty-nine major European air routes showed that in 1975 35·8 per cent of the traffic on those routes was pro-rated traffic (ECAC, 1981). The dilution arising from pro-ration can therefore be quite significant.

The impact of pro-rate dilution is frequently distorted by exchange rate fluctuations which produce gains or losses when converting revenues earned abroad into the national currency of the airline concerned. The greater volatility of exchange rates since the early 1970s has increased the risks of revenue dilution from sudden movements in exchange rates. While currency adjustment factors are introduced to allow for this they tend to be too small or to come too late to insure airlines against short-term exchange rate losses.

The final source of revenue dilution is that arising from long-haul passengers even where there is no interlining involved. This is because of the taper of unit fares with distance. An airline carrying its own passenger on a 6,000 km sector with two stops *en route* will earn less than if it had carried three separate short-haul passengers, each of whom flew only on one of the three sectors on the route. Thus Qantas, each of whose passengers travels on average around 6,900 kms, has a distinct revenue disadvantage while the shortness of many European sectors is one explanation as to why European airline yields are so high (Table 9.4).

The yields which an airline achieves on each of its routes will depend partly on the level of the normal fares, on the availability and level of promotional fares and on the degree of illegal discounting, if any. Within that framework of fares it is the traffic mix which ultimately determines the total revenue earned and thereby the unit yield. But that revenue will be diluted by pro-ration of interline tickets and possibly by exchange rate fluctuations. The proportion of interline traffic is therefore a further important determinant of the yield. The final yield will bear little relationship to any single published fare. This further complicates the issue of airline pricing. In deciding on its pricing strategy and in working out the tariffs for different market segments, airlines must balance and juggle with all these factors which transform the various fares into an average yield. It is the yield in conjunction with the achieved load factor and the costs which will determine whether an airline's financial targets can be met.

10

The Economics of Air Freight

10.1 Air freight trends

Many of the concepts and principles of airline economics discussed so far apply equally to the cargo side of the industry. At the same time there are particular issues and difficulties which arise in the carriage of air freight which require separate analysis and treatment. The importance of freight is too often underestimated yet one-third of the output of the international airline industry is generated by freight rather than passengers and for some airlines it is considerably more than this (Table 1.5). The contribution of freight to total revenue is much less than a third but it makes a significant contribution to the profitability of many air services. In order for it to continue to do so airline managers need to have a clear understanding of the air freight industry and of the particular problems facing it.

During the 1960s the rate of growth of international air freight had been very high averaging close to 20 per cent per annum and outpacing passenger growth by several percentage points. In the decade that followed annual growth rates were halved falling to an average of around 10 per cent and in the first four years of the 1980s growth rates declined further. Although air freight continues to grow faster than passenger traffic the discrepancy between the growth rates of the two sides of the industry has recently been much smaller. Until a decade ago European and North American airlines were dominant in the carriage of international air freight carrying between them three-quarters of the freight traffic (Table 10.1). Since then their dominant position has been eroded by the exceptionally rapid penetration into the freight markets by Asian and Pacific region airlines. These airlines in recent years have achieved annual growth rates in freight traffic approaching 20 per cent or about twice the world average. As a group Asian and Pacific carriers now out-perform North American airlines in the carriage of international freight and they are rapidly overtaking their European counterparts. One of the Asian carriers, JAL, is by far the largest international freight carrier. A further characteristic of international air freight is the degree to which it is dominated by three major route groups, namely the North Atlantic, the Europe to the Far East and Australasia routes and the North and mid-Pacific routes. These three route groups together generate around two-thirds of the

Table 10.1   Regional distribution of international air freight

Region of Airline Registration	Regional share of international freight tonne-kilometres 1972 (%)	Regional share of international freight tonne-kilometres 1982 (%)	Average annual growth in freight tonne-kilometres, 1972–82 (%)
Europe	44·8	38·3	+ 8·7
Asia and Pacific	12·3	28·1	+19·9
North America	29·0	17·8	+ 5·2
Latin America/Caribbean	5·8	6·1	+10·9
Middle East	5·0	5·5	+11·5
Africa	3·1	4·2	+13·9
World	100	100	+10·4

Source: ICAO (1983c).

total freight tonne-kilometres performed on international air services, with the North Atlantic route being the most important single freight market. Interestingly the very largest freight carriers such as JAL, Air France, Lufthansa or Northwest are all heavily engaged in at least two of these three route groups. This seems to be a prerequisite if an airline aims to be really big in air freight.

While in the early days air freight was considered essentially as a way of filling up spare capacity on passenger aircraft its very high rate of growth in the 1960s induced many airlines to introduce scheduled all-cargo services. Narrow-body aircraft in a passenger configuration had relatively little capacity available for freight and it was in any case unsuitable for large or awkward shipments. All-cargo aircraft, even narrow-body ones, facilitated the carriage of large unit loads and consignments and accelerated the introduction of specialized handling and sorting equipment which speeded up the movement of freight. Improved handling and the flexibility to ship freight independently of passenger aircraft which, among other things, permitted the use of night hours, allowed airlines flying all-cargo aircraft to reduce freight transit times while offering considerably more capacity. As a result, scheduled all-cargo operations generated new traffic and captured a growing proportion of it. On most major routes the proportion of freight carried on scheduled freighter aircraft grew rapidly till the early to mid-1970s and has declined steadily since then to a level of 30 per cent or less. The North Atlantic route illustrates this trend clearly.

In 1969 as much as 62 per cent of freight on the routes across the North Atlantic was being carried in freighters. This was the peak year for freighters. By 1983 their share of the market had declined to 31 per cent (IATA, 1984a). Routes across the North and Mid-Pacific are an exception to this trend. The share of the freight traffic carried by all-cargo scheduled services has remained consistently high at around 75 per cent for many years. Elsewhere the relative decline of scheduled freighter services has continued. Many airlines, British Airways, British Caledonian and TWA among them, have ceased to operate freighters altogether while other airlines which are major freight carriers, such as KLM or Lufthansa, have been reducing the number of freighters in their fleets.

One aspect of the relative decline of all-cargo services has been the eclipse, especially within Europe, of non-scheduled cargo services. Traffic rights for scheduled cargo services are governed by the bilateral air service agreements whereas cargo charters like passenger charter flights have been outside the regulatory structure and subject only to *ad hoc* permits from the two countries at either end of the route. The freedom to operate outside the bilaterals together with the growing deregulation of freight operators in the United States, the UK and some other European countries led to a rapid development of cargo charters from the mid-1970s.

Charter airlines such as Cargolux, IAS Cargo (later British Cargo Airlines) and Transmeridian grew rapidly to serve markets such as those of Nigeria, the Middle East or parts of the Far East where the rapid growth of demand for freight services could not be adequately met by the scheduled airlines. These charter airlines offered a 'firefighting' service coming in to ease major problems created by port congestion or by sudden surges of demand in particular countries. In addition, their greater pricing flexibility and their low costs based on operating fully depreciated narrow-bodied aircraft enabled them to undercut the cargo tariffs of the scheduled airlines. By 1980, however, many of the cargo charter airlines were in difficulties and British Cargo Airlines, one of the largest, collapsed, to be followed by several others. The fuel price increases of 1978–9 hit these airlines particularly badly as they were operating older narrow-body aircraft. Many of their markets also declined as economic recession began to bite. At the same time scheduled airlines began making serious inroads into these markets by more flexible and competitive pricing and by offering considerably greater freight capacity as they introduced wide-body passenger aircraft on more and more routes.

More recently Third World countries that had previously welcomed cargo charters have wished their own national airlines to share in the air freight market and have restricted charter operations. Thus in 1983 when Cathay Pacific launched its scheduled Boeing 747 freighter service to Europe the Hong Kong government cut back the freight tonnage uplift previously permitted to charter airlines such as Cargolux. As a result of all these pressures the specialist cargo charter airlines have declined in number and relative importance. Those remaining are finding it difficult to survive under the pressure of so much belly-hold freight capacity on scheduled passenger flights. Cargo charters are still needed to meet sudden surges of demand or awkward or bulky shipments but increasingly they tend to be provided by scheduled airlines such as Air France, El Al, or Saudia operating freighters that are otherwise used on scheduled cargo flights.

10.2 The demand for air freight services

Since air freight is much more heterogeneous than passengers there are several ways of categorizing it. One may, for instance, consider the commodities being shipped or one can classify freight by the weight of individual consignments or by the speed of delivery required. As with passenger traffic it is valuable to try to segment the freight market in terms of the motivation of the shipper since this has implications for the type of air freight services which need to be provided and for their pricing.

The most obvious role for air transport is for the carriage of *emergency* freight. This includes urgently required medicines such as vaccines and spare parts for machinery or equipment of various kinds which may be immobilized until the arrival of the replacement parts. Air is also used in emergency when surface communications become congested or are disrupted by natural or other causes. In all such circumstances speed is of the essence and cost of shipment is relatively unimportant. Demand to meet emergencies is irregular, intermittent and unpredictable in volume and in the size of individual consignments. It is, therefore, difficult for airlines to plan for. The need of shippers for high frequencies and good last-minute space availability means that, if adequately catered for, emergency freight demand results in low freight load factors and high unit costs. Goods with an *ultra-high value* in relation to their weight are also normally carried by air primarily because of the much higher security offered. Speed is important not in its own right but because it reduces the time during which the goods are at risk. Gold, jewellery, diamonds, valuable metals and rare furs or works of art fall into this category. Security is of overriding importance, while cost of air freighting, given the high value of the goods being shipped, is unimportant.

Both emergency and high value freight require a high quality of service. Shippers of such consignments normally want to reserve space on specific flights with a guarantee of on-time arrival, they demand preferential handling and clearing through customs and up-to-date information on the progress of their shipments. From this point of view too, such freight is more costly to handle.

The majority of air freight shipments involve what is called *routine* freight, where the shipper's decision to use air transport is based on an assessment of available transport options and is not a response to a sudden and unexpected problem; nor is it imposed by security considerations. There are many categories of routine air freight. A simple and widely used division is into perishable and non-perishable freight. In the case of *perishables* the market for the commodities being shipped is dependent on air transport. The commercial life of the products – fish, out of season vegetables, newspapers, newsfilm, high fashion textiles to name but a few – is short and the gap between producer and consumer must be bridged before that commercial life expires. Only freighting by air can do that. The freighting costs are quite high in relation to the price of the product but they can be justified if the final consumers are prepared to pay a premium because no local substitutes are available. In the case of foodstuffs the premium consumers are willing to pay for unusual or out of season produce is limited. As a result, the demand for air freight is fairly price sensitive. For all foodstuffs being shipped by air there is a tariff level at which the demand virtually dries up since the final market price of the products is no longer attractive to consumers. Since the initial price of many foodstuffs is quite low that critical tariff level may itself be quite low. Airline pricing strategy then becomes criticial. To develop new flows of perishable freight airlines may need to offer tariffs well below prevailing levels on the routes in question. The bulk of perishable freight movements are highly seasonal with very marked and often short-lived demand peaks followed by long periods when demand dries up completely. This happens with the movement of early grapes from Cyprus to the UK where the period during which air freighting is viable may last only 2–4 weeks. The seasonality of much routine perishable freight means that high year-round load factors are difficult to maintain. On the other hand, the demand patterns are known in advance and airlines can try to stimulate off-peak demand.

Routine *non-perishable freight* is shipped by air because the higher transport costs are more than offset by savings in other elements of distribution costs. Any one of a variety of costs may be reduced as a result of shipment by air. Documentation and insurance costs will normally be lower but the biggest direct cost savings are to be found in packaging, ground collection, delivery and handling. These are all transport-related costs. There may also be savings in other areas from reduced stock holdings, and therefore lower warehousing costs, and from the lower capital tied up in goods in transit. These indirect benefits tend to be more marked on long-haul routes where a shipment which may take 20–60 days or more by sea and land may reach its destination by air in an elapsed time of 2 days or less. Taken together, the total distribution costs by air should be lower than or close to those of competing modes for air to be competitive. Routine non-perishable freight consists largely of fragile high value goods such as delicate optical and electrical goods, clothing and machinery of various kinds. These benefit not only from the higher speed but also the increased security provided by air transport in terms of reduced damage and loss. This, together with the high value of these commodities, sometimes means air may be preferred even when its total distribution costs are not the lowest. For instance, some shippers or manufacturers may use air freight as a way of breaking into and testing new and distant markets without the need to set up expensive local warehousing and distribution systems. If they are successful they may then switch to lower cost surface modes. Shipments of routine non-perishable freight tend to be regular, known in advance and often of relatively constant size. Although speed is important small delays of a day or two in collection or delivery can be coped with by the shippers. Non-perishable freight is less price sensitive than perishable freight because of its higher value, but it is nevertheless responsive to the total distribution costs of air transport, especially in relation to the costs of competing surface modes.

Most goods being shipped by air have a high value to weight ratio. Since cargo rates are generally based on weight, the higher the value of an item in relation to its weight, the smaller will be the transport cost as a proportion of its final market price. Therefore, the greater will be the ability of that good to absorb the higher air transport tariffs. This tendency for high value goods to switch to air transport is reinforced if they are also fragile and liable to damage or loss, if subject to excessive handling or if the surface journey times are very long involving the tying up of considerable capital in transit. Consumer demand in many industrialized countries is switching more and more towards goods with high value to weight ratios such as cameras, video machines, home computers, calculators, expensive shoes and so on. It is goods such as these that lend themselves to shipment by air so the future prospects for air freight must be good. More importantly from the airline's point of view, it is the countries manufacturing such goods that will become the largest generators of air freight demand. This is one reason why the growth of freight traffic among South East Asian airlines has in recent years far outstripped that of other regions and why JAL, Korean and Singapore Airlines are now among the top ten airlines in terms of international freight tonne-kilometres.

While freight can be categorized and split into market segments in terms of shippers' motivations, it remains very heterogeneous with a wide range of different manufactured and semi-manufactured goods, raw materials and agricultural products that may have little in common. The commodity mix will vary from route to route but some broad generalizations can be made. Worldwide, about one third of total international air freight is composed of manufactured goods (Groups 6 and 8 in the Standard International Trade Classification) and another third is machinery and transport equipment (SITC Group 7). The remaining third or so is made up of a variety of commodities among which fresh foodstuffs and other agricultural products, medical and pharmaceutical goods and chemicals are all relatively important. The heterogeneity of goods going by air poses numerous marketing problems for airlines, particularly when trying to identify and develop new markets. Another aspect of this heterogeneity is that freight comes in all shapes, sizes, densities and weights. There is no standard unit or size for a freight consignment or any standard unit of space such as a seat. Freight density is crucial to the economics of air freight. Cargo payload on an aircraft is limited by weight but also by volumetric capacity. Since tariffs are based on weight an airline can maximize freight revenue on a flight by carrying dense heavy freight that fully utilizes its weight payload. Low density shipments may fill up the cargo space with a low total weight and a lower total revenue. Surcharges are frequently applied to shipments having a density below a certain level. An airline must try to achieve an average density in its freight carryings which makes maximum use of the volumetric capacity and payload of its aircraft. Because of the variety of goods being shipped the risk is that volumetric capacity is used up before the payload capacity.

The difficulties of handling large numbers of relatively small individual shipments of different size, shape, weight and density created considerable pressures towards unitization of air freight, both as a way of speeding up its handling and in order to reduce handling costs. As a result, most air freight now moves in a variety of unit load devices (ULDs) which fall into four major groups. There are various built-up or half-pallets which may be rigid or flexible. Some are no more than a rigid base with netting to cover the goods being shipped. Secondly, there are IATA-approved lightweight fibreboard or plywood containers or boxes which fit on to full-size or half-pallets. The third group are rigid containers which come in a number of standard sizes designed to fit into the holds of wide-body aircraft. These rigid airline containers now account for a growing proportion of total air freight since much of that freight is being moved on wide-body passenger aircraft or freighters. Finally, there are the ISO inter-modal type containers which can only be used on wide-body freighters such as the Boeing 747F. These various unit load devices may be used and filled by the shippers or the forwarders and presented for carriage to the airline. On many routes the lower costs of handling such ULDs may be passed on to them through low tariffs related to particular ULDs. The fact that much of the freight comes forward in ULDs, each perhaps packed with a variety of different goods, perhaps originating from different shippers, is an added complexity in the marketing of air freight services.

While passengers generally fly round trips or at least return to their origin, freight clearly does not. As a result, considerable imbalances in freight flows can arise. While freight flows on some major international freight routes such as Amsterdam to New York are more or less balanced in each direction on most routes there is a marked imbalance. On major freight routes it is common to find that the traffic in the densest direction is twice or almost twice as great as in the reverse direction as was the case on the Hong Kong to Bangkok or the Paris to Abidjan routes in 1982 (ICAO, 1983d). On secondary but still important freight routes the imbalances tend to be even more marked with the dense flows sometimes as much as four or five times greater than the return flows, as happens on the Los Angeles to Sydney route.

On many routes the tonnage imbalance is aggravated by pricing policies that try to stimulate demand on the low density direction by offering low tariffs. The result may well be an even more marked revenue imbalance as the low tonnages in one direction end up paying the lower cargo rates. Where freight is being carried largely on passenger aircraft, weight and revenue imbalances are easier to absorb, though sometimes airlines may find themselves with inadequate belly-hold capacity in one direction. But large imbalances are particularly detrimental for the operation of all-cargo services since they result in low overall load factors with no possibility of compensating revenue from passenger sales. The absence of assured return loads creates marketing and pricing problems which are unique to the cargo side of the industry.

10.3 The role of freight forwarders

The process of moving freight is considerably more complex than that of moving passengers, involving packaging, more extensive and complex documentation, arranging insurance, collection from the shipper, customs clearance at origin and destination and final delivery. The complexity involved has encouraged the growth of specialist firms who carry out some or all of these tasks on behalf of the shipper and provide an interface between shipper and airline. Such firms may be relatively small IATA-approved or non-IATA agents who feed their shipments directly to the airlines or to large freight consolidators. The latter will be handling freight directly for their own customers but may also be collecting and consolidating consignments from smaller agents. There is considerable fragmentation within the industry with shippers, forwarders, consolidators and airlines all involved to varying degrees with different consignments. Such fragmentation has made the marketing and product planning of freight particularly difficult for the airlines. Any one of the chain of activities necessary to move freight by air may go wrong and undermine the total service being offered, yet the airline may have no control over that activity. It is also frequently torn between marketing and selling its service direct to the shipper or concentrating its selling efforts on the forwarders.

Large forwarders and consolidators have expanded vertically to develop new markets and sources of freight, since they deal directly with the shippers, and to provide more and more services such as ground collection and delivery, which were previously often done by the airlines themselves. Large forwarders may publish their own flight schedules and tariffs. In many markets, such as the UK to North America, a handful of large consolidators may come to control over half the freight being shipped. This gives them considerable market power. By consolidating numerous small shipments into large consignments they can obtain substantial bulk discounts. In other words they buy in bulk and sell retail. On certain routes they can go even further. If the tonnage they ship is high, they can play off the airlines against each other and obtain very low special rates, particularly on routes where there is over-capacity. In this process airline yields are pushed down but the ultimate shipper may not be given the full benefit of the lower rates the consolidators obtain.

As over-capacity on many major air routes has spread so airlines have tried to stimulate total demand or to increase their market share by offering special discounted rates to large forwarders or consolidators. Large numbers of small agents could not generate sufficient freight to take advantage of these special low rates. They were also wary of shipping via large consolidators for fear of losing their customers to them. Economic pressures from smaller agents eventually led to the establishment of a new specialist, the freight wholesaler. They are a relatively recent but growing phenomenon. They buy space in bulk at rates comparable to those of the large consolidator and resell to smaller agents. Unlike consolidators they provide none of the ancillary services such as surface distribution or packaging and therefore pose no threat to their customers. They are simply brokers of freight capacity.

The growing concentration of freight demand in the hands of small numbers of consolidators and wholesalers creates two key difficulties for the airlines who supply freight services. Firstly, it cuts them off from the ultimate customers with the result that they may be less aware of and less responsive to customer needs and new opportunities. Some airlines have tried to overcome this by establishing their own freight forwarding subsidiaries. Secondly, and potentially more

Table 10.2 Impact of consolidators and wholesalers on airline revenues: London–Nairobi case, 1984 (500 kg low density consignment London to Nairobi; volumetric weight for charging = 700 kg)

		Price per kilogram
A	*Tariff structure*	
	Normal general cargo rate	£5.22
	Quantity general cargo rate for 100 kg plus	£4.11
	Lowest specific commodity rate (motorcycles)	£1.67
	Contract rates	£0.90–£1.60
B	*Selling rates*	
	Airline's contract rate to consolidator/wholesaler	£0.90
	Consolidator/wholesaler resale rate to forwarder	£1.00
	Forwarder's rate to shipper	£1.20–£1.50
C	*Revenues earned*	
	Shipper pays forwarder for 700 kg at, say, £1.50 per kilogramme	£1,050
	Forwarder 'splits' volumetric weight with consolidator/wholesaler; pays 600 kg at £1.00 per kilogramme	£600
	Consolidator/wholesaler consolidates with dense cargo to lose volumetric weight penalty; pays airline 500 kg at £0.90 per kilogramme	£450

Airline revenue as percentage of shipper's payment = 43%.

damaging, is the downward pressure on cargo yields which results from the activities of consolidators or wholesalers. The impact on airline yields can be gauged from the example of a 500 kg consignment on the London to Nairobi route illustrated in Table 10.2. The ready availability of low contract rates on this route in August 1984, well below the lowest specific commodity rates, encouraged consolidators and wholesalers to buy space at these rates which could be sold to shippers at much higher rates, although these were still lower than the general or specific commodity rates. The result was that the airlines were often receiving less than half of the monies paid by the shippers for the transport of their goods. The balance was going to the middlemen. The dilution of freight revenue in this way clearly undermines the profitability of air freight. The growing power of these middlemen and in particular their ability to force down cargo tariffs when and where there is spare capacity is a continuing problem for international airlines.

10.4 The economics of supply

10.4.1 BELLY-HOLD CAPACITY

Most air freight travels in the belly holds of the passenger aircraft and traditionally it has been regarded as a by-product arising from the supply of passenger services. Provided that freight revenues covered those costs, such as ground handling, sales and marketing or extra fuel burn, which could be directly attributed to carriage of freight, then any revenue in excess made a contribution towards offsetting the costs of passenger services. The significance of this contribution can be gauged from the fact that in 1982 British Airways estimated that 51 per cent of its freight revenues on passenger aircraft went to cover freight-related costs, while the balance of 49 per cent could be used to cover other costs which would be incurred whether or not freight was carried on the aircraft (Table 10.3). On this basis, belly-hold freight appears to make a valuable contribution to airline profitability. This is confirmed by an IATA study which estimated that in 1983 cargo revenue minus direct cargo-related costs made a net contribution to passenger services of over $2 billion (IATA, 1984b).

The by-product approach to costing, however, leaves open the question of whether freight should bear its share of other costs. Should the major costs of operating a flight be considered to be joint costs which need to be split and allocated in some way to both passengers and freight? This argument is strengthened by the fact that lower freight

Table 10.3 Distribution of revenue from cargo carried on passenger aircraft: British Airways 1982

	%
Revenue needed to cover direct cargo costs	
Cargo handling	21
Additional fuel	11
Sales and cargo promotion	8
Insurance and commission	5
Other overseas costs	4
Administration	2
Sub-total	51
Cargo contribution to other costs	49
Total cargo revenue	100

Source: Bass (1983).

decks of wide body aircraft have possible alternative uses as galleys or lounges. Freight must at least cover the opportunity cost of foregoing these alternative uses. But the allocation of joint costs inevitably involves some arbitrariness. The IATA study mentioned above apportioned aircraft direct operating costs between passengers and freight proportionally to the usable volume allocated to each. It added to these the costs directly imposed by the handling and carriage of air freight on passenger aircraft. Finally administrative overhead costs were split between passengers and freight proportionally to the sum of the other costs. On this basis, cargo on passenger aircraft in 1983 was marginally profitable if interest charges were excluded but only covered 96 per cent of its total costs including interest. Thus if joint costs are allocated to freight the contribution of belly-hold freight becomes marginal. But few airlines think of it in this way. They prefer to consider it as a profitable by-product rather than a joint product.

From the suppliers' and consumers' points of view belly-hold freight offers numerous advantages. It is certainly low cost if costed on a by-product basis. The higher frequency of passenger services is attractive to shippers, particularly for emergency type freight, and they are prepared to pay a premium for the better service. This, together with the fact that passenger aircraft tend to carry a higher proportion of small shipments which do not get bulk or quantity discounts, means that average freight yields from belly-hold freight on most routes are markedly higher than average yields on freighters. Narrow-body passenger aircraft had relatively little capacity for freight and even that was sometimes restricted by take-off limitations. The ability to generate an additional 10–15 per cent of revenue from freight has been an additional incentive for many carriers to switch to wide-body aircraft. Passengers benefit from this switch because the seat-kilometre costs of the larger aircraft are much lower than those of the aircraft they replace. In the process, however, there are indications that too much belly-hold capacity is now available on many routes with the result that there are strong downward pressures on cargo tariffs.

10.4.2   ALL CARGO AIRCRAFT

The carriage of freight on passenger aircraft, particularly narrow-body ones, faced a number of operational problems. Passenger aircraft could not handle large or outsize consignments and, since passengers were given priority, freight was more likely to be off-loaded if take-off weight limits were exceeded. Moreover, the timings and routeings of passenger services did not always match the needs of freight shippers. To overcome these problems and to stimulate freight demand many airlines introduced freighter aircraft. The penetration of such aircraft into the freight market and their subsequent decline was described earlier but not the causes of that decline.

The major economic advantage of the freighter is that it increases its payload by half or more compared to the same aircraft in a passenger configuration. By stripping out unnecessary passenger-related facilities, thereby saving weight, a Boeing 747 freighter may carry a cargo payload of 100–110 tonnes, yet the same aircraft with a main passenger deck and belly-hold freight has a typical payload of around 60–70 tonnes. The greater payload should reduce the tonne-kilometre costs of a freighter by a third or more. Yet all-cargo services have generally been unprofitable and have declined in relative importance because the airlines have been unable to maintain the fine balance between costs, yields and load factors which is essential to profitability.

In the first instance, the costs of all-cargo services were more adversely affected by the fuel price increases of 1974 and 1978–79 than those of passenger aircraft. This was because fuel costs for freighters are a higher proportion of total costs, particularly if they are narrow-body aircraft. On scheduled freighter services, fuel and other variable operating costs may represent around 50 per cent of total costs but may go up to 60 or 70 per cent. Consequently, costs can be significantly reduced in the short term by cutting the number of services. As fuel prices escalated airlines found that they could save money by switching their freight to passenger aircraft or even to road trucks and reducing their freighter services. Within two years of the 1974 fuel crisis Lufthansa had cut its freighter fleet from seventeen to six aircraft and all freight travelling less than 600 km was carried by road or in Airbus belly-holds. KLM followed the same policy in 1983 when it started phasing out its DC-9 freighters. The full costs of carrying freight on all-cargo aircraft can be readily identified so that, in theory, tariff strategies could be adopted to ensure that revenues exceeded costs. In practice, the economic recession apparent in many countries since the late 1970s, together with an excess of belly-hold capacity as airlines introduced more wide-body passenger aircraft, led to the collapse of cargo rates in many important markets such as the North Atlantic route. Moreover, yields on all-cargo freight, much of it travelling at bulk discount or contract rates, have been appreciably lower than those from freight on passenger aircraft. As a general rule airlines have found that yields from all-cargo services have been about 10–25 per cent lower than the yields achieved from the carriage of freight on passenger aircraft (Table 10.4). As a result, where airlines have managed to sustain high load factors on freighter services, as on the North and Mid-Pacific where they have been around 75 per cent, then freighter services have proved profitable. This route is a major exception. On most international air routes

Table 10.4 International freight yields: IATA airlines 1983

Route group	US cents per revenue tonne-kilometre on: Passenger or combi aircraft	Freighters	Freighter as a percentage of pax combi yield (%)
1 *Regional services*			
Within Europe/ Mediterranean	75·2	75·4	100
Within Africa	61·8	n.a.	
Within Middle East	42·5	n.a.	
Within Far East	38·9	28·3	73
2 *Long-haul services*			
Europe–Middle East	42·0	37·0	88
North to South America	30·4	28·0	92
Europe/Middle East– Far East	30·2	22·8	75
North and Mid–Pacific	28·1	23·9	85
Europe–Southern Africa	27·8	25·8	92
South Atlantic	23·4	20·1	86
North Atlantic	22·2	19·1	86
3 *All IATA services**	30·2	24·2	77

*Including routes not listed in table.
Abbreviation: n.a., not available.
Source: IATA (1984b).

all-cargo load factors have not been high enough to compensate for the low yields with the result that freighter services have tended to be unprofitable. Losses have been particularly marked on the North Atlantic route where in 1983 the break-even load factor for all-cargo services was 84·4 per cent but the achieved load factor was only 69 per cent (IATA, 1984a).

Fuel price increases, below average and falling yields and insufficiently high load factors have in recent years destroyed the economic viability of all-cargo services on many routes. The result has been the abandonment of freighter services by many airlines and an increase in the proportion of freight travelling in belly holds. Some routes have baulked the trend. Many trans-Pacific routes have done this largely because the buoyant export-oriented economies of Japan and some of its neighbours have generated a rapid growth in demand for freight space, especially for high value consumer goods, which could not adequately be met by belly-hold capacity. Yields and load factors have consequently held up better.

While all-cargo services generally will continue to be unprofitable, particular carriers or routes may achieve profitability because yields or load factors are sufficiently high. Even when that it not the case, many carriers will continue to operate freighters as a necessary adjunct to their overall freight service. They need them to provide a better overall service for their customers by using them to transport the 10 per cent or so of freight that is too large or dangerous for belly holds as well as the larger consolidations. All-cargo schedules can also be geared to the needs of shippers. On some routes where the demand for passengers is thin belly-hold capacity may in any case be insufficient to meet cargo needs. This may also be so on routes where payload or range restrictions reduce the effective cargo capacity on passenger flights. Finally, carriers may use all-cargo services which may not be viable in their own right to carry cargo on trunk routes for onward distribution on passenger flights, where the revenue generated may make a contribution to overall profitability.

10.4.3 COMBI AIRCRAFT

There are routes where the enormous payload of wide-body aircraft in an all-cargo configuration is too large for the potential freight demand, while belly-hold capacity may be insufficient or unable to cope with bulky consignments. In such circumstances, the wide body 'combi' aircraft on which passengers and freight are both carried on the main deck may prove a commercially attractive proposition. By adjusting the main deck space allocated to passengers or freight in response to the demand mix and seasonal variations of each route total revenue can be maximized. For instance, at times of peak passenger demand the whole cabin may be used for passengers. In a combi operation the allocation of joint costs to the freight side is essential. Freight revenue must be seen to cover its share of capacity costs since without freight on the main deck the passenger service would use a smaller aircraft or a lower frequency and reduce its total costs. This means that pricing must move towards a full cost recovery basis rather than be based on the by-product pricing strategy adopted for belly-hold freight. Market conditions will determine whether this can be done. The method of allocation varies between airlines but a number of airlines, KLM and British Caledonian among them, have done the exercise and have convinced themselves of the commercial advantages of combi aircraft. It is likely that combi aircraft will have a continuing role to play, particularly on the thinner long-haul routes.

In earlier years much greater use was made of convertible or quick change (QC) aircraft which were used for passengers for most of the time and were then re-configured for freight services during the night or at off-peak periods. While at one time they were quite widespread, especially within Europe, QC operations are now less common. They have been adversely affected by airport night bans, by the high costs of changing the aircraft's configuration, particularly when done twice within 24 hours, and by the ready availability of so much belly-hold capacity.

10.5 Pricing of air freight

10.5.1 STRUCTURE OF CARGO TARIFFS

As with passenger fares international cargo tariffs have traditionally been agreed by the airlines through IATA and subsequently approved by governments. With the liberalization of tariffs, especially on routes to the United States, and with over-capacity in many markets, the IATA cargo tariffs have tended to become less significant worldwide though for most countries, especially in the Third World, they provide the basis for the pricing of air freight. The IATA cargo tariffs used to be based on the 'rate construction units' with artificial exchange rates for conversions from one currency to another and with 'currency adjustment factors' to allow for sudden changes in exchange rates. In August 1984, all that was abandoned in favour of publishing fares in the local currency of the point of origin.

The majority of international city pairs involving major and secondary cities have an IATA *general cargo rate*. Like all air freight rates it is expressed as a rate per kilogram or on US routes per pound and there may be a minimum charge per consignment. Originally general cargo rates were one-eightieth of the passenger fare on the same route on the grounds that a passenger and his baggage were estimated on average to weigh 80 kg. An examination of general cargo rates around the world shows that the rate per kilometre tapers with route distance. But the taper, which in theory is cost related, is neither regular nor always evident. In addition there are significant variations in the general cargo rate for opposite directions on the same route. Thus the general rates from African points south of the Sahara to Europe have traditionally been as low as two-thirds or less of the rates for cargo originating in Europe. Similar north–south imbalances in rate levels have also existed on air routes between North and South America. Such rate variations have clearly been aimed at reducing the imbalances in freight flows and more particularly at generating more northbound traffic.

On the majority of routes, one or more additional tariffs may be available which will be lower than the normal general cargo rate. First, there may be *quantity general cargo rates* where the rate per kilogram or per pound decreases as the size of the consignment increases beyond certain agreed weight break-points. While most routes may have only one or two quantity rates, 45 kg and 100 kg are common break-points, routes to and from the United States tend to have many more break-points with successively lower rates as consignment weight increases. While the quantity general cargo rates encourage consolidation into large consignments, they fail to stimulate the air freighting of particular goods or commodities. This is done by *specific commodity rates* which are individual low rates for specific and clearly defined commodities. Some routes may have only one or two commodity rates while others may have forty or more. Such rates will reflect and encourage the types of goods most likely to be shipped by air on each route. Many commodity rates also include quantity discounts with lower rates as shipment size increases. The level of the commodity rates varies widely but on occasions they may be as low as 20 per cent or less of the general cargo rate. While the original aim of specific commodity rates was to attract goods which would otherwise not travel by air, commodity rates are now frequently agreed to even for high value, low weight goods which could bear the cost of the general cargo rates. The third type of discount rates are those related to particular unit load devices, known as *ULD rates*. Such rates are not available in all markets. There is a fixed minimum charged per ULD which declines proportionally as the size of the pallet or container increases. The minimum charge is for a given weight known as the pivot weight. If the contents in the ULD weigh more than the pivot weight then they are charged on a per kilogram basis but the rates are normally lower than the quantity general rates or most of the specific commodity rates. The tariff structure based on a minimum charge and low rates above the pivot weight encourages shippers and forwarders to pack as much into the ULDs as possible. Moreover, by mixing shipments of different weight and density in a container they can reduce the average cargo rate they pay to the airline. The aim of ULD rates is also to encourage shippers to use containers or other unit load devices which, from an airline viewpoint, are easier and cheaper to handle than disparate consignments. A somewhat different category of cargo tariffs were the so-called *class rates* which involve a rebate (for unaccompanied baggage or newspapers) or a surcharge (for gold or human remains, for example) on the general commodity rate. They have been applied to certain commodities whose carriage calls for special treatment. They are expressed as a percentage discount or surcharge on the general cargo rate, though such discounts and surcharges seem to reflect demand elasticity rather than the costs of the special treatment these shipments require. Only a small proportion of freight travels at these class rates.

In recent years, pressure from cargo charters on a few routes, excess cargo capacity on many routes and the trend towards liberalization of airline pricing have together produced significant changes in the structure of tariffs in several major markets. *Freight-of-all-kinds* (FAK) rates have become widespread on the North Atlantic route since about 1980. These are low rates based on weight, not the commodity or the type of ULD. Originally they applied only to large consolidated shipments but in very competitive markets minimum weight limits have often been abandoned. FAK rates are published separately, their main purpose being to simplify the profusion of commodity and other rates. Even more significant is the increasing use of *contract rates* directly negotiated by airlines with large shippers or forwarders guaranteeing to provide a minimum tonnage over a given period. The growing market power of freight forwarders and the competitive pressure on airlines to sell excess capacity has created a situation on the North Atlantic, the North Pacific and some other routes where very low contract rates dominate the market and where freight pricing bears little relevance to published IATA tariffs. Contract rates may fall to 20 per cent or less of the general cargo rate (Table 10.3). In competitive markets with considerable spare freight capacity slushing around, it is likely that only small and emergency consignments move at published freight rates, while well over half the freight tonnage is shipped at contract rates.

10.5.2 PRICING STRATEGIES

The preceding review of the structure of cargo tariffs suggests that they bear only a tenuous relationship to cargo costs. Different commodities on the same route may be charged at widely different rates with no marked differences apparent in the costs of handling and freighting them. General cargo rates vary markedly between sectors of similar length being operated with similar aircraft. Rates on the same route differ in opposite directions. The taper of rates per kilometre with distance is neither consistent nor closely related to costs. While IATA and some airlines have tried to dress up the cargo tariffs as being somehow cost related, there can be little doubt that the underlying philosophy, especially for commodity rates, is ultimately one of 'charging what the traffic will bear', that is market-oriented pricing. Such a pricing strategy was encouraged by the by-product view of air cargo. As a by-product of passenger services the carriage of freight appeared to impose low additional costs and any revenue in excess of these low costs made a contribution to the overall profitability of the services.

It could be argued, as the UK Civil Aviation Authority has argued (CAA, 1977b), that market pricing is discriminatory since it entails charging some shipments more than the costs they impose and others less. This is undoubtedly the case, but it is difficult to see how market pricing could be avoided given the nature of the air freight market. It has two distinctive characteristics which bedevil any attempt to establish cost-related tariffs. First, the existence of freight consolidators and wholesalers not only cuts off the airlines from their true customers and distorts the pricing mechanism but also gives such large freight agents considerable market power. Secondly, the carriage of freight is inherently more competitive even in regulated markets than is the carriage of passengers. This is because most freight, except for emergency freight, is indifferent to the routeing it is offered in order to move from its origin to its destination. A shipper is unconcerned if his shipment goes from New York to Lisbon via Amsterdam or Frankfurt or Copenhagen with a six-hour trans-shipment at one of those airports, provided that it gets to Lisbon within the expected time. Yet few passengers would put up with such circuitous and lengthy journeys. Thus in most cases there are numerous routeings (and airlines) that freight can use to get to its destination. This ensures a degree of inter-airline competition which may be absent for passengers on the same routes. If one superimposes on these market characteristics the availability on most air services of surplus belly-hold capacity then any attempts to establish cost-related cargo tariffs will inevitably be futile. Airlines have little choice but to pursue a strategy of setting rates aimed at maximizing revenue. In prevailing market conditions this means on most major routes charging what the traffic will bear.

In an environment of market-oriented pricing where consolidators and wholesalers have a major influence on what the shippers ultimately pay, current trends indicate that cargo tariffs are moving towards a three-tier pricing structure related to the speed of delivery. First, the highest or premium cargo rates are being charged for services guaranteeing overnight delivery. Effectively this means that shipments move on the next available passenger flight. The target market is emergency freight. Secondly, the special commodity, FAK or contract rates are being used for belly-hold cargo and occasionally all-cargo services offering a 2–4 day delivery. The trend here is increasingly towards FAK or contract rates that reflect the market conditions on each route. It is only on routes where belly-hold capacity is limited in relation to the demand for freight space and alternative routeings are difficult or costly that the structure of complex and relatively high specific commodity rates is likely to survive. Finally, the lowest charter competitive rates are likely to be available for large and regular shipments where delivery may be delayed for up to a week or so. Some of this traffic may go on scheduled all-cargo services. With all three tariff types lower quantity rates may additionally be offered for larger shipments.

10.5.3 FREIGHT YIELDS

The prevailing cargo tariff levels in the major markets served by an airline and that airline's traffic mix are clearly the major determinants of an individual airline's freight yields. Particularly important is the degree to which the general cargo rates have been eroded by the introduction of low specific commodity rates, FAK rates and ultimately by contract or other deep discount rates. This will be determined by market conditions, notably the availability of spare capacity and the degree of inter-airline competition. Commodity mix and consignment size are important in determining the rates paid to the airline. The length of haul of those consignments also impacts on yields since cargo rates per kilometre tend to decline with distance. Similar factors will also affect the freight yields achieved in different parts of an airline's network. The wide range of freight yields in different geographical areas is illustrated in Table 10.4. This shows that the lowest yields in 1983 were being achieved in the long-haul markets where there was most over capacity, namely the North and South Atlantic. Conversely, it is evident that on the relatively short European routes where surface transport is very competitive yields are exceptionally high. This suggests that much of the international air freight within Europe is composed of relatively small and high rated consignments often of an emergency nature.

As a general rule, yields per freight tonne-kilometre are less than half those generated per passenger tonne-kilometre. In 1983 the average yield per passenger tonne-kilometre on the international scheduled services of the IATA member airlines was 69·9 US cents. The average freight yield was 27·9 cents per tonne-kilometre, equivalent to 40 per cent of the passenger yield (IATA, 1984a). A similar relationship between the two yields has existed for many years. The relatively low freight yields explain why worldwide freight represents about one-quarter of airline production but generates only around one-ninth of airline revenues (Table 1.5).

11

Future prospects

Prospects for the international airlines during the second half of the 1980s look more hopeful. Already by the end of 1984 IATA was predicting several years of profit though the profits would not be sufficient to finance the industry's re-equipment plans. Fuel prices are moving downward and a continued decline seems likely. This together with other cost reductions should lead to a renewed fall in the real level of costs. Lower costs mean lower fares. Falling fares and cargo tariffs together with an improvement in the general economic climate should lead to a resurgence in the demand for air transport, although the growth rates are unlikely to match those of the 1960s. But will rapid growth be plagued by poor financial performances as in the past or is there a brighter future ahead for the international airlines?

Renewed opportunities for growth will occur within a less stable market environment as regulatory controls are further loosened. Continued liberalization of international regulations will come through bilateral or regional action rather than multilateral accord. The focus of deregulation will switch from the United States to Western Europe. The very liberal bilateral agreement signed between the United Kingdom and the Netherlands in June 1984 will be followed by others between pairs of European states and occasionally too between European states and countries outside Europe. More importantly, within the European Economic Community the pressure for liberalization emanating from the Commission, whose aims were outlined in its Civil Aviation Memorandum No. 2 (CEC, 1984), will probably result in the progressive abandonment of revenue pooling agreements and a relaxation of tariff controls. The trend will not always be towards liberalization. Many governments, particularly those whose airlines are in difficulties, will try to maintain a protectionist environment. Even governments who champion a more 'open skies' approach will take occasional protectionist measures. This apparent contradiction occurred in 1984. In October 1984 the Singapore government which had frequently berated other countries for limiting SIA's access to new markets refused to give Air Lanka the fifth freedom rights it requested on services beyond Singapore. In the meantime the UK government had become involved in an acrimonious dispute with the Philippines after the UK had refused PAL's request to operate a third weekly frequency on Manila–London even though under its then existing operating permit PAL was permitted three services. When PAL won its case in the courts the UK government abrogated the bilateral air services agreement. Other governments will also find themselves following contradictory policies.

The thesis argued in this book is that airlines must husband their resources carefully in matching supply, which they control, with demand which they do not. Several ways of improving this matching process have been suggested. To operate profitably in the growing but potentially less stable markets of the future scheduled airlines must do more than this. They have to learn some hard lessons from their charter competitors and from the new airlines that sprung up in the United States following deregulation. The charter airlines' success has been based on reducing indirect costs to a minimum, on higher seating densities and on very close matching of supply to demand so as to achieve very high load factors. The new scheduled US carriers such as People Express have introduced dramatically higher labour productivity through a tight control of staff numbers who are employed at significantly lower wage rates and with much greater flexibility in work practices.

To ensure their future profitability international airlines must first of all significantly reduce their labour costs to levels that are comparable to those of People Express or the newer Asian carriers. This means major increases in labour productivity. For many European and North American airlines, who have not done so already, this may require large cuts in staff numbers and an easing of job demarcation between different categories of staff. Many Asian and some other Third World airlines which already have low wage costs and high labour productivity together with new airlines such as People Express stand poised to capture a larger share of major international markets unless established European and American carriers can match them on the labour front. British Airways is one airline which set out to do just this. The second area of concern must be that of indirect operating costs. Considerable cost savings can be achieved, as the charter airlines have shown, through a simplification of reservations and ticketing procedures. Automation of ticket sales and of baggage and passenger check-in can reduce staff numbers and costs and facilitate air travel at the same time. Administrative overheads must also be cut to a minimum. Finally, scheduled airlines must strive to achieve higher year-round load factors. Currently average load factors tend to be in the mid-sixties for the better airlines and low sixties or less for the others. Airlines must aim for year-round load factors in the mid-seventies or higher. To achieve them they will need to introduce sophisticated planning of the seat capacities that will be sold at different fares together with a system of reservations control which ensures that the revenue on each individual flight is maximized. This may also require increased expenditure on marketing and promotion. This is the one item of indirect costs which may actually increase. These lessons may not be easy to accept but ignoring them will not just mean flying off course. It may well mean going to the wall.

Appendix A: Freedoms of the Air

Negotiated in bilateral air services agreements

First freedom   The right to fly over another country without landing.

Second freedom   The right to make a landing for technical reasons (e.g. refuelling) in another country without picking up/setting down revenue traffic.

Third freedom   The right to carry revenue traffic from your own country (A) to the country (B) of your treaty partner.

Fourth freedom   The right to carry traffic from country B back to your own country A.

Fifth freedom   The right of an airline from country A to carry revenue traffic between country B and other countries such as C or D. (This freedom cannot be used unless countries C or D also agree.)

Supplementary rights

Sixth 'Freedom'   The use by airline of country A of two sets of third and fourth freedom rights to carry traffic between two other countries but using its base at A as a transit point. For example, ALIA carries sixth freedom traffic between London and Middle East points via its base at Amman even though it has not been granted fifth freedom rights between these points and London.

Sixth freedom rights are not formally recognised in air services agreements, though several confidential memoranda of understanding make implicit reference to them, especially when dealing with capacity issues.

Cabotage rights   The right of an airline of country A to carry revenue between two points in country B. For example, Air France for many years had cabotage rights between various points within Morocco.

Cabotage rights are very rarely granted. Nevertheless, several Asian carriers currently flying to the United States via Hawaii are pressing the US government for cabotage rights between Hawaii and Los Angeles and San Francisco.

Appendix B: Definition of Airline Terms

Payload capacity   Total of aircraft capacity available for the carriage of passengers, baggage, cargo or mail; measured in metric tonnes.

Capacity or available tonne-kilometres (ATK)   This is a measure of airline output; ATKs are obtained by multiplying the payload capacity on a flight by the stage distance flown.

Revenue tonne-kilometres (RTK) or tonne-kilometres performed or carried   This measures the output actually sold; RTKs are obtained by multiplying the number of tonnes carried on a flight by the stage distance.

Weight load factor   Measures the proportion of the output actually sold; it is the RTKs expressed as a percentage of the ATKs.

Capacity or available seat-kilometres   This is obtained by multiplying the seats available on a flight by the stage distance.

Passenger-kilometres   The number of passengers on a flight multiplied by the stage distance; passenger-kilometres are normally converted to revenue or passenger tonne-kilometres by assuming that one passenger with baggage equals 90 kg (i.e. passenger-kilometres divided by 11·111 equal passenger tonne-kilometres).

Seat factor or passenger load factor   On a single sector this is obtained by expressing the passengers carried as a percentage of the seats available for sale; on a network of routes the seat factor is obtained by expressing the total passenger-kilometres as a percentage of the total seat-kilometres available.

Tonne-kilometres per hour   This measures an aircraft's hourly productivity; it is the payload capacity multiplied by the average speed; the latter may be the average block speed or the cruise speed.

Stage or sector distance   Ideally this should be air route distance between two airports; many airlines (and IATA) use the great circle distance, which is shorter than the distance actually flown.

Average stage length   The weighted average of stage or sector lengths flown by an airline; this is most easily obtained by dividing an airline's total annual aircraft-kilometres by the number of aircraft departures or flights recorded during the year.

Aircraft-kilometres   The distances flown by aircraft; they are derived from the stage lengths and the frequencies operated over each stage.

Length of (passenger) haul   The average distance flown by an airline's passengers; this is obtained by dividing an airline's total passenger-kilometres by the number of passengers carried.

Block time   This is the time for each stage between engines being switched on at departure and off on arrival.

Block speed   The average speed for each stage calculated from the block time.

Flying or airborne time   The time from aircraft lift-off to touch-down on the runway.

Aircraft hours   The cumulative time that each aircraft is in use calculated usually from the block times. Airborne or flying hours might also be calculated.

Aircraft utilization   The average number of block hours that each aircraft is in use; utilization may be measured on a daily or an annual basis.

Yield   Measures the average revenue obtained per ATK or RTK; it is obtained by dividing an airline total revenue by its total ATKs or RTKs.

Passenger yield   The average revenue per passenger-kilometre or passenger tonne-kilometre. It is obtained by dividing total passenger revenue by the total passenger-kilometres or passenger tonne-kilometres. Freight yields are obtained in the same way.

Flight crew   Refers to the pilot, co-pilot and flight engineer if any.

Cabin crew   Refers to stewards and stewardesses.

Seat pitch   This is the standard way of measuring seating density on aircraft. It is the distance between the back of one seat and the same point on the back of the seat in front.

References and Further Reading

AEA (1982), *Standard File on Civil Aviation in Europe* (Brussels, Association of European Airlines).

Aeroshell (1984), *Products and Prices Guides 2/1984* (London, Shell).

ATA (1983), *The Frequency of Flying among the General Public 1983* (Washington, D.C., Air Transport Association of America).

Avmark (quarterly), Quarterly Aircraft Operating Costs and Statistics (Arlington, Va, Avmark Inc.).

BAA (1978), *Long Term Airport Traffic Forecasting* (London, British Airports Authority).

BAA (1981), *BAA Traffic Forecasts: Methodology* (London, British Airports Authority).

Bass, T. (1983), 'Passenger Aircraft have Competitive Edge'. Special Report: Air Cargo, in *Transport*, Vol. 4, No. 4, July–August 1983.

Business Monitor (1983), *MQ6 Overseas Travel and Tourism: Quarterly Statistics* (London, Business Statistics Office, HMSO).

CAA (1975), *International Air Freight Services: A Consultative Document*, CAP 379 (London, Civil Aviation Authority).

CAA (1977a), *European Air Fares: A Discussion Document*, CAP 409 (London, Civil Aviation Authority).

CAA (1977b), *Air Freight Demand: A Survey of UK Shippers*, CAP 401 (London, Civil Aviation Authority).

CAA (1977c), *Freight Policy – A Consultation Document*, CAP 405 (London, Civil Aviation Authority).

CAA (1980), *Passengers at the London Area Airports in 1978*, CAP 430 (London, Civil Aviation Authority).

CAA (1981), *Air Navigation: The Order and Regulations*, CAP 393 (London, Civil Aviation Authority).

CAA (1982), *Annual Statistics 1982*, CAP 484 (London, Civil Aviation Authority).

CAA (1984a), *UK Airlines: Annual Operating, Traffic and Financial Statistics 1983*, CAP 492 (London, Civil Aviation Authority).

CAA, (1984b), 'Passengers at Aberdeen, Edinburgh, Glasgow, Prestwick Airports 1982. CAP 497 (London Civil Aviation Authority).

CAA (1984c), *Airline competition policy*, CAP 500 (London, Civil Aviation Authority).

CAA (1984d), *Deregulation of air transport. A perspective on the experience in the United States* CAA Paper 84009. (London, Civil Aviation Authority).

CAA (1985), *Statement of policies on air transport licensing - January 1985*, CAP 501 (London, Civil Aviation Authority).

CAB (1969), *Charter Travel and Economic Opportunity*. (Washington, D.C., Civil Aeronautics Board).

CAB (1975), Report of the CAB Special Staff on Regulatory Reform. July 1975. (Washington, Civil Aeronautics Board).

CAB (1976), *Uniform System of Accounts and Reports for Certified Air Carriers.* (Washington, D.C., Civil Aeronautics Board).

CAB (1982), *Aircraft Operating Cost and Performance Report*, Vol. XVI (Washington, D.C., US Government Printing Office) (see also Avmark).

Cambau, D. and Lefevre, G. (1981), *Panorama of World Non-scheduled Passenger Transport* (Paris, Institut du Transport Aerien).

CEC (1975), *Action Programme for the European Aeronautical Sector*, R/2461/75 (Brussels, Commission of the European Communities).

CEC (1981), *Scheduled Passenger Air Fares in the EEC*, COM (81) 398 Final (Brussels, Commission of the European Communities).

CEC (1983), *Council Directive Concerning the Authorisation of Scheduled Inter-Regional Air Services between Member States* (Brussels, Commission of the European Communities).

CEC (1984), *Civil Aviation Memorandum No. 2. Progress Towards the Development of a Community Air Transport Policy*, COM (84) 72 Final (Brussels, Commission of the European Communities).

CTC (1981), *The Basic Economics of Air Carrier Operations*, Report No. 40-81-04. (Ottawa/Hull, Research Branch, Canadian Transport Commission).

de Neufville, R. (1976), *Airport Systems Planning* (London, Macmillan).

Department of Trade (1978), *United Kingdom Air Traffic Forecasting: Research and Revised Forecasts* (London, Department of Trade).

Department of Trade (1981), *Report of the Air Traffic Forecasting Working Party 1981* (London, Department of Trade).

Doganis, R. (1973), 'Air Transport – a Case Study in International Regulation', *Journal of Transport Economics and Policy*, Vol. 7, No. 2, May 1973.

Doganis, R. (1977), 'Current Trends in the International Regulation of Air Transport', *ITA Bulletin*, Nos 40 and 41, 28 November and 5 December 1977 (Paris, Institut du Transport Aerien).

Eads, G. G. (1975), 'Competition in the Domestic Trunk Airline Industry: Too Much or Too Little', in *Promoting Competition in Regulated Markets*, edited by Almarin Phillips (Washington, The Brookings Institution).

ECAC (1981), *Report on Intra-European Scheduled Air Fares*, ECAC Doc. No. 23 (Paris, European Civil Aviation Conference).

ECAC (1982), *Report on Competition in Intra-European Air Services*, ECAC Doc. No. 25 (Paris, European Civil Aviation Conference).

Garcia-Fuertes, J. A. (1980), *A Proposed Air Freight Forecasting Methodology* (Los Angeles. Flying Tigers Line).

Green, J. H. T. (1978), *United Kingdom Air Traffic Forecasting* (London: Department of Trade).

Hammarskjold, K. (1975), *The State of the Air Transport Industry*. (Geneva, International Air Transport Association).

HMSO (1946), *Final Act of the Civil Aviation Conference and Agreement between the Government of the United Kingdom and the Government of the USA relating to Air Services between their Respective Territories*, Cmnd 6747 (London, His Majesty's Stationery Office).

HMSO (1956), *Multilateral Agreement on Commercial Rights of Non-*

Scheduled Air Services in Europe, Cmnd 1099 (London, Her Majesty's Stationery Office).

HMSO (1969), *British Air Transport in the Seventies*, Report of the Committee of Inquiry into Civil Air Transport (Chapters 5 and 13) (London, Her Majesty's Stationery Office).

HMSO (1971), *Agreement between the Government of the United Kingdom and the Government of the Republic of Singapore* (see Article 9), Treaty Series No. 20 (1971), Cmnd 4619 (London: Her Majesty's Stationery Office).

HMSO (1977), *Agreement between the Government of the United Kingdom and the Government of the United States of America concerning Air Services*, Treaty Series No. 76, 1977, Cmnd 7016 (London, Her Majesty's Stationery Office).

Horn, K.W. (1982), 'The Frequency of Air Travel', in *Airline Economics*, edited by George W. James (Lexington, Mass., Lexington Books), pp. 23–24.

IATA (1974), *Agreeing Fares and Rates: A Survey of the Methods and Procedures Used by the Member Airlines of the International Air Transport Association* (Geneva, International Air Transport Association).

IATA (1982a), *International User Charges* (Geneva, International Air Transport Association).

IATA (1982b), *World Air Transport Statistics 1981* (Geneva, International Air Transport Association).

IATA (1983), *Annual Report 1983* (Geneva, International Air Transport Association).

IATA (1984a), *World Air Transport Statistics 1983* (Geneva, International Air Transport Association).

IATA (1984b), *Airline Economic Results and Prospects 1982–1986*, Report by the IATA Cost Committee (Geneva, International Air Transport Association).

ICAO (1974), *A Review of the Economic Situation of Air Transport 1963–1973* (Montreal, International Civil Aviation Organisation).

ICAO (1978), *Standard Bilateral Tariff Clause*, Doc. 9228-C/1036 (Montreal, International Civil Aviation Organisation).

ICAO (1980), *Convention on International Civil Aviation*, 6th edn, Doc. 7300/6 (Montreal, Civil Aviation Organisation).

ICAO (1983a), *Survey of International Air Transport Fares and Rates*, Circular 176-AT/66 (Montreal, International Civil Aviation Organisation).

ICAO (1983b), *Regional Differences in Fares, Rates and Costs for International Air Transport 1981*, Circular 180-AT/69. (Montreal, International Civil Aviation Organisation).

ICAO (1983c), *A Review of the Economic Situation of Air Transport 1972–1982*, Circular 177-AT/67 (Montreal, International Civil Aviation Organisation).

ICAO (1983d), *On-Flight Origin and Destination Year Ending December 1982*, Digest of Statistics No. 299, Series OFOD, No. 24 (Montreal, International Civil Aviation Organisation).

ICAO (1983e), *Financial Data 1981*, Digest of Statistics No. 290, Series F, No. 35 (Montreal, International Civil Aviation Organisation).

ICAO (1984a), *Survey of International Air Transport Fares and Rates*,

September 1983, Circular 182-AT/70 (Montreal, International Civil Aviation Organisation).

ICAO (1984b), *Regional Differences in Fares, Rates and Costs for International Air Transport 1982*, Circular 188-AT/72 (Montreal, International Civil Aviation Organisation).

ICAO (1984c), *Financial Data, 1982*, Digest of Statistics No. 298, Series F, No. 36. (Montreal, International Civil Aviation Organisation).

ICAO (1984d), *Civil Aviation Statistics of the World, 1983* Document 9180/9 (Montreal, International Civil Aviation Organisation).

ICAO (1984e), *Fleet-Personnel 1983*, Digest of Statistics No. 308, Series FP, No. 37 (Montreal, International Civil Aviation Organisation).

ICAO (1984f), Traffic 1979–1983, Digest of Statistics No 303, Series T, No. 43 (Montreal, International Civil Aviation Organisation).

ICAO (1985), Financial Data 1983, Digest of Statistics No 310, Series F No. 37 (Montreal, International Civil Aviation Organisation).

Ippolito, R. A. (1981), 'Estimating Airline Demand with Quality of Service Variables', *Journal of Transport Economics and Policy*, Vol. XV, No. 1, Jan. 1981, pp. 7–15.

Kanafani, A., Sadoulet, E. and Sullivan, E. C. (1974), *Demand Analysis for North Atlantic Air Travel*. (Berkeley, Calif., Institute of Transportation and Traffic Engineering, University of California).

Lansing, J. B., and Blood, D. M. (1984), *The Changing Travel Market* (Ann Arbor, Mich., Survey Research Centre, University of Michigan).

Martin, P. et al. (1984) *Shawcross and Beaumont Air Law*, 4th edn, Vol. 2, Section A, pp. 411–417 Standard Bilateral Agreement (London, Butterworth).

McDonnell-Douglas (1968), *US Supplemental Air Carriers*, Market Research Report No. Cl-804-1313 (Long Beach, Calif., McDonnell-Douglas Corp.).

McDonnell-Douglas (1980), *World Freight Outlook, Tenth International Air Cargo Forum, Amsterdam, September 30–October 3, 1980* (Long Beach, Calif., McDonnell-Douglas Corp.).

Nammack, J. (1984), 'Labour vs Management', *Airline Executive* February 1984, pp. 21–25.

Nguyen Dai Hai (1982), 'The Box and Jenkins Approach: A Recent Short-Term Forecasting Technique Applied to Air Transport', *ITA Bulletin*, September 1982 (Paris, Institut du Transport Aerien).

Pearson, R. J. (1976), 'Airline Managerial Efficiency', *Aeronautical Journal*, November 1976.

Pearson, R. J. (1977), 'Establishing a Methodology for Measuring Airline Efficiency', PhD Thesis, Polytechnic of Central London.

Peguillan, B. (1981), 'Trends in Air Freight Rates on the North Atlantic', *ITA Bulletin*, No. 24, 22 June 1981 (Paris, Institut du Transport Aerien).

Presidential Documents (1978), *Weekly Compilation of Presidential Documents*, Vol. 14, No. 34, 28 August 1978, pp. 1462–1465.

Raben, H. (1980), 'The Real Test: Does a Liberal Bilateral Work? *ITA Bulletin*, No. 18, 12 May 1980 (Paris, Institut du Transport Aerien).

Reid, S. R. and Mohrfeld, J. W. (1973), 'Airline Size, Profitability, Mergers and Regulation'. *Journal of Air Law and Commerce*, Vol. 39.

Richmond, S. B. (1971), *Regulation and Competition in Air Transport* (New York, Columbia University Press).

Shaw, S. (1982), *Air Transport. A Marketing Perspective* (London, Pitman).

Sletmo, G. K., (1972), *Demand for Air Cargo: An Econometric Approach.* (Bergen, Institute for Shipping Research, Norwegian School of Economics and Business Administration).

Smith, A. B. and Toms, J. N. (1978), *Factors Affecting Demand for International Travel to and from Australia* (Canberra, Bureau of Transport Economics).

Smith, P. (1974), Air Freight: Operations, Marketing and Economics (London, Faber and Faber).

Straszheim, M. R. (1969), *The International Airline Industry* (Washington, D.C., The Brookings Institution).

Straszheim, M. R. (1978), 'Airline Demand Functions in the North Atlantic and their Pricing Implications', *Journal of Transport Economics and Policy*, Vol. 12, No. 2, pp. 179–195.

Taneja, N. K. (1976), *The Commercial Airline Industry* (Lexington, Mass., Lexington Books).

Taneja, N. K. (1978), *Airline Traffic Forecasting* (Lexington, Mass., Lexington Books).

Taplin, J. H. E. (1980), 'Price Elasticities in the Vacation Travel Market', *Journal of Transport Economics and Policy*, Vol. 14, No. 1, pp. 19–36.

Tillinghast, C. C. (1983), 'Airline Deregulation: Some Comments on its Impact on Labor and on Financing of Airlines', in *Airline Deregulation: Lessons for Public Policy Formulation*, edited by J. Rhoads Foster *et al.* (Washington, D.C., Institute for Study of Regulation).

US Government (1973), *Air Charter Services: Agreement between the USA and the Federal Republic of Germany*, 13 April 1973, Treaties and Other International Acts Series 7605 and 7804 (Washington, D.C., US Government Printing Office).

Wassenbergh, H. A. (1978), 'Innovation in International Air Transport Regulation (The US-Netherlands Agreement of 10 March 1978)', *Air Law*, Vol. III, No. 3.

Wheatcroft, S. (1956), *The Economics of European Air Transport*, (Manchester, Manchester University Press).

Wheatcroft, S. (1964), *Air Transport Policy* (London, Michael Joseph).

Wheatcroft, S. (1982), 'The Changing Economics of International Air Transport', *Tourism Management*, June 1982, pp. 71–82.

White, L. J. (1979), 'Economies of Scale and the Question of Natural Monopoly in the Airline Industry' *Journal of Air Law and Commerce*, Vol. 44.

Index

Index